S0-BZT-412

Contents

Preface

Despite a plethora of excellent books on budgeting and public finance, there is a void connecting theory and practice. The purpose of this textbook/workbook is to provide public budget and finance students with basic budgeting and financial management tools. From the perspective of a bureaucrat, students walk through various concepts and then work on exercises and problems to reinforce those concepts.

Chapter one begins with a discussion of the basic concepts, types of budgets, and the various types of accounting techniques. Chapter two follows with a discussion of the budget cycle, budget calendars and actors involved in the process. Chapters three and four examine personal services, operating and capital budgets. Chapter five takes a close look at the different ways to fund public budgets. Chapter six looks at the major budgeting techniques and analytical models and shows students how these methods are useful in answering important policy questions. Chapter seven discusses financial management issues that are important in the 21st century. This includes a discussion of cash management, risk management, procurement, debt management and cutback management strategies. Chapter eight examines: data sources, data quality and appropriateness; and the different ways to communicate budget data effectively using charts, graphs, and power point slides.

Each chapter provides the student with a list of important terms phrases and exercises that require the students to apply what they have learned in the chapter. These exercises assume that the students are proficient in a word processing program and Excel.

Charles E. Menifield
Memphis, TN
April 2008

Acknowledgements

First and foremost, I am very thankful to the budget and finance students that I taught at Murray State University, Mississippi State University, Howard University and the University of Memphis from 1996-2008. This book is the direct result of their encouragement. I am particularly thankful to Brenda Frantz, Vashun Coles, Julienne Watkins-Young, Yohance Duff, Heather Walker, Frank Robertson, Shayla Guy, Jana Jones, Eric Raymond, Gerard Wellman, and Kwame Antwi-Bosiako. Special thanks go to Tomeika Blackwell and Yiesha Thompson, two Ph.D. candidates at Howard University. I sincerely appreciate the encouragement that both of you have given me to complete this book.

In addition, I would like to thank all of my colleagues, both past and present, at Murray State University, Mississippi State University, Howard University, and the University of Memphis. Specifically, I would like to thank: Dannie Harrison, former Dean at Murray State University, who provided funding for me to work on the project while I was employed at Murray State, Winfield Rose, Mark Wattier, Mfanya Tryman, Nicholas Amponsah, Cal Clark, Joseph McCormick, and Joy Clay. I would also like to thank the staff at University Press of America and Linda Jackson for preparing the book for publication. A special thanks to Pete Rose for reading the book and making numerous suggestions based on his experience in the Ohio budget office.

Lastly, I dedicate this book to my wife Angela, and daughters Amber and Tiffany.

General Book and Class Guidelines, Suggestions, and Pointers

1. There are several problems at the end of each chapter that require you to use Excel. Copies of partially completed Excel tables are located in the appendix of each chapter. You can also find a complete downloadable Excel spreadsheet for each problem on my website (http://cas.memphis.edu/padm/charles_menifield.htm). Just click on the Budgeting Book Spreadsheets link.

2. Always use Excel formulas to complete mathematical functions in the spreadsheets. Do not use a calculator and plug the numbers into the spreadsheet.

3. Round dollar amounts to the nearest cent unless you are told otherwise. For example, $34.5690 should be rounded to $34.57 and $43.212 should be rounded to $43.21. When using Excel, format dollar amounts using the Excel functions. Dollar amounts should look like a dollar amount rather than just a number. Follow the formats used in the text.

4. Always bring two hard copies and a disk/flashdrive/cd copy of your work to class (whichever is applicable in your setting). Be prepared to share you work on a computer with your class.

5. Make sure that you visually inspect the math in your spreadsheets to ensure that Excel is recalculating any changes that you make.

6. Excel will round numbers differently when different formulas are used. That is, two different students can insert two correct formulas and get slightly different results. Normally, these differences are very minor.

7. When completing an assignment in Excel, you should first type the question (use the crux of the question for longer questions rather than retyping the entire question) and then paste Excel spreadsheets (without the lines), graphs, charts, etc directly into MS Word.

Chapter 1
The Context of Public Sector Budgets

Chapter One Overview

One of the most important facets of a government is the ability to tax and spend. Conceptually, this appears to be an easy to understand phenomenon. However, it is not that simplistic. Budgeting is a two-fold process at the very least. First, someone has to decide how much money the government needs to function. Second, someone has to determine how much funds to allocate to each program/department. Since budgeting involves the allocation of scarce resources it can be a difficult process. While elected officials decided how to allocate funds, collecting revenue is an administrative function. Both procedures can be very complicated, sophisticated, and crucial to the very existence of governments.

The first chapter provides the reader with a general overview of budgets and the processes that go along with them. This includes, but is not limited to: the purpose of a budget, the different types of budgets, sources of revenue and expenditures, government accounting techniques, and audits.

What is a Budget?

A *budget* is a fiscal policy document that outlines revenues and expenditures an organization needs to carry out some specific functions during the course of a set period of time. With respect to the government, this period of time is called a *fiscal year* (FY), a twelve-month period where funds are collected and spent. For example, FY 2009 for most states begins on July 1, 2008 and ends on June 30, 2009. At the end of this period, the budget must be (legally) balanced and available for public scrutiny. The legal requirement for a balanced budget is the primary definitional difference between a public and private budget. States and local governments should not carry *deficits* over to the next fiscal year. However, in many instances, particularly at the fund level, deficits are carried over on the budget basis.

According to Richard Musgrave (1959), three roles emanate from budgets: allocation, distribution and economic development. First, governments have to decide what services will result from the allocation of funds. Second, they determine who will benefit from the distribution of these funds and who will pay for the services. Lastly, they determine what levels of income and job growth are required to maintain stability.

Functions of a Budget

The single most important function of a budget is *accountability*. It is one of many tools that can be used to determine if an organization has accomplished its objectives as laid out by legislative and executive institutions. Legislators and city councilmen alike use these documents when reviewing the activities of public agencies. A budget can also be used to *control* an agency. Legislators and councilmen appropriate funds to an agency based on their strategic priorities. However, if they are dissatisfied with the agency, they have the legal right to withhold funds. A third function of a budget is to *plan*. By organizing costs around some function or activity, agencies have some estimate of what their tasks will cost and how to go about carrying out those tasks. It also forces the agency to meet deadlines and behave in an efficient and effective manner. In harmony with planning are good management skills. Agencies can organize and best utilize personnel by indicating performance standards and objectives. At the end of the fiscal year, an agency can review the year's activities to determine if goals and objectives were met. If resources were not spent in the best manner, changes can be made to remedy the problems (Schick 1966; Bland and Rubin 1997; Howard 2002; Mikesell 2003; Solano 2004; Rubin 2006). In our system of government, no expenditure can be made unless the governing authority-legislature, city council- authorizes it.

Budget Formats

Generally speaking budgets come in three formats: line-item, program, and performance. However, there are also budgeting techniques that can be applied. One seldom used example is *zero-based budgeting*.[1] In this technique, each unit submitting a budget has to justify all of their budget requests from beginning to end without assuming a guaranteed allocation by defacto (see also chapter 7). An agency can also use an *incremental* approach to budgeting where they simply add or subtract from the previous years spending. Although a state or local government may require an agency to submit a certain type of budget, they do have some discretion as to the type of budget that they prefer (Axelrod 1995; Gianakis and McCue 1999; Thurmaier and Willoughby 2001; Smith and Lynch 2004).

First, there is *a line item* or a *traditional budget,* which allocates funds to specific commodities or objects of cost. Emphasis is placed on personnel, supplies, equipment, utilities, contractual services and capital expenditures. Each of these major categories can be broken down into individual items. For example, within personnel cost, there are salaries, fringe benefits (Pensions, social security, health care, etc), retirement, and so on. Capital outlays are for higher costs items that have value for a number of years. This would include items such as buildings, busses, bridges, and equipment (see also chapter 4). Capital outlay equipment also falls into the high cost item category and therefore is not equivalent to equipment used as a major category. Equipment as a major category is for low cost items such as a single computer, a typewriter or a desk (see also chapter 3).

Line-item budgets are probably the easiest of the three types to prepare. They are quick and simple. The major shortcoming of a line item budget is its inability to describe the activities that will be performed by the agency. This type of budget is used for control and accountability. Legislators determine salaries and benefits and can clearly delineate the differences between the various categories. Salaries and benefits constitute the greatest portion of a line item budget. Line-item budgets are useful in that that they provide the exact cost of specific items. This is useful if a budget needs to be cut. Exhibit 1.1 provides a partial example of a line item budget for the Street Department in the city of Clay.

Column one has each of the major categories of expenditures. Even though there is no category for equipment, it is possible to have this category. Whether or not a category is used depends on how the budget staff wants to categorize those items. Again, equipment that does not reach high levels of cost that reoccur over several fiscal years is not included in the capital category. The second column in Exhibit 1.1 represents *actual spending* for fiscal year 2008, while the third column has *estimated spending* for the up-coming fiscal year. In estimating cost, expenditures are rounded to the nearest dollar. However, rounding cannot be used when calculating actual costs. Every last penny must be accounted for in a public budget. Given this detail, line-item budgets should always be placed in a spreadsheet program to ensure fewer mathematical errors. This requirement does not necessarily hold for performance and program budgets due to the vast amount of dialogue that goes into the budget. In these cases, great care should be taken to ensure that there are no math errors.

Mikesell (2003) indicates that the policies of governments dictate using traditional budgets that do not develop long term profiles. This in effect makes it easier to control the agency, but it does not allow for good planning of activities that may be occurring over several years.

The second type of budget is a *program budget*. This budget allocates funds to programs or activities within an organization. A budget of this type would list items in categories by division, department or agency such as public works and public safety along with the cost of operating the agency. Program budgets are advantageous in that they allow programs of a similar nature to be combined rather than split into separate budgets. Program budgets can allow administrators and legislators to plan for not only the current fiscal year, but also for future years. A good program budget lists the goals and objectives of an agency along with the funds that are allocated to achieving those objectives. These goals and objectives should be clear, concise and self-explanatory. This also serves the dual function of preventing redundancy among agencies as well as ensures that the annual review process will flow smoothly. Lastly, program budgets allow for the use of analytical tools to measure costs and benefits.[2]

Exhibit 1.1 Line-Item Budget
Street Department, City of Clay
FY 2008 & FY 2009 Expenditures

Personnel	FY 2008 (Act.)	FY 2009 (Est.)
Salaries	$165,459.78	$179,000.00
Fringe Benefits	22,410.56	25,000.00
Retirement	9,521.13	12,000.00
Insurance	6,510.87	7,000.00
Training	2,750.09	3,000.00
Sub-total	$206,652.43	$226,000.00

Supplies	FY 2007 (Act.)	FY 2008 (Est.)
Disposable Trash Cans	$25,230.25	$29,000.00
Uniforms	6,298.69	7,530.00
Mechanical Brooms	10,498.91	12,300.00
Subtotal	$42,027.85	$48,830.00

Capital Outlay	FY 2007 (Act.)	FY 2008 (Est.)
Equipment	$23,789.90	$28,987.08
Desks	2,987.32	.00
Trucks- F 350	49,874.23	84,890.54
Subtotal	$76,651.45	$113,877.62

TOTAL	$325,331.73	$388,707.62

Program budgets can be written using a variety of different formats. Exhibit 1.2 provides two basic examples for the city of Mitchellville. First, let's take a look at the city's Department of Transportation. Initially, the goal of the organization is stated followed with objectives to accomplishing that goal. This is followed with the budget allocation for the Department.[3]

Exhibit 1.2 Program Budget
City of Mitchellville, 2008-2009 Expenditures

<u>Department of Transportation</u>
The goal of this agency is to provide transportation within the city of Mitchellville in the most effective and efficient manner as possible.

Objectives:
a. Improve the public transit system by evaluating the needs of riders.
b. Maintain the mechanical needs of the buses.
c. Keep the streets clear of snow and other debris.

TOTAL: $454,370.00

Public Works is the second example of a program budget (Exhibit 1.3). Notice how the budget directs attention towards the subject of the expenditure rather than the object of expenditure. In this example, there are two divisions within the department: solid waste and recycling. Although each division has a separate budget, their combined budgets make up the total budget for Public Works. If the budget director requests estimates for future years, you can create a separate budget and modify your objectives and expenditures. If your objectives are the same, you can simply add another column next to the existing expenditure column with the appropriate year.

Exhibit 1.3 Program Budget
City of Graystown, 2008-2009 Expenditures

<u>Department of Public Works</u>
The goal of this agency is ensure that the city can continue to dispose of solid waste in the most effective and efficient manner as possible.

Objectives:
a. Provide for the removal of all solid waste in a cost efficient manner.
b. Establish a recycling program for each community within the city.
c. Enhance public property.

Divisions:
-Solid Waste $100,000.00
-Recycling   75,000.00
TOTAL $175,000.00

The last type of budget discussed is a *performance budget*. A performance budget classifies funds based on some activity and the direct output created by that activity rather than the purchase of resources. This type of budget relies heavily on strategic planning, operational planning and performance accountability. *Strategic planning* is a future oriented process of diagnosis and strategy building. It closely monitors an agency's mission, capacity, and the environment in which it exists. *Operational planning* monitors the allocation of resources on a task-by-task basis in order to ensure that goals and objectives are met. Lastly, *performance accountability* measures progress by results, for example, measuring graduation rates, documenting the number of students in a classroom or measuring the amount of snow removed from streets. The Governmental Accounting Standards Board (GASB) has a concept statement and provides examples and a framework that governments are encouraged to use when formulating accountability measures (see Smith and Lynch 2004, p. 156).

An advantage to using a performance based budget is the direct correlation between spending and services provided (i.e. results). Performance budgets can be very useful for management and accountability for both agency heads and legislators. This, however, is a double edged sword. On the one hand, agency heads must be very specific in detailing their operations. Legislators on the other hand must *appropriate* funds based on performance rather than the normal line-item format (Gianakis and McCue 1999). In a nut shell, this means greater effort on the part of legislators. Unless they have some level of expertise with that particular agency, they may find themselves ignorant of the details of spending and the long-term repercussions of their act. The main benefit of a performance budget is that it allows for the outcomes of spending to be monitored every fiscal year. Hence, they are tied directly to performance reviews. Performance budgets date back to the early 1900s in New York City where attempts were made to bring greater accountability to agency heads and politicians (Mendosa 1983; U.S. General Accounting Office 1993; Lynch 1995).[4]

Exhibit 1.4 provides an example of a performance budget for the city of Angels. Note the exact functions that are to be carried out as a result of the expenditures. In addition, a performance budget can list the result of previous activities. For example, Exhibit 1.4 shows that the number of children using drugs has decreased along with the number of crimes involving children. Also, note that the performance objectives are tied to the performance review.

Unfortunately, one of the problems with performance-based budgets is the inability to relate cause to effect. Why did the crimes decrease? Was it because more emphasis was placed on crime prevention or because people stopped reporting crimes because they do not see any benefit in doing so? These problems are not necessarily limited to performance-based budgets. Similar problems exists with line item and program budgets.

One thing that the reader should recognize is presentation of the budget is very important. It is important that the user examines the budget and navigates through it with relative ease. If items are ambiguous and hard to find, it is a clear sign that the budget should be revised. If it is within their power, legislators and council members do not spend their days and nights working with budgets. As a result, you want the budget to be understandable to the user. You can highlight important items by using the bold function, italics, underlining, and shading functions in your spreadsheet programs. In performance and program budgets, carefully placed words and explanations are also very useful (Seckler-Hudson 2002; Smith and Lynch 2004; see also chapter 8).

Exhibit 1.4 Performance Budget
City of Angels Police Department, FY 2008-2010 Expenditures

Program/Division: D.A.R.E.
Description: Drugs Abuse Resistance Education

Operating Expenses	FY 2008 Actual	FY 2009 Recommended	FY 2010 Projected
Personnel Services	$189,467.23	$199,050.00	$225,000.00
Supplies	32,512.00	39,000.00	45,000.00
Equipment	54,650.15	59,000.00	65,000.00
Printing	20,000.34	25,000.00	28,000.00
TOTAL	$294,629.72	$322,050.00	$363,000.00

Program Performance Objectives:
1. Expand the D.A.R.E. Program to remaining ten additional schools.
2. Involve 40% of the senior police core in the after school program.
3. Increase the number of interactions/meetings with students by 10%.
4. Decrease the number of drug offenses by at least 10% each year.
5. Increase the number of teenage volunteers by at least 10% each year.

Performance Review:

	FY 2008 Actual	FY 2009 Estimated	FY 2010 Projected
1. Number of Teen Participants	159	230	320
2. Number of Teen Volunteers	20	45	55
3. Number of Teen Drug Offenses	120	70	43

Reading a Budget

A good budget should be very user friendly. The lay reader at the very least should be able to determine how much the government intends to collect (revenue), how much the government plans to spend and on what (expenditures). As previously mentioned, there are three basic budget formats and they provide different types of information. However, there are several things that each of these have in common.[5]

1. *Budget Message/Budget Highlights/Executive Summary*: A good budget always has a message, usually in the form of a letter from the governor of the state or mayor of the city directed to the state legislature or city council. This message should indicate the law or statute that requires the submission of the budget and the time period that it covers. The message should also indicate the amount of revenue that is expected during the fiscal year and whether or not this is an increase or decrease. If the legislative body governing the state or locality has recommended changes in budget allocations, those items should be indicated. If cuts were made, the reader should see what departments were cut in the message. If new programs were established or expanded, these should be highlighted. The letter should be followed with a table of contents outlining the remainder of the budget (see Appendix 1A for an example of a Budget Letter).

2. *Budget Summary*: The budget summary is normally a spreadsheet document indicating all of the revenue sources by type (includes: property taxes, sales taxes, user fees, etc.) and the expenditures by type (each agency or department should be listed). Small cities with limited revenue sources will frequently use this format. It is important that each fund is clearly labeled (see Appendix 1B for an example).

3. *Source of Revenue*: This section should detail to the reader exactly where all the revenue came from and the changes that occurred from previous fiscal years. Each source of revenue should be listed with, at a minimum, the actuals for the previous fiscal year, estimates for the current year, and the projections for the budgeted year. This page allows the reader to see not only the overall growth of the budget over the past years, but also which revenue source is growing and which is decreasing (see Appendix 1C for an example).

4. *Source of Expenditures*: This section lists the major expense categories: personnel, operating, capital expenditures, and special appropriations for the entire government. You can also list the various departments by fiscal year along with the expenditures. A program or performance budget can follow the same format by listing the program or activity that is in use. Again, each of these categories show the comparisons between the current fiscal year and the previous two fiscal years with a column for the actual dollar amount change and the percent change from the previous fiscal year (see Appendix 1D for an example).

5. *Department/Agency Budget Information*: The bulk of the budget contains the individual budget requests for each department. There are several good ways to prepare this information in an efficient manner. The first way is to list the various line item expenditures of the department in the right hand column and then

indicate the changes in the budget by fiscal years. On a second page, you should list the fund sources for that department and the changes that have occurred over the previous fiscal years. Again, the presentation of this information will vary with respect to the type of budget. To say the least, the reader should be able to determine exactly how much revenue is coming into the department and what it is used for. Since most agencies are balancing the budget from previous fiscal years, the spreadsheet should provide the reader with the amount of allocations from the previous two fiscal years along with the percent change in both dollar amount and percentage change (see Appendix 1E for an example).

6. *Supplemental Budgeting Information*: The budget document should provide the reader with any new laws, statutes, rules, or ordinances that affect the budget document. This is particularly true for capital improvement projects. Again, if necessary, a spreadsheet should be created for these projects in a format similar to the previous documents.

Public Versus Private Budgets

Although there are many common themes that exist in all budgets, public budgeting does differ from the private sector in many respects. First, public budgeting often involves the interaction of many actors involved with a variety of different agendas. Private budgeting may involve one or a few personnel regardless to the size of the organization. Second, funds that are spent and collected in the public sector are collected from tax payers who may or may not want the monies to be collected and spent and may not receive any direct services as a result of paying the tax. On the other hand, monies collected in the private sector are not compulsory and services are directed accordingly. Third, public budgets are public documents and therefore are open to be scrutinized by citizens, while private budgets are not. Fourth, public budgets are well designed documents that are written to last an entire fiscal year (or two). Hence, they are not very flexible. When crisis or other unplanned events occur, it can be catastrophic to budget analysts as well as elected officials. Private budgets are very flexible and can be changed at a moments notice in order to move with changes in the economy, budget shortfalls, etc. Fifth, the number of rules and actors involved in public budgeting far surpasses that in the private sector. For example, there may be rules affecting expenditures, tax collection, balancing the budgets, assessments, mandates, etc. While there may be rules applied in the private sector, the process does not tend to be overly bureaucratized (Rubin 2006). Last, appropriation acts and ordinances are legal documents that place limits on spending. Many governments have severe penalties for overspending appropriations, including jail time.

Overview of Revenues and Expenditures

State and local revenues come from a variety of sources.[6] *Revenues* are the monies collected by all levels of government to pay for the operation of government. *Expenditures* are financial obligations that flow from the operation of government. The major source of revenue for state and local governments is taxes. For some states, *income taxes* make up the greater proportion of taxes collected. Unlike state governments, some local governments have the option of collecting payroll taxes (income taxes). These taxes can be used for special purposes or serve as additional income for the local government. Income taxes are deducted directly from individual earnings and are compulsory. State income tax rates tend to be lower than federal income taxes. They are *progressive taxes*. That is, higher income individuals pay more taxes than lower income individuals. Although corporations pay income taxes, they tend to be a much lower percentage of all taxes collected. Individual income taxes make up about one-third of all taxes collected in a state. All states do not have state income taxes (Mikesell 2004; Bland 2005).

The second major source of revenue in a state (and in some localities) comes from *sales and use taxes*. These are taxes placed on goods and services. Sales taxes are considered *regressive taxes*. Citizens pay the same rate regardless of their income level. Each state sets its own sales tax rate. States and localities also have some discretion as to what items will be assessed sales taxes. For example, sales taxes are not applied to the sale of un-prepared foods in Kentucky. Other sources of revenue for the state include: tobacco, alcohol, petroleum product taxes, inheritance taxes, automobile taxes, and public utility taxes.

States also get a large amount of revenue from the federal government in the form of *grants*. Grants come in two major forms: categorical and block. *Categorical grants* make up the largest type of grants that a state receives. A categorical grant is used for a specific program and has very strict guidelines for the activities to be carried out within a specific time period. Categorical grants exploded during Johnson's Great Society programs in the 1960s. Formula and project grants fall within the umbrella of categorical grants. *Formula grants* use a distribution formula to determine the amount to be allocated to the state or locality. Population, geography, income and education are variables that are used in formula grants. A *block grant* is used for broad policy areas. It can be used for a variety of programs and activities by state and local governments.

A major source of revenue for local governments is *property taxes*. These are taxes levied against real property, perhaps personal property and private utilities. Many local governments have the ability to impose sales taxes. The taxes are piggy-backed onto state sales taxes for collection efficiency. Many local government have the ability to impose license fees on motor vehicles. Another source of revenue for local governments is licenses and permits, franchise fees and user charges. A *license fee* is a flat rate tax for business entities. The cost of the license fee differs by activity. For example, the cost of a hunting license is different from that of a license to operate a restaurant. Without a license, an individual or business is forbidden to engage in the activity legally. The owner of a license does not receive any specific government service by having the license. Under normal circumstances, everyone who applies for a license receives it (Bland 2005; Raphaelson 2004).

A *franchise fee* appears to be closely related to a license fee, but there are some subtle differences. Franchises are provided on a very limited basis. A franchise presupposes that the business will serve the entire community, operate with a certain quality and rate, and outlines the responsibility of the owner and the government. A *user charge* is a fee charged to individuals who voluntarily use a publicly provided service. For example, large municipalities may implement a toll charge to pay for the construction of a new road. If you do not use the new road, then you do not pay the charge. The purpose of a user charge is to relieve the financial burden placed on the general revenue system. In most cases, user charges are geared toward the population that is benefiting from the public service. User charges are useless if they are not enforceable (Bierhanzl and Downing 2004).

Another source of revenue for local governments is the proceeds from *public utilities*. Public utilities are government owned business. These include but are not limited to water utilities, gas utilities, electric utilities, sewers, and intercity transit. These government businesses have little or no competition (*monopoly*). One of the newest forms of revenues for states and local governments are the revenues collected from casinos, lotteries, and other forms of gambling.

Although *bonds* are not considered a source of revenue in most cities and states, they do serve as a major source of funds for the construction of public buildings, schools and other bid ticket items. A bond is basically money that is borrowed from an individual with the assurance that the bond can be cashed in a given period of time for a sum of money (principal and interest). State and local governments use bonds to finance projects that cannot be financed from the current revenue sources. The interest earned on bonds is not taxable by the United States government. There are two types of bonds: full faith and credit bonds (general obligation bonds) and non-guaranteed bonds. General obligation bonds are paid for out of the general revenue fund and are guaranteed by the state or local government that issued them. Non-guaranteed bonds have a limited backing, usually from a revenue source such as water and sewer revenue. The only backing is the revenue stream that is pledged to repay the debt. (Lee and Johnson 1998; Vogt 2004; Bland 2005).

Taxes and other sources of revenue are used to pay for government *expenditures*. An expenditure is "the disbursement of money to cover the costs of a governmental agency's operation" (Riley and Colby 1991). The majority of revenues collected by local governments are used toward the payment of salaries and fringe benefits to employees. In addition to personnel cost, supplies, equipment, contractual services and *capital outlays* make up the vast amount of the budget. Capital outlays are monies allocated for big ticket items that cannot be completed in a single fiscal year. Normally, personnel cost will range from 65%-75% of a local budget. States typically have large expenditures for transfer payments to local governments or individuals, such as primary and secondary education allocations to school districts, payments to institutions of higher education, and Medicaid payments for low income individual. The operating expenditures for states typically make up only 35%-45% of total spending. The percentage change would depend on the function of an agency. For example, police and fire departments have higher equipment cost than an auditor's office.

Tables 1.1 and 1.2 provide examples of a revenue and expenditure summary for the city of Dresden and the state of Nowhere respectively. Table 1.1 shows that property taxes tend to make up the greater portion of all taxes collected by local governments, followed by sales taxes. In the expenditure column, the Executive and Highway and Streets departments have the largest budgets. A line item budget for each of these divisions would reveal that the majority of the budget is used for personnel services.

Table 1.1 Estimated Revenues and Expenditures
City of Dresden (FY 2009)

Sources of Revenue	Amount
1. Property Tax	$361,250.00
2. Local Sales Tax	232,979.00
3. Beer Tax	59,752.00
4. State Sales Tax	153,000.00
5. State Petroleum Tax	59,500.00
6. Automobile Registration	15,725.00
7. Minimum Business Tax	21,482.00
8. Corporate Excise Tax	12,750.00
9. Solid Waste Fund	154,445.00
10. Debt Service Fund	65,025.00
11. Water and Sewer Fund	642,485.00
12. Other	120,210.00
TOTAL	$1,899,450.00

Sources of Expenditures	Amount
1. Executive Department	$282,455.00
2. City Recorder	133,790.00
3. Police	199,494.00
4. Fire	56,396.00
5. Highways and Streets	292, 570.00
6. Playgrounds	64,770.00
7. Solid Waste	136,000.00
8. Water Utilities	218,926.00
9. Non-Operating Exp.	95,200.00
10.Bond Principal	60,106.00
11. Libraries	12,750.00
12. Other	346,993.00
TOTAL	$1,899,450.00

Table 1.2 shows that half of the revenue collected by the State of Nowhere comes from taxes. It is also noteworthy to mention that expenditures are typically listed by department in a "line-item" format. However, in a summary expenditure sheet, such as this one, there is no need to break down expenditures into sub-categories that detail personnel, equipment and capital outlays (Bahl 2004). That information would be provided in the individual agency line-item budget sheets (see Appendix1A).

Table 1.2 Estimated Revenues and Expenditures, FY 2009
State of Nowhere (in billions)

Sources of Revenues		Sources of Expenditures	
1. Tax Collections	$43.5	1.General Government	$2.1
2. Federal Funds	25.4	2. Health and Human Services	26.1
3. Licenses and Fees	7.4	3. Public Education	26.4
4. Lottery	4.4	4. Higher Education	11.9
5. Interest Income	3.9	5. Public Safety	7.0
6. Other Revenue Sources	2.7	6. Natural Resources	1.7
TOTAL	$87.3	7. Business and Economic Dev.	10.3
		8. Other	3.7
		TOTAL	$87.1

Governmental Accounting

One of the most important functions of state and local governments is to maintain a meticulous accounting record. Unlike individuals who are paid a certain amount of dollars at some set period, governments receive various amount of money throughout the course of a fiscal year. Hence, they must allocate and manage funds in order to cover all expenditures. State and local governments typically use a *fund accounting system*. The Governmental Accounting Standards Board (GASB) establishes accounting and reporting standards for state and local governments. This board created what is called Generally Accepted Accounting Principles (GAAP). Audits of state and local governments are performed based on GAAP and an opinion is rendered by an auditor. The federal government requires all governmental units receiving federal funds to adhere to the principles outlined in GAAP.[7] The GASB provides standards for reporting but not budgeting. There are no standards for budgeting unless they are established by state law.

Governmental accounting normally takes three forms: cash basis, modified accrual and full accrual. A *cash basis* system is very comparable to your checking account system. Budget officials basically add the revenue to an account when they literally receive the funds in their hands. On the expenditure side of the equation, funds are subtracted from an account as soon as they are spent. This technique will work for all sorts of accounts, but is not necessarily the best system for all accounts (Table 1.3).

Similar to a cash basis system, a *modified accrual* system records revenue when the funds are measurable and available. Measurable means the amount is known and available means that it is received during the year or soon enough after the end of the year so that obligations for that year can be paid. This period is typically 60-120 days. However, expenditures are recorded when a fund liability is incurred. A *full accrual* system records revenue as it is earned regardless to whether the revenue has been received. For example, property taxes are recorded when the bill is mailed (earned) rather than when the bill is paid. A full accrual system records expenses when a financial obligation is incurred. The accrual basis of accounting is used primarily for matching revenues to the cost of production. The basis of accounting for state and local governments is prescribed by the GASB based on the fund type that is involved.

Budgeting takes place on a prospective basis. That is, funds are deducted as soon as a commitment is made. For example, the Transportation Department gave a contract to Whitley's Construction Company to repair the city's streets. As a result, the dollar amount of the contract is immediately deducted from the department's budget even though the payment has not been made. The accounting system will not record an obligation until services have been rendered.

Table 1.3
Accounting Methods

Cash Basis System:
a. Revenue is recorded when the funds are received.
b. Expenditures are recorded when the funds are spent.

Modified Accrual:
a. Revenue is recorded when the funds are measurable and available.
b. Expenditures are recorded when a fund obligation is made.

Full Accrual:
a. Revenue is recorded when actually earned or when the government established a claim.
b. Expenses are recorded when a financial obligation is made.

Governments tend to be financially conservative when it comes to estimating or forecasting revenue. For example, local governments do not count on collecting 100% of the property tax, so they normally estimate anywhere from 90-95% based on the collection trend.

As a result, most governments use the cash basis for budgeting taxes in general, although some use the modified accrual method. Some use a hybrid system—modified accrual for some sources and cash for others. The federal government uses the cash basis system except for interest and credit programs (Analytical Perspectives: Budget of the U.S. Government, 2004, 470). Private entities tend to use the accrual method since the objective is to match expenses to revenue. As revenue comes in, it is placed into separate *funds*. GAAP sets up three classes of funds—governmental, proprietary and fiduciary. Governmental funds are those that are used to carry out basic government services and are primarily supported through taxes and shared revenues. Proprietary funds are business-type in nature and are similar to those used in the private sector. Fiduciary funds are used to account for assets that are held by the government as an agent or trustee. Fiduciary funds are not used to carry out government activities. Within each class of funds, there are several types of fund. Funds act as fiscal control agents. That is, they force governments to spend the money for the purpose that it was created.

The largest classes of funds are *governmental funds*. There are five types of funds within this class: General Fund, Special Revenue Funds, Debt Service Funds, Capital Project Funds, and permanent. With regard to the number of funds a government can have, the only limit involves the General Fund—there can only be one. GASB recommends that only the minimum number of funds needed for legal and operating requirements should be established. It is common for governments to have more funds for budgeting purposes than for external reporting purposes. For external reporting, governments tend to combine like funds, such as federal grant funds (GASB Codification Section 1100).

Basic Types of Funds

- *General Fund* includes all revenue not designated in another fund. It is the largest fund. An example of revenue that goes into this fund is property taxes, license fees, and income taxes.
- *Special Service Funds* are designed for earmarked revenue. Revenues that are designated for special purposes. Taxes on petroleum products would go into this fund. Governments frequently use grant funds in special revenue funds to ensure that monies are *allocated* for the designed purpose. A government is not limited to the total number of special revenue funds that it may have.
- *Debt Service Funds* are funds designed to collect revenue for the repayment of long term debt. Revenue in this fund frequently comes from transfers from the general fund. The purpose of the fund is to ensure that revenues are set aside for the repayment of debt. General obligation bonds are included in this fund. There are no limits on the number of debt service funds.
- *Capital Project Funds* are designed to collect revenue for the purchase and construction of capital projects. The proceeds from the issuance of bonds would go into this fund.
- *Permanent Funds* are used to report resources that are legally restricted to the extent that only earnings, and not principal, may be used for purposes that support the government's programs. For example, money may be donated to the government to maintain a cemetery and provides that only the earnings from investments can be used for that purpose.

Proprietary funds are for public service activities that resemble those of the private sector, proprietary or business like activities. This would include for example the use of a public gas company or a golf course. There are two types of proprietary funds: enterprise funds and internal service funds.

Proprietary Funds

- *Enterprise Funds* contain revenues collected from individuals external to the government. These are collected on a fee basis.
- *Internal Service Funds* contain revenue from agencies within the government for services rendered.

Enterprise funds operate much like that of a private sector business. They collect most of their revenue from user charges. For example, drivers pay a fee to cross the Bay Bridge from Oakland to San Francisco. Other examples would include public utility companies, public transportation, and government owned public radio and television stations. The purpose of this fund is to determine if the entity is collecting enough revenue to maintain its existence.

Unlike enterprise funds, internal service funds are used within the government and provide a service to other government agencies rather than the public at large. For example, the city of Birmingham, Alabama has a central motor pool that provides transportation services for all of the cities agencies. When a car needs to be repaired, the city garage repairs it. Revenues are shifted to this department from other departments when services are rendered. Since most agencies have funds dedicated for this service, they are likely to use it. There is no charge unless the service is used.[8]

The distinction between an enterprise fund and internal service fund is the primary customer. If the primary customer is outside the government, an enterprise fund is used. If it is within the government, an internal service fund is used.

There are also other types of funds that may be used by state and local governments. The first type is fiduciary funds. *Fiduciary funds* are essentially revenue held for other individuals or government organizations. There are four types of fiduciary funds: pension trust funds (and other employee benefit trust funds), investment trust funds, private-purpose trust funds and agency funds.

Fiduciary Funds

- *Pension (and other Employee Benefit) Trust Funds* hold monies for government employee's pension plans, other post employment benefits, or other employee benefit plans. This is usually the largest type of fiduciary fund.
- *Investment Trust Funds* are used to report the external portion of investment pools reported by the sponsoring government.
- *Private-purpose Trusts* are used to report trust arrangements under which the principal and interest benefit individuals, private corporations, or other governments.
- *Agency Funds* hold monies in a purely custodial capacity for individuals or other governments.

Conclusion

As the chapter shows, elected officials can use the budget as a tool to control the bureaucracy, as a plan of action, and to create accountability. The type of budget used plays a significant role in the information that is conveyed.

Elected officials frequently do not have in depth knowledge of all the agencies that they ultimately govern. As a result, the type of budget used can serve several purposes. Similarly, the type of accounting methods used can affect how the monies can be spent. The next chapter will show the reader how elected officials close this information gap.

Important Terms and Phrases

Accrual Accounting	General Obligation Bonds
Agency Fund	Grant
Allocation	Income Tax
Audits	Internal Service Fund
Appropriations	License Fee
Balanced Budget	Line Item Budget
Block Grant	Modified Accrual Accounting
Bonds	Monopoly
Budget	Non-Expendable Trust Fund
Cash Basis Accounting	Outlay
Capital Project Fund	Performance Accountability
Capital Outlay	Performance Budget
Categorical Grant	Program Audit
Debt Service Fund	Program Budget
Deficit	Progressive Tax
Earmarked Fund	Project Grant
Economy and Efficiency Audit	Property Tax
Enterprise Fund	Proprietary Fund
Expendable Trust Fund	Public Utilities
Expenditures	Regressive Tax
Fiduciary Fund	Revenue
Financial Audit	Sales Tax
Fiscal Year	Set Asides
Franchise Fee	Single Audit
Formula Grant	Special Revenue Fund
Fund	Tax
Fund Accounting System	User Charge
General Fund	Zero Based Budgeting

Chapter 1 Homework Exercises

Directions: Please read each question in its entirety prior to completing the assignment.

1. You have been chosen by Mayor Moses to direct the newly created Recycle Department for the City of Port Arthur. She has also requested that you provide budget estimates for FY 2009 and budget projections for FY 2010. Design a simple line-item, performance, and program budget for the department using the directions that are listed below. Treat each of your budgets as separate entities. Your budgets cannot exceed: $350,000.00 in FY 2009; and $390,000.00 in FY 2010.

A. *Line Item Budget*: In your line-item budget, I want you to use the categories (personnel, operating and capital outlay) that are listed in the text. You are free to spend the funds any way that you see fit. However, remember that personnel costs usually consume the majority of a budget.

B. *Program Budget*: Consider the different types of activities (divisions) that a recycling department would be engaged in (recycling glass, paper, plastic, aluminum, etc). If your goals or objectives change in the second year, you will need another column or a separate budget with the new divisions, etc.

C. *Performance Budget:* Set some specific goals that you can attain for any of the divisions that you created in your performance budget (i.e., collect 6 tons of paper during the first year of operation).

Suggestion: In addition to staff, a Recycling Department may need the following: recycling bins, aluminum compressors, trucks, marketing brochures, and trailers.

2. Based on the information in the text and the goals and objectives that you have established for the Port Arthur Recycle Department in Question 1 respond to these questions.

A. Which one of these three budgets best describes what the Recycle Department does? Explain your answer.

B. Which one of these three budgets gives: the director of the department/agency; the mayor; and the legislative body, the most

discretion/latitude in making decisions about the agency?
Think about the roles of these persons prior to answering the
question. Explain each response separately.

3. From the perspective of a bureaucrat, which government accounting method
is more feasible for each revenue source? Cash Basis, Modified Accrual or Full
Accrual. Explain your response. The key to your response should be stability of
the revenue source over time. For example, if user fees are not stable over time
or over a short period, a cash basis system would be better. However, if the user
fee is stable, then an accrual system may be better. Further, you should consider
whether the revenue source can be broken down into components parts. For example, user fees collected from a street meter may differ in stability from user
fees collected at a toll. Further, you should realize that the amount and percentage of revenues collected from each source can vary from year to year depending on any number of social, political and economic factors. In any event, be
specific and justify your response. It may be useful to review Chapter 5, "Funding State and Local Budgets" prior to responding to this question.

   A. Property Taxes   D. Block Grants   G. Gaming Fees
   B. Sales Taxes   E. Licenses and Fees   H. Motor Fuel Taxes
   C. Donations   F. Public Utility Fees I. State Income Taxes

4. Define each of the following terms:

   A. Recommended Budget   D. Appropriated Budget
   B. Projected Budget   E. Actual Budget
   C. Estimated Budget

5. Go to a local or state government budget office and request a copy of their
budget (some local and state budgets are on the Internet, see Appendix 1F for a
list of state government websites). Based on the contents of the budget, decide
whether or not it is "good" using the information in the section titled "Reading
the Budget" in the text. A summary of the headings is provided at the end of the
question. In addition, the Government Finance Officers Association
(http://www.gfoa.org/) has a Distinguished Budgeting Awards program where
they award governments for budgets that meet "best practices." Feel free to utilize their criteria as well. Justify your responses and attach a copy of pertinent
sections of the budget your homework assignment that support your responses.
Do not copy and turn in the entire budget. Pertinent sections should not exceed 7
pages. Note: This question should be answered using the headings provided below along with any other items that you deem worthy from the GFOA web site.

Budget Evaluation

    A.   Budget Message/Budget Highlights/Executive Summary
    B.   Budget Summary
    C.   Source of Revenue
    D.   Source of Expenditures
    E.   Department/Agency Budget Information
    F.   Supplemental Budgeting Information

References

Analytical Perspectives: Budget of the United States Government. 2004. U.S. Government Printing Office.

Axelrod, Donald. 1995. *Budgeting for Modern Government.* 2nd Edition. New York: St. Martins Press, Inc.

Bahl Jr., Roy W. 2004. "Local Government Expenditures and Revenues." In J. Richard Aronson and Eli Schwartz's *Management Policies in Local Government Finance.* 5th Edition. Washington, D.C.: ICMA.

Bierhanzl, Edward J. and Paul B. Downing 2004. "User Charges and Special Districts." In J. Richard Aronson and Eli Schwartz's *Management Policies in Local Government Finance.* 5th Edition. Washington, D.C.: ICMA.

Bland, Robert L. 2005. *A Revenue Guide for Local Government.* Washington, D.C.: ICMA.

Bland, Robert L. and Irene S. Rubin. 1997. *Budgeting: A Guide for Local Governments.* Washington, D.C.: ICMA.

Carney, James D. and Stanley Schoenfeld. 1996. "How To Read a Budget." In *Budgeting Formulation and Execution.* Eds. Jack Rabin, W. Bartley Hildreth, and Gerald J. Miller. Athens, GA: Carl Vinson Institute of Government, University of Georgia.

Gianakis, Gerasimos A. and Clifford P. McCue. 1999. *Local Government Budgeting: A Managerial Approach.* West Port, CT: Praeger.

Government Finance Officers Association. http://www.gfoa.org.

Howard, S. Kenneth. 2002. "Planning and Budgeting: Who's On First." In Albert C. Hyde's *Government Budgeting: Theory, Process, and Politics.* Toronto, Canada: Wadsworth.

Kittredge, William P. and Sarah M. Ouart. 2005. *Budget Manual for Georgia Local Government.* Athens, GA: Vinson Institute.

Lee, Robert D. and Ronald W. Johnson. 1998. *Public Budgeting Systems.* 6th ed. Gaithersburg, MD: Aspen Publishers.

Lynch, Thomas D. 1995. *Public Budgeting in America.* 4th ed. Englewood Cliffs, NJ: Prentice Hall.

Mendosa, Arthur A. 1983. "Budgeting." In *Budget Management: A Reader in Local Government Financial Management.* Eds. Jack Rabin, W. Bartley Hildreth, and Gerald J. Miller. Athens, GA: Carl Vinson Institute of Government, University of Georgia.

Mikesell, John L. 2003. *Fiscal Administration: Analysis and Applications for the Public Sector*. 6th Ed. Belmont, CA: Harcourt Brace Publishers.

Mikesell, John L. 2004. "General Sales, Income, and Other Nonproperty Taxes." In J. Richard Aronson and Eli Schwartz's *Management Policies in Local Government Finance*. 5th Edition. Washington, D.C.: ICMA.

Mills, Patti A. and Jennie L. Mitchell. 1997. "Cash Basis Financial Reporting for Local Government: A Comparison with GAAP. In *Case Studies in Public Budgeting and Financial Management*. Eds. Aman Khan and W. Bartley Hildreth. Dubuque, IA: Kendall Hunt Publishing.

Musgrave, Richard. 1959. *The Theory of Public Finance: A Study in Public Economy*. NY: McGraw Hill.

Novick, David. 2002. "What Program Budgeting Is and Is Not." In Albert C. Hyde's *Government Budgeting: Theory, Process, and Politics*. Toronto, Canada: Wadsworth.

Raphaelson, Arnold H. 2004. "The Property Tax." In J. Richard Aronson and Eli Schwartz's *Management Policies in Local Government Finance*. 5th Edition. Washington, D.C.: ICMA.

Riley, Susan L. and Peter W. Colby. 1991. *Practical Government Budgeting: A Workbook for Public Managers*. Albany NY: State University of New York Press.

Rubin, Irene S. 2006. *The Politics of Public Budgeting: Getting and Spending, Borrowing and Balancing*. 5th ed. Washington, D.C.: CQ Press.

Schick, Allen. "The Road to PPB: The Stages of Budget Reform." *Public Administration Review*. 26: 245-256.

Seckler-Hudson, Catheryn. 2002. "Performance Budgeting in Government. In Albert C. Hyde's *Government Budgeting: Theory, Process, and Politics*. Toronto, Canada: Wadsworth.

Smith, Robert W. and Thomas D. Lynch. 2004. *Public Budgeting in America*. 5th ed. Upper Saddle River, NJ: Pearson/Prentice Hall.

Solano, Paul L. 2004. "Budgeting." In J. Richard Aronson and Eli Schwartz's *Management Policies in Local Government Finance*. 5th Edition. Washington, D.C.: ICMA.

Thurmaier, Kurt M. and Katherine G. Willoughby. 2001. *Policy and Politics in State Budgeting*. Armonk, NY: M.E. Sharpe.

Vogt, A. John. 2004. *Capital Budgeting and Finance: A Guide for Governments.* Washington, D.C.: ICMA.

Appendix 1A
Budget Letter

January 26, 2005

TO THE GENERAL ASSEMBLY AND THE PEOPLE OF MISSOURI:

It is critical for the future of this state that we move Missouri in a new direction. We must move Missouri toward conscientious stewardship of the hard-earned tax dollars that Missourians send to their state capitol. The wisdom, energy, innovation, thrift, and commitment to service that are demonstrated by the citizens of this state must be reflected in their government. It is my greatest hope that this budget and enactment of meaningful legislation designed to strengthen our schools and foster job creation will chart a new course for our state- one of hope and prosperity for all.

The spending that this budget does define focuses on several key priorities:

- Increased funding for education. Missouri's Constitution declares that public education must be our first commitment. Even if we were not legally bound, we would be morally bound to serve the children of our state and the families who have placed their confidence in us. My budget reflects with commitment by increasing funding for education by $170.6 million.

- Achieve a structural balance for state government. Past budgets have relied heavily on special one-time monies without addressing a deep structural imbalance that existed. This budget matches incoming state revenues with expenditures. This, the first of several significant steps towards restructuring state government, improves and solidifies Missouri's financial position.

- Foster economic development. If our state's revenue is to grow to meet our needs, then we must increase the number of quality employment opportunities for Missourians. Future budgets will rely upon economic growth. The budget also reflects my interest in developing nationally leading industries in numerous areas, including technology, biomedical research, life sciences, and renewable fuels.

The budget I submit to you is build around my belief that Missourians pay enough taxes. I am opposed to increasing the tax burden imposed on the people of this state and my budget reflects that. Our state government must live within its means. This budget rededicates state government to the noble idea that it should function as an innovative, efficient, and conscientious servant of the people.

I am grateful for the confidence Missourians have placed in me and look forward to working with the General Assembly to enact my Fiscal Year 2006 budget and legislative initiatives.

Sincerely,

Matt Blunt, Governor of Missouri

Fiscal Year 2007 Annual Report of the Comptroller on Capital Debt and Obligations Executive Summary

December 07, 2006

Debt is issued by the City of New York (the "City"), or on behalf of the City, through a number of different mechanisms. This report assesses the debt condition of the City of New York in accordance with Section 232 of the City Charter. The Charter requires the Comptroller to report the amount of debt the City may incur for capital projects during the current fiscal year and each of the three succeeding fiscal years.

New York City's general debt limit, as provided in the New York State Constitution, is 10 percent of the five-year rolling average of the full value of taxable City real property. The City's FY 2007 general debt-incurring power of $53.34 billion is projected to rise to $59.8 billion in FY 2008, $63.43 billion in FY 2009, and $65.15 billion in FY 2010. The City's General Obligation (GO) debt was $35.07 billion at the beginning of FY 2007. After including contract and other liability and adjusting for appropriations, the City's indebtedness that is counted toward the debt limit totaled $39.71 billion at the beginning of FY 2007, as shown in the Debt-Incurring Power table (on page iv). The City's indebtedness is expected to grow to $55.04 billion by the beginning of FY 2010. New York City has the largest population of any city in the U.S., and it is obligated to maintain a complex and aging infrastructure. The City bears responsibilities for more school buildings, firehouses, health facilities, community colleges, roads, bridges, libraries, and police precincts than any other municipality in the country. Capital bond proceeds are used for the construction and rehabilitation of these facilities. Bond proceeds are also used for financing shorter-lived capital items such as comprehensive computer systems.

In addition to GO bonds, the City maintains several additional credits, including bonds issued by the New York City Transitional Finance Authority (NYCTFA) and TSASC, Inc. The debt-incurring capacities of NYCTFA and TSASC total $17.3 billion of which $12.8 billion has been utilized to finance the City's capital program. Also included in the $17.3 billion capacity is $2.0 billion of recovery bonds issued for general fund expenses in the aftermath of the World Trade Center disaster. After adjusting for the benefit of the remaining NYCTFA debt-incurring power, the City was below its general debt limit by $13.62 billion on July 1, 2006 and is projected to have remaining debt-incurring capacity of $15.79 billion on July 1, 2007, $14.17 billion on July 1, 2008, and $12.11 billion on July 1, 2009.

Debt per capita, which amounted to $2,490 in FY 1990 grew to $6,801 by FY 2006, an increase of 173 percent. Over the same period, the cumulative growth rate in debt per capita exceeded the rate of inflation by 112 percentage points and the growth rate of City tax revenues by 45 percentage points. Based on an analysis of financial statements released by other jurisdictions, New York City leads a sample of large U.S. cities in debt burden per capita by a margin of 2.5 to one.

The City continues to have good access to the public credit markets. The City's credit ratings are A1 by Moody's Investor Service, AA- by Standard & Poor's, and A+ by Fitch Ratings.

Source: http://www.comptroller.nyc.gov/bureaus/bud/Summary_budget_report.shtm

Appendix 1B

City of Cambridge
Budget Summary
FY 2008-2009

	General Fund	Central Garage	Water &Sewer	Sanitation	Grand Total
FUNDING SOURCE					
Property Taxes	$1,483,000	$0	$0	$0	$1,483,000
Insurance Taxes	885,000	-	41,500	-	926,500
Vehicle Stickers	420,000	-	-	-	420,000
Business Licenses	350,000	-	-	-	350,000
User Charges	-	116,250	3,421,500	1,884,000	5,421,750
Special Assessments	-	-	195,000	50,000	245,000
Other & Misc.	662,779	-	-	-	662,779
Fund Transfers	-	-	-	-	-
TOTAL Revenues	$3,800,779	$116,250	$3,658,000	$1,934,000	$9,509,029
Beginning Fund	650,000	-	-	50,600	700,600
TOTAL Available Funds	$4,450,779	$116,250	$3,658,000	$1,984,600	$10,209,629
EXPENDITURES					
General Government	$1,309,454	$0	$0	$0	$1,309,454
Public Safety	2,781,100	-	-	-	2,781,100
Public Works	360,225	-	-	-	360,225
Central Garage	-	116,250	-	-	116,250
Sanitation	-	-	-	1,984,600	1,984,600
Water &Sewer Oper.	-	-	3,658,000	-	3,658,000
Cemetery Operations	-	-	-	-	-
Gas System Oper.	-	-	-	-	-
Capital Expenditures	-	-	-	-	-
TOTAL Expenditures	$4,450,779	$116,250	$3,658,000	$1,984,600	$10,209,629

Appendix 1C

San Pablo
Sources of Revenue

	FY 2007 Est.	FY 2008 Est.	FY 2009 Est.	Net Change	% Change
BALANCE FORWARD	$525,756.30	$174,868.50	$50,621.10		
Sales and Use Tax	$2,555,557.00	$2,715,000.00	$2,875,500.00	$160,500.00	5.91%
Income Tax-Ind.	2,095,499.10	2,299,760.00	2,472,728.00	172,968.00	7.52%
Income Tax-Corp.	496,023.90	512,000.00	512,000.00	0.00	0.00%
Other	708,760.60	657,882.90	674,568.80	16,685.90	2.54%
TOTAL Base Revenue	$6,381,596.90	$6,359,511.40	$6,585,417.90	$350,153.90	5.51%

Appendix 1D

Source of Expenditures
Nowhere Mississippi (amounts in millions)

	FY 2008 App.	FY 2009 Request	Net Change	% Change
General Government	$2,345.00	$2,498.00	$153.00	6.52%
Public Safety	7,129.00	7,893.00	764.00	10.72%
Health and Human Services	27,189.00	31,890.00	4,701.00	17.29%
Public Education	28,000.00	30,000.00	2,000.00	7.14%
Higher Education	13,685.00	14,589.00	904.00	6.61%
Judiciary	386.00	399.00	13.00	3.37%
Natural Resources	1,693.00	1,785.00	92.00	5.43%
Business & Economic Dev.	10,456.00	11,000.00	544.00	5.20%
Regulatory	456.00	469.00	13.00	2.85%
Article IX	721.00	732.00	11.00	1.53%
Other	250.00	255.00	5.00	2.00%
DEPARTMENT TOTAL	$92,310.00	$101,510.00	$9,200.00	9.97%

Appendix 1E

City of Hardin
Fire Dept

	FY 2007 Actual	FY 2008 Budg.	FY 2009 Est.	Net Change	% Change
SALARIES	$658,939.00	$731,000.00	$765,000.00	$34,000.00	4.65%
Education	150.00	500.00	500.00	0.00	0.00%
Life Insurance	1,268.00	2,150.00	1,500.00	-650.00	-30.23%
Medical Insurance	110,467.00	120,000.00	120,000.00	0.00	0.00%
Social Security	51,689.00	57,500.00	57,500.00	0.00	0.00%
State Incentive	70,054.00	72,500.00	72,500.00	0.00	0.00%
Workmen's Compensation	38,660.00	36,000.00	40,000.00	4,000.00	11.11%
Kentucky Retirement	126,853.00	137,000.00	145,000.00	8,000.00	5.84%
Subtotal	$1,058,080.00	$1,156,650.00	$1,202,000.00	$45,350.00	3.92%
OPERATING EXPENSES					
Station II Facility	$5,575.00	$3,500.00	$3,500.00	$0.00	0.00%
Fire Hydrants	23,414.00	23,500.00	24,250.00	750.00	3.19%
Water, Sewer & Gas	3,344.00	3,500.00	3,500.00	0.00	0.00%
Electricity	1,641.00	2,000.00	2,000.00	0.00	0.00%
Office Supplies	1,581.00	1,500.00	1,500.00	0.00	0.00%
Gasoline	4,854.00	5,000.00	5,000.00	0.00	0.00%
Uniforms	15,554.00	12,000.00	12,000.00	0.00	0.00%
Training School & Supplies	703.00	2,500.00	2,500.00	0.00	0.00%
Vehicle Repair and Maint.	8,514.00	15,000.00	15,000.00	0.00	0.00%
Housekeeping Supplies	1,130.00	1,000.00	1,000.00	0.00	0.00%
Travel & Meetings	1,262.00	1,500.00	1,500.00	0.00	0.00%
Dues & Subscriptions	280.00	300.00	300.00	0.00	0.00%
Miscellaneous	5,014.00	5,000.00	5,000.00	0.00	0.00%
Fire Marshall Office	3,707.00	3,500.00	3,500.00	0.00	0.00%
Reappropriations	1,223.00	1,500.00	1,500.00	0.00	0.00%
Subtotal	$77,796.00	$81,300.00	$82,050.00	$750.00	0.92%
CAPITAL EXPENDITURES					
Equipment	$8,209.00	$39,000.00	$10,000.00	-$29,000.00	-74.36%
Fire Truck Payment	24,369.00	24,500.00	24,500.00	0.00	0.00%
Subtotal	$32,578.00	$63,500.00	$34,500.00	-$29,000.00	-45.67%
TOTAL	$1,168,454.00	$1,301,450.00	$1,318,550.00	$17,100.00	1.31%

Appendix 1F
State Budget Offices

1. AL: http://www.budget.state.al.us/
2. AK: http://www.gov.state.ak.us/omb/
3. AZ: http://www.state.az.us/ospb/index.cfm
4. AR: http://www.arkansas.gov/dfa/budget/budget_facts_brochure_fy05.html
5. CA: http://www.dof.ca.gov/HTMLBUD_DOCS/Bud_link.htm
6. CO: http://www.colorado.gov/dpa/eo/bfu.htm
7. CT: http://www.opm.state.ct.us/publicat.htm#Budget
8. DE: http://www.state.de.us/budget/
9. FL: http://www.ebudget.state.fl.us/govpriorities.asp
10. GA: http://www.legis.state.ga.us/legis/budget/index.htm
11. HA: http://www.hawaii.gov/budget/
12. ID: http://www2.state.id.us/dfm/index.html
13. IL: http://www.state.il.us/budget/
14. IN: http://www.in.gov/sba/
15. IO: http://www.dom.state.ia.us/state/budget_proposals/index.html
16. KS: http://da.state.ks.us/budget/
17. KY: http://www.osbd.state.ky.us/
18. LA: http://senate.legis.state.la.us/FiscalServices/Default.htm
19. ME: http://www.state.me.us/budget/homepage.htm
20. MD: http://www.dbm.maryland.gov/
21. MA: http://www.mass.gov/eoaf/
22. MI: http://www.michigan.gov/budget
23. MN: http://www.finance.state.mn.us/
24. MS.: http://www.mississippi.gov/frameset.jsp?URL=http%3A%2F%2Fwww.df
    a.state.ms.us
25. MO: http://www.oa.state.mo.us/bp/
26. MT: http://www.discoveringmontana.com/budget/
27. NE: http://www.budget.state.ne.us/
28. NV: http://www.budget.state.nv.us/
29. NH: http://admin.state.nh.us/budget/
30. NJ: http://www.njleg.state.nj.us/legislativepub/budget.asp
31. NM: http://www.state.nm.us/clients/dfa/index.html
32. NY: http://www.budget.state.ny.us/
33. NC.: http://www.osbm.state.nc.us/osbm/index.html
34. ND: http://www.state.nd.us/fiscal/
35. OH: http://www.obm.ohio.gov/
36. OK: http://www.osf.state.ok.us/budget.html
37. OR: http://www.bam.das.state.or.us/
38. PA: http://www.oit.state.pa.us/budget/site/default.asp?
39. RI: http://www.budget.ri.gov/
40. SC.: http://www.state.sc.us/osb/
41. SD: http://www.state.sd.us/bfm/
42. TN: http://www.state.tn.us/finance/bud/budget.html
43. TX: http://www.lbb.state.tx.us/
44. UT: http://www.governor.utah.gov/gopb/budget.html

45. VT: http://www.state.vt.us/fin/
46. VA: http://www.dpb.state.va.us/
47. WA:http://www.ofm.wa.gov/
48. WV:http://www.wv.gov/Offsite.aspx?u=http://www.state.wv.us/admin/finance/
49. WI: http://www.doa.state.wi.us/section_detail.asp?linkcatid=38&linkid=
50. WY:http://ai.state.wy.us/budget/index.asp

If one of these cites does not function, go to the state's home page. The vast majority of state government internet home pages are: http://www.state.??.us. For example, the home page for the state of Tennessee is: http://www.tn.us. If you want to go to another state, just use the two-letter abbreviation for that state.

Chapter 2
Preparation of the Budget Proposal

Chapter Two Overview

In the previous chapter you learned the basic terms, phrases and devices used in budgeting systems. This chapter centers on budget preparation. On the surface, this may seem to be an easy task. However, budgeting is not as simple as it appears. For instance, at any given time, a state or local government may be working on three separate budgets: the current year, previous year, and the up-coming fiscal year. This process requires the cooperation and efforts of a lot of individuals and agencies, including various groups and individuals that may have completely separate agendas.

The chapter begins by first examining the budget cycle and the phases that occur. This section is followed with an analysis of the role of individuals involved in the process, determining agency needs, and writing agency policy statements.

Budget Cycles

Repetition of events essentially drives the *budget cycle*. A budget cycle is a period of time in which the budget has to be prepared and executed. This cycle or system ensures greater accountability for decisions. It also allows decision makers to modify the budget for greater *efficiency* and *effectiveness*. The budget cycle has three phases: executive preparation, legislative approval, and budget execution. However, there is also an audit/evaluation phase that occurs after the execution phase

Phase 1. *Executive Preparation*: The chief executive of a state or local government is the one person who sets the tone for the policy issues that will be addressed during the budget preparation phase. Guidelines are generally prepared by the chief budget/fiscal officer and given to agencies laying out key issues that will be addressed for the upcoming budget year, along with the timetable for submission. These would include items such as policy priorities and proposed new legislation affecting the budget. A good budget should be very comprehensive in describing anticipated revenues and proposed expenditures, provide accountability for spending, avoid *earmarking funds* which could hinder new priorities, and indicate the purpose for new spending and the desired result (Mikesell 2003; Kittredge and Ouart 2005). Agencies in turn use this information when preparing their budget requests. In addition to preparing spending requests, agencies that have dedicated funding sources, such as federal grants, licenses and permits, and charges for services, provide estimates of revenue for the forthcoming budget year in their submission.

These requests are then forwarded to the chief executive's budget office to be reviewed and analyzed. Often, hearings will be held with the agency to clarify the budget request. The chief budget/fiscal office is responsible for the preparation of revenue estimates, particularly for the General Fund. In analyzing the requests, the revenue that will be available is a key factor during the internal budget deliberations. More often than not, the sum total of the budget requests for the General Fund exceeds the available revenue. As a result, decisions have to be made regarding the amount that will appear in the budget submission for each agency. It is not uncommon for department heads to be upset with the final recommendation. Some will try to get more money by lobbying the legislature/council, or will use special interest groups for that purpose.

Many state and local governments are legally bound to have a balanced budget pursuant to state law, local charter, or ordinance. The problem with most balanced-budget legislation is that it does not specify what "balanced" means. Usually, it is on the budget basis, which is most often cash. A cash budget can be manipulated by simply not paying bills at the end of the year. If the budget has to be balanced on the modified accrual basis, then more discipline is added to the process since liabilities cannot simply be passed on into the future. Some balanced budget laws state that revenues have to equal expenditures (without stating the basis that is to be used). This means that available balances are not able to be used to fund a deficit.

Once the requests have been received and analyzed, they are assembled into a single document. The budget is then submitted to the legislative body and also released to the public. Some governments prepare a budget-in-brief, which is intended for the citizens. It contains summaries of the requests along with an explanation as to what will be accomplished during the upcoming year.

Phase 2. *Legislative Approval*: Similar to other legislation, a legislative body has to approve the budget. The chief executive forwards the budget to the legislative body and when it approves the document, it has the force of the law. This process seems very simple, but in reality it is not. Negotiations between the executive and members of the legislature or city council are very common. In some cases, these negotiations can be very stressful given partisan differences. Party politics plays a smaller role at the local level when compared to the federal and state governments (Smith and Lynch 2004).

For every state except Nebraska (which only has one house), the budget is submitted to the lower house, similar to the process used by the federal government. The Finance Committee is in charge overall. However, other committees will be involved. For example, the Transportation Committee will hear the request for the Department of Transportation. After they conclude the hearing, the recommendation will be forwarded to the Finance Committee. During the course of the hearings, many parties will comment on the request. The department head will provide an overview of the request. Public interest groups will offer their comments as well. Most states have legislative budget offices that provide projections independent of the executive, which are used by the legislature in formulating the appropriations. Once the lower house completes its hearing, they vote on the measure. It is then sent to the upper house (Senate), and the process starts all over again. Once the upper house completes its process, more often than not changes are made from the version passed by the lower house. As a result, a conference committee is formed with representatives from both houses. The responsibility of the conference committee is to come up with a single appropriation act that is acceptable to both houses. Although it is desirable to have the budget passed before the start of the next fiscal year, it often does not pass quickly because of political differences. In that case, a *continuing resolution* is passed, so that government can operate while the problems are worked out. Eventually, an appropriation act is passed and sent to the governor for signature. Many governors have the ability to use a line-item veto, by which specific appropriations can be vetoed. The legislative body has the ability to override the veto if it can muster the necessary votes.

The process is much simpler in local governments. The legislative body is the council, board, or commission. The executive branch still presents information regarding the request. The public and special interest groups still have the ability to testify and offer ideas. Eventually, an appropriation ordinance is passed and signed by the chief executive officer. Many local governments have charter or ordinance provisions that require the budget to be enacted before the start of the fiscal year.

Phase 3. *Budget Execution*: At the beginning of the fiscal year, agencies carry out or execute their approved budgets. Spending is monitored by the agencies and the executive budget office in order to ensure that appropriations are not overspent. This is usually done through the use of accounting software that is designed to ensure that spending is within the authorized amounts. Monthly, quarterly, and midyear budget reports are issued to that provide comparisons between actual revenue received to date and revenue projections and actual expenditures compared to appropriations (see Appendix 2A for an example). If revenue projections are off the target, modifications should be made to ensure that the budget is balanced. Budget short falls can cause serious operating and personnel problems for agency heads (Nice 2002; Smith and Lynch 2004). Many state and local governments have legislation that requires the chief executive officer to take action to reduce spending if revenue projections are not met.

Most states and large local governments use an allotment process to help control the budget. At the start of the year, each agency is required to allot the annual appropriation by quarter. This, in effect, means that agencies are managing quarterly budgets. Another budget control tool is the *encumbrance*. When an agency enters into a contract or purchase order, an encumbrance is established setting aside that amount so that when the goods and services are received, funds are available to pay the bills.

Audit/Evaluation Phase: The purpose of this phase is to determine if the budget was executed in the manner that was set forth in the legislation (Nice 2002). That is, does the approved budget and actual budget match up? An audit occurs after the fiscal year has ended and can be done internally and externally. Individuals working within the agency conduct *internal audits*, and *external audits* are done by paid professionals outside of the organization. Audits vary according to the type of budget that is used by agencies. Generally speaking, there are two types: financial and performance. A *financial audit* checks to ensure that an agency's financial statements fall within the principles of GAAP and gauge whether an agency has followed the laws and statutes regulating its spending.

A *performance audit* concentrates its efforts on efficiency and effectiveness, by examining procurement, duplication, utilization of staff, legal compliance and measuring and reporting performance (Lee and Johnson 1998; Solano 2004; Smith and Lynch 2004). Basically, what was accomplished with the funds that were spent? There are two types of performance audits: economy and efficiency and program audits. "*Economy and efficiency audits* determine whether the governmental unit is acquiring protecting, and using its resources economically and efficiently and whether it has complied with laws and regulations on matters of economy and efficiency. *Program audits* determine the extent to which desired results are being achieved and analyze related compliance issues" (Holder 2004, p. 221). There are also *single audits* that "focus more closely on the expenditure of grant resources than do other types of audits" (Holder 2004, p. 221). A single audit is required by the federal government for all state and local governments that have $500,000 or more in federal grant awards and requires auditors to test to see if grant provisions are being followed.

Pariser and Brooks (1997) highlight some generally accepted government auditing standards that administrators should have in place as a follow up to determine the effectiveness of the audit. That is, were the recommendations followed and did they achieve desirable results? They suggest that the following items should be included in an audit recommendation follow up system (p. 337).

- Firm policy basis for following up on audit recommendations
- Organizational commitment to implementation
- Evaluation of recommendations including budgetary and organizational impact
- Clear assignment of follow up responsibilities
- Preparation of corrective plans
- Special attention to key recommendations
- Periodic review to evaluate the adequacy of actions taken on recommendations
- Preparation and distribution of periodic status reports
- Use of status reports for oversight and management evaluations

Further, management should be fully committed to implementing the suggestions from the audit and this should be evidenced by formal policies or a procedures manual that describes the details of the audit recommendation follow up system as well as securing individuals to be responsible for implementing the recommendations.[9]

The Budget Calendar

Since state and local governments work around a fiscal year, budget approval has to occur prior to the beginning of the fiscal year. The beginning of the budget cycle differs for most states and cities. For 46 states, the fiscal year is from July 1-June 30.

Exhibit 2.1 Budget Fiscal Years

Government	Fiscal Year Beginning
U.S. Federal Government	October 1-September 30
46 States	July 1-June 30
2 States	October 1-September 30
1 State	September 1-August 31
1 State	April 1-March 31
Local Governments	Variously January, July, September, October

Source: Axelrod, Donald. 1995. *Budgeting for Modern Government*. 2nd Edition. St. Martins Press: N.Y., NY.

A lot of local governments begin the fiscal year in January, July, September and October. The federal fiscal year begins on October 1 and ends on September 30.

Exhibit 2.2 shows the budget time frame for the city of Hutchinson. Although fiscal year 2009 begins on July 1, 2008 for the city, the process began officially on March 12, 2008. At this point, the city makes the final adjustments to close out the FY 2006-2007 budget while they are in the middle of the 2007-2008 budget season. So, they are in affect managing three budgets simultaneously. By establishing exact dates and times for forms and meetings, it brings a lot of order to the process. Unless something out of the ordinary occurs, agency personnel and elected officials tend to stick to the set times frames.

Exhibit 2.2 City of Hutchinson Budget Timetable, FY 2008-09

1. March 12, 2008, Audit & Finance Committee meets to finalize time table with agencies and departments on budget request.

2. March 13, 2008, Send out notices to agency heads that deadline to submit appropriation request will be Friday, March 31st.

3. March 30, 2008, Deadline for Agencies, Boards and Commissions to submit budget proposals to CAO for copying for elected officials.

4. April 9, 2008, A&F Committee Meeting. Preliminary revenue Projection and summary spreadsheets of requested expenses submitted to Mayor and Audit and Finance Committee from CAO and Financial Director.

5. April 16-20, 2008, Agency and Department Appropriation Hearings before Audit and Finance Committee.

   April 16th (Monday): Agencies-7:00 to 10:00 a.m.
   April 18th (Wednesday): Agencies-7:00 to 10:00 a.m.
   April 20th (Friday): Departments-6:00 to 10:00 p.m.
          Public Works-6:00 to 7:00 p.m.
          Police Dept.-7:00 to 8:00 p.m.
          Fire Dept.-8:00 to 9:00 p.m.
          Administration Dept.-9:00 to 10:00 p.m.

6. April 23, 2008, A & F Committee Meeting. Final revenue Projections submitted to Mayor and Audit & Finance Committee. Mayor and Committee discuss budgetary emphasis and priorities, and agree on strategy to handle revenue shortfalls, request overruns, etc.

7. May 7, 2008, MRA/LGEAF Budget Hearings held as required by state law.

8. May 21, 2008, Mayor's Budget and Budget Message presented to Council.

Mayor usually delivers his proposed budget at a special called meeting late in the month.

9. June 4, 2008, First Reading of the FY 08-09 Budget Ordinance.
10. June 18, 2008, Second Reading of FY 08-09 Budget Ordinance.

11. June 20-30, 2008, Publication of FY 08-09 Budget Ordinance.

The Budget Game

Making budgeting decisions can be a very complicated process given the number of individuals involved and their ideas and goals. In an executive budgeting system, the chief executive plays the major role in the budgeting process. That is, he/she initiates the process. However, there are a number of others involved in the process as well, including the budget office, legislature, and agency directors. In addition, there are some non-governmental actors that can play a role in the process such as interests groups and individuals (Rubin 2006). All governments however do not use an executive budgeting system.

County governments tend to have administrators, auditors, or someone in the legislative branch prepare the budget. Some states have legislative budget offices that expend enormous amounts of energy and paperwork on the budget (Lee and Johnson 1998). Under normal circumstances, the word game and government would not go together. These two terms tend to go hand in hand at the state level and in very large cities.

Figure 2.1
Actors and Budget Decisions

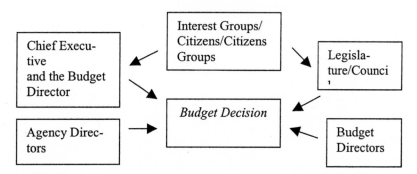

Budgeting is a bit more bureaucratic in smaller governments. However, when one considers the entire decision making process, it does display some of the same characteristics of a game. Players/decision makers use strategy and sometime they win and sometime they do not. Policy makers render decisions that are good and bad for certain individuals and agencies. Figure 2.1 illustrates the four main actors involved in the process as well nongovernmental actors (Smith and Lynch 2004; Bland and Rubin 1997; Rubin 2006).

1. Chief Executive

The chief executive is the only person responsible for the entire institution of a particular governmental entity. As a result, executives try to ensure that spending is done as harmoniously as possible in order to satisfy the greatest number of individuals and agencies. The executive, via the *budget director*, initiates the budgeting process and is responsible for sending letters to the various agencies informing them of important dates and dead lines for information.[10] Although the chief executive may appoint agency heads, this relationship may not be as friendly as it appears. The executive has the option of saying no, and does so frequently. You must also consider the role of interests groups, citizens, and citizen groups. Mayors, governors as well as legislators and councilmen are frequently bombarded with requests that may impact budget decisions. Given the nature of their position they cannot ignore the existences of these external groups and the potential impact that they could have on their electoral fortunes.

In sum, the chief executive works hand in hand with the budget director to put the initial budget together. Then, it is the legislative body responsibility to decide the final spending patterns and enact the appropriations. Last, the chief executive carries out the mandates of the legislative branch.

2. Budget Director

The budget director runs the budget office for the chief executive. This office is the center for the city or state's budget processing. Budget requests are generally sent to the budget office rather than directly to the executive. Once this office receives all of the requests, it goes about balancing expenditures against expected revenues. This effort can be eased when the executive informs the agencies of expected increases or decreases in revenue prior to their submitting budget requests. However, budget projections are not finalized until the last possible moment. Given the constraints of limited revenues, the budget office must ensure that items of high priority, as deemed by the chief executive and legislative body, be provided for. However, this process can cause a lot of friction between the budget office and the agency directors. Although there are many different reasons why an agency may be denied funding for some program, common reasons would include the following: 1.) The money is not available; 2.) Items were not adequately justified; 3.) Items do not fit the goals and objectives of the agency; and 4.) Items are not in harmony with the executive's priorities (Bland and Rubin 1997; Mikesell 2003; Smith and Lynch 2004; Kittredge and Ouart 2005).

3. Legislator/Council Member

This group of persons is responsible for approving the budget. They are always looking for an opportunity to bring in programs and projects that will benefit their constituents. Most legislators/councilmen do not have a good grasp of the budget process from a micro perspective. This is not necessarily a bad thing given their role in the budget process. They are often given dense information with little time to react to it. As a result, they tend to center their efforts on their individual pet projects. Legislators on powerful committees and party leaders can use their influence to secure pet projects a lot easier than less senior legislators. Unlike the chief executive, the decisions made by legislators and councilmen are more likely to be impacted by interest groups, citizens, and citizen groups.

4. Agency Directors

Agency directors head the various departments within the *bureaucracy*. These departments provide the services that affect the well-being of the citizens. Since their efforts gravitate towards the individuals that they serve and the agency's goals and objectives, agency directors are constantly defending their budget requests from both a technical and political perspective. However, it is not clear as to whether agency directors engage in a *budget maximizing strategy* (Sigelman 1986; Smith and Lynch 2004; Wildavsky and Caiden 2004). That is, do they ask for the greatest increase in their budget as possible? However, it is clear that agency directors attempt to maintain the existence of their agency. They do this by maintaining a good relationship with legislators and the chief executive. Particularly, they need proponents in the legislature or the city council that will defend them in times of severe budget cuts. Rubin (2006) points out, agency directors often engage in strategies to improve budget passage. First, they may instill a sense of urgency. That is, if the request is not funded then x, y, and z might occur. Second, they may indicate how the request may be cost efficient and effective and thus save money over time. Third, the agency head may ensure that the chief executive or key legislators/councilmen are getting their individual demands met in the request.

Agency Roles Expanded

While requesting budget statements from an agency, the budget office project revenue collections for the up-coming year based on available data (previous tax collections, inflation, interest rates, population movement, etc.). This increase (or decrease) is compared with the *baseline* for agencies to continue at their current rate and the new demands brought on by new legislation and priorities that have been set by the chief executive. If there are gaps between expected revenues and expenditures the chief executive (first line) and the legislative body (second line) have to decide where cuts should be made to compensate for the disparity.

In most cases, budget requests are denied rather than raise taxes. As a result, each agency has to essentially defend its budget in a formal hearing. In preparing for a hearing, each agency should submit to the budget office a narrative explaining the purpose, goals and objectives of the agency, a budget request, and a detailed explanation justifying new requests. This would include items such as a request for a new employee. It is much easier for an agency to defend spending new monies when they can show that it fits the goals of the agency, the mission of the chief executive, and the priorities set by new legislation. If an agency cannot elaborate in detail why it needs to expand a program or hire a new secretary, it will be extremely difficult for that agency to receive new funding during a period of budget constraint. A request for spending is not limited to one occasion. An agency may request additional funding during the course of the fiscal year (Mikesell 2003; Smith and Lynch 2004; Solano 2004).

Justifying and Defending the Budget

Ideally, the best news for an agency is to find out that their entire budget was approved. Unfortunately, agencies frequently find that the chief executive and the legislative body demand more services with less money. Rarely is a budget completely funded without some changes. As a result, it is imperative that agency heads are completely prepared to justify their budgets. If they are not prepared, they may quickly find the agency on the short end of the revenue stick. There are two basic ways to sell your budget. The phrases *political budget* and *technical budget* are two methods that characterize the process. Generally speaking, all budgets are political in nature given that government is political. However, some budget processes are more political than others. Likewise, all budgets should be technical in nature. That is, contain budgetary facts. However, the stance used to sell the budget can vary.

-Political Budgets

An agency director who uses a political budget strategy plays the political game. Rather than concentrate on the numbers, they use other slight of hand tricks in an effort to out maneuver the politicians. Wildavsky (1979), Meyers (1999), Rogers and Brown (1999) and Wildavsky and Caiden (2004) offer several budget maximizing strategies that an agency director may employ. Using these methods are not sure fire methods to selling your budget. Policy makers are not ignorant of these "tricks".

- Cultivate a clientele in the legislative and executive branch.

- Serve a specific clientele and encourage them to contact their elected officials and sing your praises.
- Build confidence in your agency by not covering up bad deeds.
- Cut or eliminate programs that are popular with complete knowledge that they will be reinstated.
- Shift the blame of cutting the program onto the policy maker.
- Combine new programs with old programs so that they do not appear as new programs.
- Argue that new programs are modified old programs.
- Lower the budget levels for new programs with the assumption that you will get more funds later.
- Maintain your base line and use the funds for other purposes.
- Argue that some of your expenditures are short term.
- Study the political scene and use crisis to expand or create new services.
- Show how expenditures will save money later.
- Show how a program will pay for itself in user charges.
- Use workload data to build up the budget base.

There are no guarantees that these or any other strategies will work. Agency directors should assess the political environment and proceed from there. If revenues increase, it may be easier to use the technical strategies. In some cases, legislators and executives may take it upon themselves to cut or limit agency programs despite the efforts of the agency director. In some cases, they may simply cut a program. This is particularly true when resources are limited. In fact, legislators and councilmen may quickly find that their pet projects will disappear. It is a lot easier to cut a program that is utilized by one district rather than the entire jurisdiction (Meyers 1999; Mikesell 2003).

-Technical Budgets

A technical budget concentrates on the numbers or budgetary facts. Expenditures can be split into two categories: mandatory, and discretionary spending. A baseline (Base) is a technique that can be used in both categories.

Mandatory expenditures are reflected in state and local law. That is, the agency is legally required to conduct the service. These expenditures include: salaries, FICA, pensions/retirement, unemployment compensation, and any other legal obligations. While there are always questions surrounding how many employees are actually needed to provide services, eliminating an employee or cutting the personnel budget is the last thing that a politician wants to do. Under normal circumstances, elected officials honor mandatory spending.

Discretionary spending constitutes the smallest part of the overall budget.

These funds often only represent increases in the budget and are sought by everyone. While not necessary for the general operation of the agency, these funds will allow the agency to expand services and operate more efficiently and effectively. Due to limited funding, agency heads should put a lot of effort into justifying spending. Data indicating population shifts, economic up swings, legal requirements are all useful in justifying new positions and an expansion in services (see also Le Loup 1977).

Base expenditures are expenditures that an agency needs to maintain the same level of services. This includes operating expense items such as office supplies, printing, equipment, utilities, vehicles, tools, and other related items. Agency directors can justify these items using previous year budgets, the current year's budget, ongoing projects, or projects for the upcoming year. In any case, the director should be able to justify the request given any change in the amount of the request. This would include an increase or decrease in any part of the budget. By highlighting productivity, a budget is much less likely to be cut.

Conclusion

By now the reader should have concluded that preparing a budget is an arduous task. While there are time frames established to make the process logistically more efficient and effective, any number of problems may come up. In fact, establishing the time frames may be the easiest part of the process. Unfortunately budget decisions are not always technical in nature, budget games are real and are played throughout the fiscal year. If an agency wants to achieve the most for the organization, the wise decision is to be completely prepared to argue for the political or technical budget.

Important Terms and Phrases

Audit
Baseline/Base Expenditures
Budget Calendar
Budget Cycle
Budget Game
Budget Director
Budget Execution
Budget Maximizing Strategy
Bureaucracy
Chief Executive
Discretionary Spending
Earmarking Funds
Efficiency
Effectiveness
Economy and Efficiency Audits

Encumbrance
Executive Preparation
Evaluation
External Audit
Financial Audit
Hearings
Internal Audit
Legislative Approval
Mandatory Spending/Expenditure
Performance Audit
Political Budget
Program Audit
Stakeholders
Single Audit
Technical Budget

Chapter 2 Homework Exercise

Directions: Please read the entire assignment prior to beginning the assignment. You can retype the forms or go to the website and download the forms. Use the Budget Request Form as a template to completing step 1 of the assignment. This assignment is not limited to one page, so feel free to expand the individual sections to accommodate your needs.

-Step One: Homework

First, each student should obtain a line-item budget for an agency/department, within a city, using the internet or by going to a local city and requesting a hard copy of the budget. After you locate the budget, select an agency/department. Using the *original budget request form* that is provided at the end of chapter two, your job is to decide how you (the Agency Director) can improve that agency/department by adding a new program or task to the agency. You are free to choose any agency that is listed in the budget that you selected. For example, you could create a new Child Care Program within the Department of Human Services for the City of Jonesboro. After you decide whether to add a new program or function in the agency/department, you should type your responses on the *original budget request form* in the book or use a word processing program to duplicate the *original budget request form* and type in your information. This request should not exceed two pages in length. Your main job is to create a budget for your new program/function using the information that is listed below as well as project future costs. From the role of Agency Director, justify your program/function/activity (sell the idea and think about potential questions).

- You are limited to $250,000.00 in your initial request.
- Budgets rarely decrease.
- Agencies that bring in revenue are more likely to receive more revenue.
- Indicate why this program is efficient and effective.
- Indicate the overall benefits of this program.
- Give special attention to items that are unusual.
- Provide justifications for substantial increases or decreases in spending.

Note: The brief description (text, not the dollar amounts) of future year cost should only address substantive increases in your request. It is assumed that inflation and other factors will drive incremental changes in your budget. Only address major increases in this section.

Provide your instructor with a copy of the pertinent sections of the city or state budget that you retrieved and a copy of your original budget request form. You will need *three additional copies* of your original budget request form for the second step of the assignment.

-Step Two: In Class Games

As pointed out earlier, there are four main individuals/groups involved in the budget process. Hence, the class should be split into groups of four. If someone is left out, he or she can be assigned the role of a council member and added to any particular group. Each person in the group will defend his or her budget request from the role of agency head while the remaining group members will assume the other roles. Given what has been stated about each one of these actors in the text book, decide whether to approve each budget request. It is the ultimate objective of each agency head to have his/her budget request passed. Only modifications to the original budget request form should be made on the *revised budget request form*. The original unmarked and revised budget request form should be turned in to the instructor at the close of class. Each agency director has ten minutes to defend his or her budget request to the group and answer questions after the other actors have reviewed the budget request. When the time limit has expired, the three members will vote yea or nay to approving the budget. Your grade is not determined by whether or not your budget is approved by your group, but by the quality of your work.[11]

-Step Three: Evaluation

When you have finished discussing each of the budgets in your group, complete the *evaluation form*. When everyone in the class has completed this process, individual agency directors can provide the entire class an overview of their project and its ultimate outcome.

-Step Four: Completed Assignment

Give your professor the following items:
1. Original Budget Request Form (Do not write on this form after you type in your responses).
2. Revised Budget Request Form (Only include the items that you changed).
3. Evaluation (Completed)
4. The Budget sheets that you used to formulate your new program.

Agency Budget Request Form (original)

Agency:

Agency Director: Date:

Requested Item/Title of Program:

Description and Rationale for Item/Program:

Objectives Justifying the Need:

First Year Cost and Brief Description:

	Cost	Description
A. Personnel:	_____	_____
B. Supplies:	_____	_____
C. Equipment:	_____	_____
D. Capital Outlay:	_____	_____
Total Cost $		

Proposed Future Year Cost:

	FY 2	FY 3	FY 4	FY 5
A. Personnel:	_____	_____	_____	_____
B. Supplies:	_____	_____	_____	_____
C. Equipment:	_____	_____	_____	_____
D. Capital Outlay:	_____	_____	_____	_____
Total Cost $				

Measure of Success:

Group Members	Approved: Yes or No
Budget Director_____	
Council Member_____	
Council Member_____	

Agency Budget Request Form (revised)

Agency:

Agency Director: Date:

Requested Item/Title of Program:

Description and Rationale for Item/Program:

Objectives Justifying the Need:

Proposed Future Year Cost:

	FY 2	*FY 3*	*FY 4*	*FY 5*
A. Personnel:				
B. Supplies:				
C. Equipment:				
D. Capital Outlay:				
Total Cost $				

Proposed Future Year Cost:

	FY 2	*FY 3*	*FY 4*	*FY 5*
A. Personnel:				
B. Supplies:				
C. Equipment:				
D. Capital Outlay:				
Total Cost $				

Measure of Success:

Group Members   Approved:
                                                 Yes or No

*Budget Director*_____

*Council Member*_____

*Council Member*_____

Evaluation of the Role Playing Assignment

Name: Date:

1. After playing the role(s) of various budgeting officials on several proposals, do you feel that government priorities were maintained while approving the agency requests? Briefly explain your opinion.

2. Are you satisfied with the outcome of your proposal? Why? Why not? What could you have done to improve the success of your proposal?

3. Which of the four actors appear to play the greatest role in determining the outcome of a budget proposal in your opinion? Why?

References

Axelrod, Donald. 1995. *Budgeting for Modern Government.* 2nd Edition. St. Martins Press: New York, NY.

Bland, Robert L. and Irene S. Rubin. 1997. *Budgeting: A Guide for Local Governments.* Washington, DC: ICMA.

Kittredge, William P. and Sarah M. Ouart. 2005. *Budget Manual for Georgia Local Government.* Athens, GA: Vinson Institute.

Lee, Robert D. and Ronald W. Johnson. 1998. *Public Budgeting Systems.* 6th ed. Aspen Publishers: Gaithersburg, MD.

Le Loup, Lance T. 1977. *Budgetary Politics: Dollars, Deficits, Decisions.* Ohio: King's Court.

Meyers, Roy T. 1999. "Strategies for Spending Advocates." In Roy T. Meyer's ed. *Handbook of Government Budgeting.* California: Josey Bass.

Mikesell, John. L. 2003. *Fiscal Administration: Analysis and Applications for the Public Sector.* 6th ed. Belmont, CA: Thomson Wadsworth.

Riley, Susan L. and Peter W. Colby. 1991. *Practical Government Budgeting: A Workbook for Public Managers.* SUNY Press: Albany, NY.

Rogers, Jacqueline H. and Marita B. Brown. 1999. "Preparing Agency Budgets." In Roy T. Meyer's ed. *Handbook of Government Budgeting.* California: Josey Bass.

Rubin, Irene S. 2006. *The Politics of Public Budgeting: Getting and Spending, Borrowing and Balancing.* 5th ed. Washington, D.C.: CQ Press.

Sigelman, Lee. 1986. "The Bureaucrat as a Budget Maximizer: An Assumption Examined." *Public Budgeting and Finance,* Vol. 6 #1, p. 50-59.

Smith, Robert W. and Thomas D. Lynch. 2004. *Public Budgeting in America.* 5th ed. Upper Saddle River, NJ: Pearson/Prentice Hall.

Solano, Paul L. 2004. "Budgeting." In *Management Policies in Local Government Finance.* 5th Edition. Washington, D.C.: ICMA.

Performance Budgeting: State Experiences and Implications for the Federal Government. 1993. U.S. General Accounting Office. Washington, D.C.: Government Printing Office

Wildavsky, Aaron. 1979. *The Politics of the Budgetary Process.* 3rd Edition. Boston: Little Brown.

Wildavsky, Aaron and Naomi Caiden. 2004. *The New Politics of the Budgetary Process*.
    5th Edition. New York: Pearson/Longman.

Appendix 2A

City of Theodore

FY 2008-2009	Estimated Revenue	Year to Date Actual Revenue	Uncollected Balance	Uncollected Percent
GENERAL FUND				
Tax Revenue-City Portion	$ 1,780,000.00	$ 1,649,781.71	$ 130,218.29	7.32%
Auto Property Tax	225,000.00	161,377.07	63,622.93	28.28%
Prop. Tax Int & Penalty	10,000.00	13,171.73	<3171.73>	-31.72%
Prop. Tax Int/ Penalty Prior	90,000.00	7,831.06	82,168.94	91.30%
Auto Tax (State)	-	3,576.97	<3576.97>	
Prop tax Delinq 96 Prior	-	36,560.21	<36560.21>	
Prop Tax Delinq 97	-	238,490.52	<238490.52>	
Propery Taxes (State)	35,000.00	35,920.50	<920.5>	-2.63%
Payment in Lieu of Taxes	68,000.00	28,589.12	39,410.88	57.96%
Bank Deposits Tax	90,000.00	100,863.58	<10863.58>	-12.07%
Tobacco Tax	-	6.02	<6.02>	
Payroll Tax	6,225,000.00	4,693,517.87	1,531,482.13	24.60%
Payroll Tax Penalty	6,000.00	11,631.66	<5631.66>	-93.86%
Business Licneses	600,000.00	43,612.99	556,387.01	92.73%
Business Lic. Pen& Int	-	3,711.08	<3711.08>	
INS Premium Licnese Tax	1,575,000.00	1,186,939.63	388,060.37	24.64%
Liquor and Beer Licenses	19,000.00	1,693.75	17,306.25	91.09%
Cable TV Franchise	150,000.00	95,538.35	54,461.65	36.31%
Franchise Tax	65,000.00	103.24	64,896.76	99.84%
Court Revenue	125,000.00	93,696.78	31,303.22	25.04%
Severance Tax	25,000.00	24,374.24	625.76	2.50%
Insurance Payroll DED	-		-	
Investement Interest	325,000.00	250,744.95	74,255.05	22.85%
Rent Income	3,000.00	2,250.00	750.00	25.00%
Misc Inc Used Veh/Equip Sale	15,000.00	17,950.66	<2950.66>	-19.67%
Misc-Inc Police CT Sale	-	-	-	
Building Permit Fees	60,000.00	59,960.02	-	0.07%
FEMA Flood Reimbursement	-	12,690.00	<12690>	
Miscellaneous Income	25,000.00	20,091.96	4,908.04	19.63%
DARE Program Reimbursement	17,000.00	21,026.30	<4026.30>	-23.68%
HWY Safety Prog. Reimbur.	35,000.00	14,743.25	20,256.75	57.88%
Building Demo Reimbursement	10,000.00	-	10,000.00	100.00%
Houseing Authority Grant	33,000.00	24,099.02	8,900.98	26.97%
Staduium Prop Sale	9,000.00	-	9,000.00	100.00%
Circuit Court Clerk Fees	4,000.00	3,890.00	110.00	2.75%
Police Department	8,000.00	5,679.20	2,320.80	29.01%
Animail Control License Fee	20,000.00	-	20,000.00	100.00%
Parking Meters	-	-	-	
SUBTOTAL General Fund Net	$ 11,652,000.00	$ 8,864,113.44	$ 3,110,445.81	
SUBTOTAL GENERAL Fund Prior YR	$ 820,179.00	$ -	$ 820,179.00	
TOTAL General Revenue Fund	$ 12,472,179.00	$ 8,864,113.44	$ 3,930,624.81	

Chapter 3
Personnel Services and Operating Budgets

Chapter Three Overview

A budget typically has three main components: personal services, operating and capital outlay expenditures. The purpose of this chapter is to introduce the reader to the components of a standard personal services and operating budget. Specifically, the chapter provides information on writing the budget, justifying new positions, position classifications, pay ranges, and the different types of employees. The chapter also discusses calculating FICA, Medicare, and pension benefits. Lastly, the chapter considers the different formats, advantages, and disadvantages of an operating budget. Capital outlays are discussed in chapter four.[12]

Writing a Personal Services Budget

The personal services budget is normally funded out of the general fund. Personal services include salaries and *fringe benefits* for employees and can be managed in a step by step process.[13] A salary is simply the wages paid for services rendered over a given period of time. Salaries can be calculated very easily using a spreadsheet. However, many governments have software that automate the calculation of salaries and associated benefits. That is, it is very easy to increase or decrease salaries using a very simple formula. Fringe benefits are payments and services rendered by an agency in addition to normal wages. Fringe benefits can be based on a percentage of pay roll, such as *pensions, social security* (FICA) and *Medicare.* Social security and Medicare are represented as a tax on your check stub. Some argue that these two items are personnel costs and not benefits. A second group of benefits represent a flat amount that varies based on the employee's circumstances, such as life and health insurance. Non-monetary benefits include paid time off, such as holidays, vacations, sick leave and personal leave which are a component of the annual salary; take-home cars; free parking; employee incentive programs; and time off for education. Social security is required for all government employees according to federal law unless the government has its own retirement system. Medicare is required for all government employees. It is not a legal requirement to have health, life insurance, provide training supplements or any non-monetary benefits.

Another important factor in the personal services budget is overtime. This is particularly true for police and firefighters, since they are on 24/7 schedules. Overtime is normally paid at the rate of one and one-half times the hourly rate of pay. Overtime can be a significant cost for many governments. Percentage-driven benefits, such as pensions and Medicare are also a component of overtime. Many governments prefer to pay overtime rather than add employees because it keeps the headcount down. Another advantage is that new employees have to learn the job while existing employees are familiar with job requirements.

-Calculating FICA and Medicare

The federal government sets agency contributions to Medicare and social security annually. Currently, agencies match the 6.2% social security rate that employees have deducted directly from their paycheck. Hence, the employee and employer contribute a total of 12.4%. In 2008, the social security tax rate applied to earnings up to $102,000.00 (www.ssa.gov). No taxes are due from the employee or employer beyond that amount. For example, if a public administrator professor had a salary of $104,000.00 in 2008, she would pay $6,324.00 and the university would also contribute $6,324.00 on her behalf for a total of $12,648.00 in social security taxes for the year ($102,000.00 x 0.124 = $12,648.00). Note that the remaining $2,000.00 of her salary is not subject to social security taxes.

The rate for Medicare is 2.9%, and is split equally between the employer (1.45%) and the employee (1.45%). Contrary to social security, the Medicare rate applies to the full salary. Let's consider an example. A budget analyst has an annual salary of $75,000.00, so the Medicare tax is $2,175.00 ($75,000.00 x 0.029 = $2,175.00). Medicare is mandatory for all employees. If an employee is a part time or contract worker, he or she may not qualify for full fringe benefits. For example, if the agency does not pay their share of social security and Medicare benefits the employee has to pay the full amount to the federal government. Hence, the employer's contribution of half the social security and Medicare payment is considered a fringe benefit or an additional cost. So, it is important that you remember that you should only consider the government's portion of the payment on the budget rather than the total amount. Employee contributions to social security, Medicare, pensions, etc is included in a separate budget document. [14] However, when calculating these taxes in a personnel budget, both contributions should be included if you want to know that total cost of employing a staff person (see page 84 for additional comments).

-Pensions

For the most part, nearly all full time government employees participate in what is commonly called a pension plan. Some government pension plans are in lieu of Social Security while others may have both. Very small governments may only have Social Security. A *pension plan* provides financial benefits to an employee after he/she retires and/or has reached a certain age. Some plans allow an employee to retire after attaining a certain number of years of service, such as 30, at any age. Others require both an age and years of service requirement. Still others have only a strict age requirement. Both employee and the employer contribute funds to the pension plan (not necessarily at the same rate) and both receive benefits. The employee receives the monetary benefit and security of knowing that they will have funds upon retirement. The government benefits because they can serve their personnel management objectives. They want employees to make a career out of public service. The experience and training that is gained through the years contributes to a professional bureaucracy. So, in order to recruit the best people and keep them the government must provide a good retirement package (Hildreth and Miller 1996; Smith and Lynch 2004). Pension rates can range from a low of 2% up to a high of 30% or more of an employee's salary. There may be an equal contribution or the greater burden may be on the employee.

A pension resembles and behaves like social security. However, unlike social security, pension funds are invested in accounts that belong to the employee. Social Security is a "pay-as-you-go" system, whereby current contributions are used to pay the cost of past retirees. As history would indicate, it is possible for pension fund balances to suffer or grow as the economy changes. When the economy or the investment takes a turn for the worse for an extended period of time, it is important that fund managers ensure that enough funds are set aside and the tax base is stable enough to make up for the difference in lost investments (Smith and Lynch 2004). As a general rule, pension fund portfolio managers should ensure that they are making socially beneficial investments. This process is facilitated with a *pension board of directors*. Normally made up of member representatives along with outside appointments, they are responsible for implementing legal requirements (Hildreth and Miller 1996; Hildreth and Adams 1997).

Pension investments normally fall into two categories: fixed income securities and equity securities. *Fixed income securities* are obligations that provide a steady stream of interest payments barring any defaults, such as a corporate bond or corporate annuity. *Equity securities* (which are more risky) are investments in *stocks*, which may or may not pay *dividends* (Petersen 2004; see also Hildreth and Adams 1997).

As years have passed and budgets have tightened, public pension fund accounts have grown and have become more and more susceptible to fungibility issues. Again, it is important that the pension fund managers and the board of directors make sure that these funds are not transferred to other funds haphazardly (Nollenberger 2003; Petersen 2004).

Until the mid-1990's, virtually all government pension plans were defined benefit plans. When an employee began work, he/she was handed a book that stated exactly how much could be expected at retirement based on age, years of service, and final average salary. Pension fund managers have the liability for pensions calculated by *actuaries*. The actuaries determine how much the employer and employee have to contribute to fund the pensions. It is the responsibility of the managers to find investments that will yield the amounts necessary to cover all members in the system. When the economy has significant downturns, as happened in the early 2000s, investments are not able to keep pace with the required amounts. This means that the pension contributions should be increased. However, that is not easy to do. It requires legislation to raise contributions. Some pension plans have had to borrow to meet their obligations.[15] Others have had to supplement pension contributions with general fund subsidies.

Since the mid-1990's, a number of governments have established defined contribution plans. The government and employee each contribute a required amount for the pension. However, the employee is responsible for investing the funds. Employees are provided various investment options and select an option that is appropriate. Defined contribution plans are portable. That is, when the employee leaves government service, the pension stays with the employee. In a defined benefit plan, the employee may not get back any money or may receive a refund of his/her contribution. The advantage to the employer of a defined contribution plan is that there is no long term liability. Some governments, such as Orlando, Florida, have replaced a defined benefit plan with a defined contribution plan for all employees coming on board after October 1, 1998.

Calculating the Pension Benefit

While the years of service can vary, most state and local governments require their employees reach an age between 62-65 and work at least 5-10 years in order to receive a pension. However, there are a number of other factors that can take place to change that scenario. These would include things like disabilities.

There are two key factors involved in calculating the pension benefit—final average salary and the annual multiplier. The final average salary is based on the highest earning years of an employee and can vary from three, four or five years depending on the pension system. An annual multiplier is the percentage of final average salary that is applied to each year of service. For example, a pension plan provides for each year of service to be multiplied by two percent. An employee working 30 years would receive 60% of his/her final average salary. This comprises the total percentage value. An employee that works five years, which is usually the minimum vesting period, would receive 10% of their final average salary.

Exhibit 3.1 provides a model that can be used to calculate retirement benefits. In this example, Mrs. Angela Hooper worked 29 years for the city and is 64 years of age. The last piece of data needed to calculate her retirement benefit is her five highest fiscal year salaries. In order to calculate her benefit, you must first multiply her years of service times the percentage value per years of service. Second, her five highest years of service are added up and divided by five (years). Third, her average five year salary is multiplied by the total percentage value (TVPP). Based on the formula, Mrs. Hooper would receive $37,544.07 per year and $3,128.67 per month for her 29 years of service.

There are some other issues that this model does not examine, but they are still important to the employee. This includes things such as vesting, portability systems, cost of living adjustments, early retirement, and disability/survivor protections. *Vesting* occurs when an employee works a certain number of years making them eligible to receive retirement benefits. The minimum number of years required for vesting can range from 3-5, but really depends upon the system where you work. In some cases, you can move your vested status to another government job (portability). This is simple when you stay in the same system (work for the same municipality or state), but less likely to occur if you move to a different city or state. This is one of the drawbacks of the defined benefit plan and one of the advantages of the defined contribution plan.

Exhibit 3.1 Sample Calculations of Retirement Benefits

Step 1: Creditable Services and Percentage Value

	% Value Per Year of Service	Total Years Of Service	Total % Value Per Plan (TVPP)
Retirement up to age 62 or 30 Years	1.60%	x _____	= _____
Retirement at Age 63 or 31 Years	1.63%	x _____	= _____
Retirement at Age 64 or 32 Years	1.65%	x __29__	= __47.85__
Retirement at Age 65 or 33 Years or more	1.68%	x _____	= _____

Step 2: Average Final Compensation (AFC)

Mrs. Angela Hooper worked for 29 years in the same system and retired at age 64. In this step, we list her five highest fiscal year salaries and divide the total by five.

AFC = $392,310.00/ 5 = $78,462.00

$74,589.00
$76,123.00
$78,598.00
$80,211.00
$82,789.00
$392,310.00

Step 3: Monthly Benefit Calculation

AFC x TVPP =   Annual Benefit $78,462.00 x .4785 = $37,544.07

AFC x TVPP = Annual Benefit/12
= Monthly Benefit $78,462.00 x .4785 = $37,544.07 / 12 = $3,128.67

Source: Smith, Robert W. and Thomas D. Lynch. 2004. *Public Budgeting in America*. Upper Saddle River: Pearson/Prentice Hall.

Short Version of the Above Problem (in Excel)

% Value Per Year of Sevice	Total Years of Service	Total % Value PP	Average Final Compensation	Annual Benefit	Monthly Benefit
1.65%	29	47.85%	$78,462.00	$37,544.07	$3,128.67

5 Highest Years
$74,589.00
$76,123.00
$78,598.00
$80,211.00
$82,789.00
$392,310.00

$78,462.00

There is an array of issues and questions related to disability status. For example, will you be able to receive pension benefits if you become disabled prior to becoming eligible for benefits? Will your children or spouse receive your pension if you die prior to receiving benefits? Will you qualify for benefits if you permanently injure yourself outside of work? The answers to these and many other questions will vary based on where you are working. It is important that a government address all of these questions with written policies (Hildreth and Miller 1996; Smith and Lynch 2004).

Position Classifications and Salary Ranges

Exhibit 3.2 shows a simple agency budget with each of three main categories along with classification codes. The codes are for administrative purposes. They make it easier to locate a specific line in a budget. This particular budget represents a specific division within an agency. Because it is in a line item format, it essentially tells the reader the amount of funds necessary to run the division without any cost associated with a particular individual and their responsibilities. However, the budget does not tell the reader the number of persons who work in the Procurement Division, nor does it break down the fringe benefits by employee. Most budgets are typed into a computer spreadsheet. This expedites the budget process and reduces mathematical errors.

The most common employee classification is a *full time equivalent* (FTE). Full time positions are normally 35-40 hours per week. A full time employee (equivalent) is eligible to receive full fringe benefits. *Part time employees* (PTE) normally work 15-35 hours per week and are not eligible for full fringe benefits. Some part time employees may receive prorated benefits. A bus driver would be an example of a part time employee who works for the majority of the fiscal year and could be eligible for fringe benefits.

Exhibit 3.2 Simple Agency Budget

Agency: *Central Budget Office* Division: *Procurement*

Code	Item	Adopted Budget
1000	1. *Personal Services*	
1001	Salaries	$146,000.00
1002	FICA	18,104.00
1003	Insurance	6,000.00
1004	Retirement	19,578.00
		$189,682.00
2000	2. *Operating Expenses*	
2001	Contractual Services	$6,500.00
2002	Training	650.00
2003	Travel	505.00
2004	Utilities	3,000.00
2005	Printing	1,700.00
2006	Misc. Supplies	12,500.00
		$24,855.00
3000	3. *Capital Outlay*	
3001	Vehicles	$35,000.00
3002	Equipment	2,500.00
		$37,500.00
	Total Agency Budget	$252,037.00

Temporary positions may also exist. These are employees who may work full time, but are not permanent, such as summer employees of a park and recreation department. They may also be eligible for prorated fringe benefits as well. An example of a temporary employee may be a secretary or janitor hired only during the peak season (Riley and Colby 1991).

The classification FTE is used by the government in calculating the number of hours associated with a position. For example, a full time employee who works for the entire fiscal year would be the equivalent to 1.0 FTE. Four janitors, each working six months out of the year, would equal 2.0 FTE's. By using this system, the government views personnel cost in terms of the number of positions and costs needed to complete a job rather than the number of people.

State and local governments frequently use pay plans for employees. These plans normally apply to full time employees. The plan lists each position class along with the salary range for that position. It is very difficult to justify paying a particular employee a salary out of the range without raising the bar for all other employees in that classification. The *Salary Range Plan* includes the title of the position, administrative code associated with the position, and annual salary range. Exhibit 3.3 contains an example of a salary range classification.

Exhibit 3.3 Salary Range Classification

Position Code	Class Title	Min. Salary	Max. Salary
1100	Accountant	$35,000.00	$49,000.00
1101	Administrative Assistant	25,000.00	35,250.00
1102	Budget Analyst	55,000.00	65,000.00
1103	Clerk	30,000.00	40,500.00
1104	Division Director	85,000.00	99,950.00
1105	Janitor	18,000.00	23,595.00
1106	Principal Investigator	65,000.00	79,000.00
1007	Security Guard	38,000.00	54,000.00

Like most things related to government, a salary range classification is approved by a legislative body and serves many purposes. A few are listed below.

- It provides government officials data that may be useful in accounting, payroll and personnel.
- It ensures that salaries are reasonable and equitable relative to the responsibilities of the employee.
- It limits the opportunities to discriminate.
- It allows the government to remain competitive in an open market and retain experienced employees.
- It acts as a control over salaries when new positions and raises are considered.

Justifying a New Position

Growth in responsibilities of an agency and personnel are fairly standard in most governments. As a result, it is necessary on occasion to request one or more new positions. There is never a guarantee that a request for a new position will occur. Nonetheless, it is important that agency heads ensure that they adequately review the old and new responsibilities of the agency in order to make sure that they can thoroughly justify new positions and maintain the previous positions. There are several items that go into a request for a new position that will facilitate the process (Riley and Colby 1991). The agency can:

- Justify the creation of the new position(s) by outlining the responsibilities of the person(s) relative to increases in workload or expanded programs.
- Describe the qualifications of the employee(s) with a notation as to whether it fits the current salary pay classification.
- Show how this position(s) will make the agency more efficient and effective.
- Show how the new position(s) will enhance new assignments or enhance current responsibilities.

One last item to note is that newly hired staff frequently waits one year before receiving health insurance.

Calculating a Personal Services Budget

Preparing a new budget can be difficult for the budget officer. In fact, this period causes a fair amount of trepidation for the entire staff. However, the process can be eased with several items. First and foremost is accurate information. It is very important that agency directors and the personnel office provide the budget officer with reliable data that corresponds with known facts. Second, a computer can expedite the budgeting process, but it cannot read minds. Hence, it does not notice mathematical errors in data entry for example. In most cases, budgets are inaccurate because of human error. Specific items needed by the budget office include:

- A manual to review budget requests. The manual would normally contain management policy information (the direction the agency is headed and potential areas to cut or expand).
- Budget preparation forms along with instructions.
- Salary information related to personnel (includes information on projected salary increases as well as fringe benefits).
- Operating and capital outlay instructions.

Beginning with the previous year's base, the budget officer can put the new projected salary information (based on *budget projections*) into a computer spreadsheet program for each position classification. Budget projections are based on projected revenue, which are unknown versus what is known. *Budget estimates* are based on more concrete information. Assuming that no changes occurred, the computer will automatically calculate the fringe benefits associated with the salary. In some cases, the percentage or dollar amount of fringe benefits may change. Exhibit 3.4 is an example of an *Agency Salary Projection Report*.

Exhibit 3.4 Agency Salary Projection Report

FY 2009 (General Fund)
Agency: *Police Department*   Division: *Homicide*

Title	Employee	Salary	FICA	Medicare	Pension	Health	*Total*
Director	Sally Jones	$69,569.22	$8,626.58	$2,017.50	$8,108.31	$1,800	$84,799.58
Captain	Joe Smith	45,230.12	5,608.53	1,311.68	5,427.61	1,800	50,490.22
Detective	Larry Jones	38,987.39	4,834.44	1,130.64	4,678.49	1,800	48,448.42
Detective	Lisa Leslie	35,789.01	4,437.84	1,037.88	4,294.68	1,800	44,621.55
Assistant	John Day	27,123.90	3,363.36	786.60	3,254.87	1,800	34,253.75
TOTAL		$216,699.64	$26,870.75	$6,284.30	$25,763.96	$9,000	$268,041.13

This report allows the viewer to determine the exact cost associated with a position or an individual. Social security, Medicare, and retirement funds are based on formulas while health care cost for the individual employee is the same for everyone that has a particular characteristic, such as single, married with one dependent, and married with multiple dependents for health care benefits. Each of the employees listed here are current employees. Note that the FICA and Medicare costs are the full amount on this sheet. The total cost is included on this spreadsheet because the employee contribution is considered a part of the entire budget. Employee contributions can be deducted using a separate spreadsheet and is an accounting/bookkeeping function. The amount listed here includes the total dollar amount involved in the transaction.

If there are a number of employees who have the same salary, the budget officer may simply want to list the position by title and put the number of employees who correspond to that position/grade (see Appendix C3 for an example). This format saves time and space. However, this format only works when there are a number of employees who have the exact same salary.

A request for a new position along with salary projection follows the same format. However, there should be a justification for the new position at the bottom of the budget request (see Exhibit 3.5). The justification should indicate why the position is needed along with any supporting evidence that would substantiate the request. Data are particularly useful in a position justification. Since the agency is not making a verbal argument for the new position, the justification should be carefully prepared.

A separate form should be used for each new position request. If the administrative position code does not indicate whether the position is an FTE or PTE, then it should be included on the personnel request form. Since positions are based on class, the requested salary for the new employee should fall within the legal pay range that was set by the legislative body. These forms normally come with complete instructions dictating what should be included. Specifically, these instructions should indicate the current rates for FICA (12.4%), Medicare (2.9%), and retirement (18%). In addition, it should contain the cost of health insurance ($1,800.00) and any other pertinent information.

Exhibit 3.5 New Personnel Request Form

Agency Personnel Salaries
FY 2009 (General Fund)
Agency: Police Department   Division: Homicide

Position Title	Position Code	Base Salary	FICA	Medicare	Pension	Health	Total Costs
Dispatcher	1011	$22,500.00	$2,790.00	$652.50	$4,050.00	$1,800.00	$31,792.50

Justification:

Due to an expansion in 911 services the number of incoming phone calls has proved to be a burden for one person. As a result, we had to hire a temporary employee and use patrol officers to aid in this effort. Therefore, it is economically feasible to have a full time employee to carry out these responsibilities.

Preparing an Operating Budget

As stated earlier, the personnel budget makes up the bulk of expenditures in the budget process. However, operating costs are just as important. These requests are reviewed and justified each fiscal year. Operating costs include items such as travel, telephone services and other utilities, pencils, paper, adding machines, rent or any other item that recurs. In simple terms these are items needed by an agency to conduct business. Equipment, such as vehicles, can also be included as an operating expense if the agency is not requesting a large number of new vehicles every year. Further, if vehicles were to be replaced over a number of fiscal years, this might not be the best category to include them. It would depend on the policy of the government. Other exclusions would include high cost items such as super computers and buildings. These are capital expenditure items.

When making a request for operating expenditures, an agency has to indicate how these items will be used to meet the mission of the agency and any new activities that the executive or legislative body may have. The agency director submitting the budget should indicate in the budget transmittal letter how the requests are tied to the goals of the agency. In addition, data showing how expenditures are tied to programs and performance is very useful. Despite the inclusion of these items, operating budgets are not examined as much as personnel budgets. The few exceptions are training and travel.

There are three basic ways to present an operating budget proposal. The first is the incremental method. An *incremental operating budget* essentially shows a modest increase in the budget due to inflation and other naturally occurring economic factors. A lot of agencies tend to use this type of budget because it links spending directly to a service or item (see Exhibit 3.6 for an example).

Also, this budget is particularly useful when there have been no new requests in the personnel budget and when there is no indication of changes in the agency. In addition, it is easy to convey the budget in this manner when the agency can show that it has efficiently and effectively pursued the mission of the agency. The incremental operating budget has four main components: an object code, item/service, current year cost and estimated cost for the upcoming fiscal year. Where appropriate, it may also be useful to indicate the number of items requested (for example, the number of adding machines).

Exhibit 3.6 Incremental Operating Budget Proposal

Object Code	Item	FY 2008 Cost (estimated)	FY 2009 Cost (proposed)
2003	Travel	$5,000.00	$6,000.00
2004	Utilities	2,569.00	3,000.00
2005	Printing	12,904.00	15,000.00
2006	Misc. Supplies	459.00	600.00
2007	Pens	245.00	300.00
2008	Paper	2,349.00	3,600.00
2009	Adding Machine	299.00	150.00
2010	Telephone	1,349.00	2,800.00
TOTAL		$25,174.00	$31,450.00

The estimates in FY 2008 should be based on the appropriation. That is, the estimate would not exceed the appropriation but could be less based on costs as of the date of preparation of the budget. The agency could add an additional column with FY 2007 actual spending to give the reviewer a better trend analysis.

This method is also good to use when there is a drastic change in the cost of an item. For example, let's assume the cost of telephone usage has increased by 5% each fiscal year for the last five years and the amount for FY 2008 is a 15% increase over the previous year (Exhibit 3.7). This increase would require a justification since it does not follow the previous trend. Ideally, the justification would indicate what policy change precipitated the increase in phone service. Clear crisp explanations to changes expedite the approval process (Riley and Colby 1991).

Exhibit 3.7 Police Department Program Operating Budget Proposal

Program	Travel	Utilities and Fuel	Printing	Telephone	FY 2008 Cost (est.)	FY 2009 Request
911 Service	$79,999.00	$3,985.00	$175.00	$10,785.00	$80,546.00	$94,944.00
DARE	1,459.00	350.00	100.00	150.00	1,643.21	2,059.00
Patrol	359,999.00	15,899.00	150.00	987.00	338,456.09	377,035.00
Annual Ball	450.00	600.00	1,200.00	100.00	1,789.43	2,350.00
TOTAL	$441.907.00	$20,834.00	$1,625.00	$12,022.00	$422,434.73	$476,388.00

Justifications:

A.) <u>DARE Program</u>: In harmony with the Mayor and City Council's mission to expand the program into every school, we have increased the number of officers who go into the schools and the amount of information that they disseminate.

B.) <u>911 Service</u>: Due to the expansion of emergency services into the newly annexed suburbs of Mt. Vernon and Taylorville, we are requesting two new patrol officers and thus need to provide them with adequate training and other amenities.

The second and third types of operating budgets are *performance* and *program budgets*. A performance or program operating budget would link the operating expenditures to performance and programs (Riley and Colby 1991; Kelly and Rivenbark 2003). Exhibit 3.7 provides a partial example of a program budget. The budget examiner should be able to look at this budget along with the justification and see exactly where and what the funds are used for.[16]

Conclusion

Personal services and operating budgets appear to be more or less operational functions. However, there is still a degree of negotiation that takes place. Positions are not always guaranteed despite good arguments indicating the need.

Budget personnel officers should ensure that they are meticulous with their data entry skills. A computer is only as good as the operator. It is very easy to put in the wrong number and throw off the entire budget. Budgets must balance to the last dollar. Hence, rounding errors must be minimized.[17]

Important Terms and Phrases

Accrual Accounting

Budget Estimates

Budget Projections

Capital Budget

COLAs

Fringe Benefits

Full Time Employee

Grant

Health Insurance

Incremental Operating Budget

Life Insurance

Medicare

Operating Budget

Part Time Employee

Pension

Pension Board of Directors

Performance Operating Budget

Personal Services Budget

Program Operating Budget

Retirement

Salary Range Plan

Social Security

Chapter 3 Homework Exercises

Directions: A template for answering each of these questions is found in the appendix. You must use excel formulas to calculate the answers. Email your assignment to your instructor prior to class and turn in a hardcopy in class.

1. The city council of Charleston decided to create a new Tourism Department in FY 2009. The department has a director, secretary and three tourism officers. As the budget officer for the city, your job is to create a personnel budget for the department using this information. Only consider the items that are listed. Read each bullit prior to beginning the assignment.

- The director has a salary of $70,000.00 and is a FTE.
- The secretary has a salary of $28,000.00 and is a FTE.
- Each tourism officer has a salary of $20,000.00 and works part time (PTE). Although they each work 6 months out of the year, they are paid over a 12-month period.
- FICA is 12.4% and Medicare is 2.9% for all employees.
- Health insurance costs are $3,000.00 per year for each FTE.
- Each tourism officer has a clothing budget of $500.00.
- Each tourism officer is eligible for 50% of the fringe benefits (health insurance premium, life insurance and pension).
- Training costs associated with each tourism officer is $650.00.
- Life insurance premium is $25.00 per month for each FTE.
- Pensions are 9.5% of salary for each FTE. The city pays the full amount.
- Complete the FTE column.

2. Prepare a salary projection report for the Fire Department for FY 2009 using the actual budget for FY 2008 as a model along with a budget request for two new fire fighter (2a) positions. Use the following information in your FY 2009 Salary Projections and budget requests (see APPC3). Note that the budget has the number of employees in each position grade rather than listing each employee. Also, you should calculate the total cost of employment for each staff person.

- The salary of the chief increased 7% while everyone else received a 5% increase.
- FICA is 12.4% and Medicare is 2.9% for all employees.
- The cost of health insurance increased 5%.
- The cost of uniforms increased 2%.

- The fire fighter (1a and 1b) pay range is $30,000.00-$40,000.00. You will pay the new fire fighters (2a) $35,000.00
- The new fire fighters (2a) will receive the same benefits package as the other FY 2009 employees.
- The cost of training the new fire fighters is $2,000.00 per employee.
- The pension rate in FY 2009 is the same as it was in FY 2008.
- The clerical staff member works a half day schedule 12 months per year (.5 FTE).
- Complete the FTE column.

3. As the budget officer for the Glenbury State Prison you have to prepare the FY 2009 Operating Budget projections for the Security Division based on the FY 2008 budget estimates. Below you will find one portion of the budget history for the prison. Here are a few facts that you should know about the prison when preparing the operating budget. First, there are thirty staff members in the division. Twenty-seven of the staff are equal in rank (guards). The warden, budget officer and secretary are the last three staff members. Other than what is stated, why do think these changes occurred (see Exhibit 3.5)? Be rational and creative in your responses and justify the changes (see APP3C for a hardcopy). Round all of your projections to the nearest dollar amount.

- Ten of the guards need training. Thus, training cost will increase by 40%.
- Because of the Enron debacle, energy costs are expected to rise 15%.
- The cost of printing, pens, pencils, and paper decreases by 2.5% from FY 2008.
- Telephone costs are expected to increase 3%.
- No new adding machine, but we need a new printer which will cost $450.00.
- Miscellaneous supplies will increase 25%.

Glenbury State Prison Security Division
Operating Budget

Object Code	Item	FY 2007 Cost (actual)	FY 2008 Cost (est.)	FY 2009 Cost (proj.)
2004	Training	$25,000.00	$35,999.00	
2005	Utilities	12,569.16	14,999.00	
2006	Printing	9,904.12	10,899.00	

2007	Misc. Supplies	959.05	1,599.00
2008	Pens and Pencils	145.18	245.00
2009	Paper	3,749.74	4,999.00
2010	Adding Machine	299.67	150.00
2011	Telephone	3,349.42	4,500.00
2012	Printer	0	0
TOTAL		$55,976.34	$73,390.00

4. Three employees are retiring from the city of Standridge. Your job as the human resource officer is to calculate their pension using the following information. Use the model in Exhibit 3.1 to assist you in completing this problem. Turn in the short version answer to your professor.

Employee 1 Matthew Joyner
- Has 27 years of service and is 64 years of age.
- 5 highest years of salary are: $18,904; $19,398; $20,198; $22,239; & $24,908.

Employee 2 Jeremy McEntire
- Has 34 years of service and is 66 years of age.
- Five highest years of salary are: $28,504; $29,698; $30,798; $32,839; & $34,508.

Employee 3 Anna Murray
- Has 38 years of service and is 69 years of age
- Five highest years of salary are: $47,904; $49,899; $53,678; $55,742; & $57,108.

References

Bland, Robert L. 2005. *A Revenue Guide for Local Government.* Washington, D.C.: ICMA.

Friedman, Marvin. 1983. "Calculating Compensation Costs." *In Budget Management: A Reader in Local Government Financial Management.* Eds. Jack Rabin, W. Bartley Hildreth, and Gerald J. Miller. Athens, GA: Carl Vinson Institute of Government, University of Georgia.

Gruber, Jonathan. 2005. *Public Finance and Public Policy.* NY, NY: Worth Publishers.

http://www.ssa.gov.

Kelly, Janet M. and William C. Rivenbark. 2003. *Performance Budgeting for State and Local Government.* Armonk, NY: M.E. Sharpe

Mikesell, John. 2003. *Fiscal Administration: Analysis and Applications for the Public Sector.* 6th Edition. CA: Thomson Wadsworth.

Riley, Susan L. and Peter W. Colby. 1991. *Practical Government Budgeting: A Workbook for Public Managers.* NY: State University of New York Press.

Smith, Robert W. and Thomas D. Lynch. 2004. *Public Budgeting in America.* 5th ed. Upper Saddle River, NJ: Pearson/Prentice Hall.

Chapter Three

Appendix 3A

City of Charleston
Tourism Department
FY 2009

Position	FTE	Salary	S.S.	Medicare	Pension	Health	Life Ins.	Training	Clothing	Grand Total
Director										
Secretary										
Tourism Officers										
TOTAL										

Appendix 3B

Personnel Services Budget
FY 2008

Position	FTE	Salary	SS	Health Ins.	Pension	Medicare	Uniforms	TOTAL
Chief	1	$87,000	$10,788	$2,160	$17,400	$2,523	$750	$120,621
Shift Commander	3	150,000	18,600	6,480	30,000	4,350	2,250	211,680
Fire Fighter 1a	12	420,000	52,080	25,920	84,000	12,180	9,000	603,180
Fire Fighter 1b	26	650,000	80,600	56,160	130,000	18,850	19,500	955,110
Clerical (PT)	0.5	45,000	5,580	0	9,000	1,305	0	60,885
TOTAL	42.5	$1,352,000	$167,648	$90,720	$270,400	$39,208	$31,500	$1,951,476

FY 2009

Position	FTE	Salary	SS	Health Ins.	Pension	Medicare	Uniforms	TOTAL
Chief								
Shift Commander								
Fire Fighter 1a								
Fire Fighter 1b								
Clerical (PT)								
TOTAL								

New Position
Budget Request

Position	FTE	Salary	SS	Health Ins.	Pension	Medicare	Uniforms	Training
Fire Fighter 2a								

FY 2009	FTE	Salary	SS	Health Ins.	Pension	Medicare	Uniforms	Training
GRAND TOTAL								

Appendix 3C

Glenbury State Prison
Operating Budget

Object Code	Item	FY 2007 (act)	FY 2008 (est)	FY 2009 (proj)
2004	Training	$25,000.00	$35,999.00	
2005	Utilities	12,569.16	14,999.00	
2006	Printing	9,904.12	10,899.00	
2007	Misc. Supplies	959.05	1,599.00	
2008	Pens and Pencils	145.18	245.00	
2009	Paper	3,749.74	4,999.00	
2010	Adding Machine	299.67	150.00	
2011	Telephone	3,349.42	4,500.00	
2012	Printer	0.00	0.00	
TOTAL		$55,976.34	$73,390.00	

Appendix 3D

Mr. Matthew Joyner

Step 1: Creditable Services and Percentage Value

	% Value Per Year of Service	Total Years of Service	Total % Value Per Plan (TVVP)
Retirement up to age 62 or 30 years	1.60%		
Retirement up to age 63 or 31 years	1.63%		
Retirement up to age 64 or 32 years	1.65%		
Retirement up to age 65 or 33 years or more	1.68%		

Step 2: Average Final Compensation (AFC)

AFC =

Step 3: Monthly Benefit Calculation

AFC x TVPP = Annual Benefit

AFC x TVPP = Annual Beneftit / 12 = Monthly Benefit

Chapter 4
Preparing a Capital Budget and a Capital Improvement Plan

Chapter Four Overview

One of the most crucial components of a government is to provide citizens with sound infrastructure and equipment capable of helping the government to be efficient and effective. In order to accomplish this purpose, two items can be used: a capital budget and a capital improvement plan. Part one of this chapter defines and discusses the capital budget, while part two discusses a capital improvement plan and financing capital projects.

Capital Budgets versus a Capital Improvement Plan

While there is a definite correlation between a capital budget and a capital improvement plan, they are not the same. A *capital budget* is merely an expenditure list of high cost items such as buildings, bridges, highways and other large-scale items that are expected to provide benefits and services over a considerable period of time. A *capital improvement plan* (CIP) on the other hand is a spending plan that will take place over a three to five year period. In some instances, the first year or current year of the capital improvement plan can become the capital budget. This decision is determined by a number of items, including the size of the budget and the size of the government. Some governments include the capital budget in their operating budget.[18]

Capital Budgets

Unlike a personnel and operating budget, a capital budget only includes high cost non-routine items such as public buildings, equipment, infrastructure, and land purchases. Public buildings include police stations, court houses, public schools and government offices. Equipment includes vehicles, computers, and office furniture. Infrastructure includes roads, bridges, and water lines. It is possible that some of these items can be included in an operating budget. For example, the purchase of a single computer would not require a long-term plan. However, the purchase of several computers tends to be more costly and cause a greater burden on the funding source. By placing the computers in the capital budget, a budget office may be more creative in financing the item (Gianakis and McCue 1999). Further, a city can have a separate infrastructure replacement budget to replace existing sewers, streets, etc. Most often, the determination of what is included in the capital vs. operating budget is a function of the government's capitalization policies. For example, if the government requires all equipment with a unit price greater than $5,000 to be capitalized, then all equipment with a unit price less than $5,000 would be included in the operating budget.

During times of budget shortfalls equipment can and often is the first thing cut out of the budget. This occurs because it is easier to cut equipment than people. Further, budget officials assume that agencies can get by one more year with the equipment that they have rather than replacing it. These cuts are facilitated when agencies seek to replace functional equipment with the "latest and greatest equipment" which may in fact improve efficiency and effectiveness.

When an agency is preparing a budget for new expenditures, analysts should realize that start-up costs are often expensive even though additional efforts lead to lower unit costs. In these circumstances *marginal costs* may be lower. When considering a comparable increase in the budget because of the new expenditure, the analyst should remember that marginal costs should not increase proportionally.

When performing this function, expenditures should be split into one-time *fixed costs* and *recurring costs*. One-time fixed costs include the up front costs, and include: research cost, evaluations, land, construction labor, construction materials, legal fees, freight and shipping costs, and training. Recurring costs are those costs associated with providing the service on an annual basis. These include utilities, personnel, supplies, etc. As more units of service are added, recurring costs increase. As more services are added the unit cost goes down.

Let's assume for a moment that the municipal golf course is submitting their capital budget request. Since the golf course is more or less self-sufficient, funding is not a big issue. The first mistake that the golf course officials could make is to assume that since money is available that they can do a lack luster job in justifying the new requests. A budget officer should never take a surplus or a "guaranteed" increase in their budget for granted.

Unlike an operating and personnel budget, a capital budget may not be incremental in nature. The budget essentially reacts to the items within it. For example, during periods of relative inactivity a capital budget may appear to be incremental in nature. However, when agencies have large projects underway, the budgets can change drastically from year to year.

For example, take a look at Exhibit 4.1. The Post Office has been purchasing items using a capital improvement plan that began a few years earlier. In FY 2008 they estimate that they will spend $10,000.00 on computers and are requesting $20,000.00 in FY 2009 to complete their system. According to the justification, this purchase is the final stage of a multiyear plan to replace older computers with new ones. The justification for purchasing the new trucks also follows the same logic. Unlike an operating and personnel budget, it is not necessary to elaborate in detail when justifying items in a capital budget that is following a CIP. However, thorough justification is needed if the plan is changed in any way.

Exhibit 4.1 A Simple Line Item Capital Budget for the Post Office

Object Code	Item	Quantity	FY 2008 Cost (est.)	FY 2009 Cost (proposed)
3003	Computers	10	$10,000.00	$20,000.00
3004	Security System	1	500.00	34,000.00
3005	Copy Machine	1	4,000.00	4,000.00
3007	Trucks	8	75,000.00	120,000.00
3008	Office Desks	10	1,500.00	3,000.00
Total			$91,000.00	$181,000.00

Brief Description:

The Post Office is going through a normal update of its computer systems and vehicle fleet. The new security system will bring the Post Office into compliance with the last round of federal statutes. The new trucks will not only replace some of the aging fleet but also provide for two new trucks to handle our expanding population.

Justifications:

1. Installing and implementing the new security system: The old system is outdated and does not offer the level of security that we need for our new equipment. Further, over time, this new equipment is cost effective and more efficient. The monthly up keep cost is 60% less than the old system. Last, the system will bring the office into federal compliance.

2. New Computers: These computers will allow us to complete our overhaul of the computer network. Our workload capacity will increase 20%.

3. Copy Machine: This purchase is the second and last phase of our office equipment update.

4. Trucks: These five trucks are the final vehicle purchases in updating our fleet for the foreseeable future.
5. Desks: The ten desks will hold the ten new computers.

Last, agency heads must remember that operating budgets are affected by capital budgets in the long term. As capital projects come to fruition, maintenance and personnel cost fall back into operating and personnel budgets. So, it is important to ensure that staff and additional resources needed to manage the capital project are in place prior to the completion of the project. These projects often provide considerable strain on operating budgets when checks are not put in place.

Why Separate a Capital Budget from an Operating Budget?

- Capital outlays are financed and often paid from one-time, earmarked sources such as debt proceeds and grants. Segregating the funds from operating budgets ensure that they are spent for their original purpose.
- The decision making process differs in a capital budget. Frequently projects are ranked and funded as revenue becomes available. As projects are funded other projects are added to the list.
- The time frame for spending varies. Capital budgets are rarely completely executed in a single fiscal year.
- Capital budgets often exceed budget projections and thus require close scrutiny.[19]
- Capital budgets can stabilize tax rates when individual capital projects are large relative to the tax base of the city (Mikesell 2003).
- Financial mistakes (underestimation of costs) made with capital budgets can linger for many years and these errors should not be tied to operating budgets which must balance each year.[20]

Capital Improvement Plans

When cities are expanding their capital infrastructure or simply planning for the future they will frequently put together a long term spending plan called a capital improvement plan (CIP) as well as the sources for funding the plan. Doss (1993) defines a CIP as, "a comprehensive document that enables local governments to budget for immediate capital projects, evaluate the condition of existing projects, and assess the future capital needs for either expansion, renovation or construction of new capital stock" (p. 272). This plan is a list of high cost expenditures that would occur over several fiscal years. This process will often begin with a request from the budget office for project proposals (See Appendix 4A at the end of the chapter for an example). Concurrently, the chief executive officer along with the legislative body will begin to develop their list of spending priorities (Bland and Rubin 1997; Mikesell 2003; Vogt 2004; Kittredge and Ouart 2005). Why develop a CIP?

Advantages
- Establishes agency long-term priorities.
- Provides a mechanism for coordinating various agency projects.
- Helps to prevent duplication.
- Maximizes the distribution of public resources.
- Can stimulate private investment and economic development (excerpted from Riley and Colby 1983, p. 105).

Disadvantages
- Items that should be placed in the operating budget sometime end up in the CIP because of high cost.
- Assume that officials will continue to reevaluate project proposals as the environment changes.
- The amount of funds may distort the ranking of projects. Some projects create their own funding, which may make them seem more practicable and appealing than non revenue producing ventures.
- At some point, it is necessary to eliminate projects from consideration. The availability of funds play a perennial role in this process, but politics does as well. Decisions should be made objectively with the greater interest of the community.[21]

The Capital Budgeting Process

The capital budgeting process presented here occurs in three stages. The first stage is *planning*. Several important items must occur during this stage. First, some basic identification, classification and analysis of capital requests should occur. Then, a preliminary ranking of projects should occur, along with a time frame in which the work should be completed, (*capital budget calendar*).

According to Riley and Colby (1983), a budget calendar is "useful in coordinating the work of all the players and identifies who does what and when?" (p. 107). Exhibit 4.2 has an example of a capital project request form.

Exhibit 4.2 Capital Budget Project Request Form

Directions: Complete this form for each capital request (includes new projects, repairs, or modifications).

1. Title of Project: Construction of Newburg Elementary School.

2. Location of Project: Mound Bayou.

Description of Project: The school will serve the southwest part of the city. It will fit the standard model that we have used for the last five years in school construction. Should the region continue to grow at the current rate, this building model will allow the school to expand at minimal cost.

Justification of Project: The population in southwest Mound Bayou is growing at an extremely fast rate. Hence, this is the best location for the school. The other schools in the city are overwhelmed with students and the bus system is being stretched thin due to long bus rides to the schools.

Estimated Cost of Project

Project Cost Components		Projected Annual Cost	
1. Land	$10,000 .00	1. FY One	$175,000.00
2. HVAC	$35,000 .00	2. FY Two	$100,000.00
3. Construction	$315,000.00	3. FY Three	$25,000.00
4. Plumbing	$20,000.00	4. FY Four	$75,000.00
5. Equipment	$20,000.00	5. FY Five	$50,000.00
6. Other Costs	$25,000.00		
		Total Costs	*$425,000.00*

Current Status of Project: The project has not begun.

Estimated Project Life: 15-20 years once the school is open.

Possible Sources of Funding: School Bond_____

Stage two is concerned with *budget analysis, project evaluation* and *budget adoption.* In this stage, evaluators examine the status of current capital projects and capital facilities. Further, they select new projects and determine which projects require funding from the general fund or other sources, and which projects will create revenue. In addition, an assessment of infrastructure changes and the construction or purchase of buildings can be done (Bland and Clarke 1999). At this juncture, budget forecasts can be made. Vogt (1983) suggests that quantitative analysis be used in this process (see chapter 6). Once these decisions are made, *implementation* of the CIP can begin. In stage three, funds are acquired, managed, and invested in the CIP. Equipment is bought, land is purchased and the construction begins (Vogt 1983).   Lastly, a *post evaluation* has to be conducted shortly after the project has been completed (Mikesell 2003). The purpose of the evaluation is to ensure that goals and objectives were met (See Appendix 4A for an example of a Capital Improvement Program).

Identifying and Prioritizing Projects

Selecting a group of people to identify projects for a capital improvement plan is not as simple as it appears. Bland and Rubin (1997) point out that the selection of participants will largely determine what comes out of the process (Bland and Clarke 1999). Vogt (2004) argues that experience should play a major role in prioritizing projects. Experienced citizens who are in touch with citizen's need should play a vital role.[22] Bland and Rubin (1997) offer three possible plans. Plan 1 is a planning oriented process plan where priorities are assigned by the planning or capital budget office based on need or technical standards. Priorities in Plan 1 can be categorized as follows:

- **High:** These are projects that are vital and impending. They should be ranked at the top and funded in the early years of the Capital Improvement Plan. These are items that *must be* done.

- **Medium:** These are projects that are also vital but do not have to be funded immediately. They should be in the middle to latter years of the CIP. These are items that *should be* done.

- **Low:** These are projects that have great benefit to the city, but not to the extent that they should receive higher priority. That is, they will not adversely affect critical areas immediately. These are items that *could be* done. Elected officials may have a peripheral role in the plan.

Plan 2 is a less planning oriented process and may have the input of elected or bureaucratic officials as well as citizens. Hence, it becomes more politics based than strategically based on need. In Plan 3, a group of elected officials and technical staff would identify and prioritize projects. Since the implementation of a capital improvement plan is a multi faceted process involving different areas of expertise, it seems quite reasonable that the process is not limited to elected officials and bureaucrats. In fact, it may be necessary to consult with professionals in the private sector (see also Bland and Clarke 1999; Kittredge and Ouart 2005).

Nice (2002) argues that "need" should be the prevailing characteristic when prioritizing projects. For example, the building of a new landfill to offset an old one that is operating at the maximum capacity should take precedence over a new recreational park. A long-term assessment of a locality's needs would be very useful when prioritizing projects. Bland and Rubin (1997) suggest two methods for prioritizing projects. In the first method, "projects are generated and ranked through a technical planning process, possibly overseen by the planning department" (p. 179). One way to prioritize projects using this method is to address the following issues:

- Legal Mandates: Is the project required by federal or state statute, court order, etc?
- Removes or Reduces Hazards: Does it remove hazards or improve public safety?
- Legislative or Executive Goals: Does the project advance stated goals and objectives?
- Efficiency: Does the project improve productivity and lower operating costs?
- Standards of Service: Does the project maintain or extend current service levels?
- Economic Development: Does the project support or benefit economic development?
- New Service: Does the project offer new services or programs?
- Quality of Life: Does the project improve the quality of life for citizens?
- Convenience: Does the project make it easier for citizens or government officials to manage activities?[23]

At the other end of the spectrum, "projects are generated by departments and examined and ranked by variously structured committees" (p. 179). Unfortunately, politics plays a role in this process. Most projects tend to show characteristics of both methods. In either case, a level of economic and political parity much be reached (Axelrod 1995; Mikesell 2003; Aronson and Schwartz 2004).

Needs Assessments and the Selection of Projects

Prior to implementing a capital improvement plan, a *needs assessment* should be conducted. A needs assessment allows all concerned parties to examine the current status of the capital infrastructure. That is, the assessment should indicate the condition of all capital assets. By showing the positive benefits of previous investments in the infrastructure, you can legitimize new investment. Needs assessments should be comprehensive and conducted by a neutral unbiased party. Why? An agency can only look at its own needs over some period of time. Citizens and elected officials often have their own agendas and fail to see the big picture and as a result overlook conflicting or competing needs.

At the tail end of this process, someone has to decide what projects will be selected for funding. Nice (2002), Bland and Rubin (1997), Gianakis and McCue (1999), Axelrod (1995) and Millar (1988), offer a number of suggestions and questions that should be answered prior to making a final decision on capital projects. Vogt (1983) offers a two-dimensional matrix to establish priorities based on a numerical score. The matrix and the items included in Table 4.1 are quite consistent.

Table 4.1 Other Factors to Consider Prior to Selecting Capital Projects

1. Prepare an inventory of current fixed capital assets. What is the life expectancy of these assets and how much are they currently worth?

2. What is the fiscal impact of each new project for the current and future years? How will the project impact the personnel and operating budget on a year-by-year basis? Will the project generate revenue on a year-by-year basis? Is the project a continuation of an earlier project? Are there any legal liabilities that will impact the project?

3. Assess the impact of the project on the community. Are there any special energy requirements? How will the project affect the aesthetic value of the community (noise, air, commuters, households, recreation and quality of life)? Are there any health and safety issues?

4. Determine the possible health and safety effects (accidents, illness, sewage, etc).

5. Estimate how the project will disrupt day-to-day activities in the community.

6. What is the impact of the project on the various populations in the community? Consider the following factors: race, income, single parent households, age and disabled.

7. Ascertain the level of public support for the project. Is the project consistent with the master plan for the community?

8. If the project is not funded or deferred, what impact will this have on the community (i.e. higher costs, inconvenience)?

9. Will the project benefit or adversely impact other localities?
10. Will the project benefit or adversely impact other capital projects?

Financing Capital Improvement Projects

In most state and local governments where funds are limited, a decision to pursue a project and the decision to fund a project occur relatively close together. While it is possible for a project to create revenue, a lot of projects do not generate revenue. In either case, the budget officer should make at least four revenue projections relative to funding capital outlay: current operating revenue and expenditures, current outstanding debt, annual debt-service payments and intergovernmental grants and aid. Every attempt should be made to determine how the economy and other environmental and demographic changes have affected these items (Vogt 1996 2004).

How to fund a capital project, to a large extent, depends on the project. For example, it is feasible to fund the construction of a new highway from a toll on the highway. However, it would not be feasible to use a highway toll to fund the construction of a new school. This is illegal. A bond may be a better alternative.

Bland and Rubin (1997) offer two basic strategies for financing capital improvement projects. The first is *pay-as-you-go* financing. In this method, officials may use current revenues, federal or state grants, reserve funds, revenue from leases or other revenue such as utility charges to fund projects. Vogt (1983) points out several advantages to using this method. First, "it encourages responsible spending by requiring the same officials who approve projects or outlays also to levy taxes to pay for them," "it avoids paying the interest charges that are involved with bonding; and it avoids the accumulation of large, fixed principal and interest payments in the operating budget" (p. 139). It also, "side-steps bond and debt markets" as well as improves the financial position of the local government by holding down debt and lowering debt service cost (Vogt 2004, p. 144; Solano 2004). Pay-as-you-go financing is particularly effective if a government has a consistent need for infrastructure maintenance. For example, a mature state or local government needs to replace and maintain its streets, water-lines, and sewer lines. Dedicating a set amount annually for this purpose avoids the extra interest charges.

Vogt (2004) offers a second pay-as-go or cash method for financing capital projects by creating a capital reserve. Essentially revenues would be diverted from other sources into this capital fund which could be used when the time arose. Spending does not occur until a sufficient amount of revenues have been collected to meet the needs of the expenditure. For example, a city might want to construct a new city park and have a five-year plan to save the funds to pay for it. A capital reserve would be the perfect tool to facilitate this process. A note to the wise, it is better to separate the capital reserve fund from other funds. This prevents fungibility from occurring easily (Aronson and Schwartz 2004).

The second method is *pay-as-you-use* financing. This includes bonds or other debt instruments, assessments on recipients of the service, or mortgages or bank loans. Bland and Clarke (1999) point out two advantages to debt financing. First, it allows a government to acquire capital as needed yet devote a relatively stable amount of current revenue each year for debt service. Second, it also removes capital acquisition decisions from the operating budget process, which is often completed under a tight time constraint. This also allows officials to better plan for the future (see also Vogt 1983; Aronson and Schwartz 2004). Another advantage of pay-as-you-use financing is that the taxpayers who are receiving the benefit of the project are paying for it. The taxpayers are contributing annually to the payment for debt service.

Riley and Colby (1991) offer several methods to the pay-as-you-use financing method. The first method is to issue *bonds*. A bond is basically money that is borrowed from an individual(s) with the assurance that the bond can be cashed in a given period of time for a sum of money (principal and interest). State and local governments use bonds to finance projects that cannot be financed from the current revenue sources. The interest earned on bonds is not taxable by the United States government.

Bonds can be issued through public entities to assist in private development activities, if they further the objectives of a particular agency (e.g., economic development, energy conservation, affordable housing). These bonds can either be *revenue bonds*, which are a type of *municipal bond* where principal and interest are secured by revenues such as charges or rents paid by users of the facility built with the proceeds of the bond issue. The issuer of a revenue bond is not obligated to use any other funding source to pay back the bond. Projects financed by revenue bonds include turnpikes, airports, and not-for-profit health care and other facilities. The more common approach is to use *general obligation bonds* (GO), which may be taxable or tax-exempt bonds and are backed by the general "faith and credit" of the issuing entity to assure repayment of the bonds. Because the backing for revenue bonds is limited to the revenue stream that is used to support the bonds, they have a higher interest rate than general obligation bonds. General obligation bonds can make up more than a third of the long-term debt issued by state and local governments (Vogt 2004).[24]

Prior to securing any type of bond, a local government may need to be rated. *Bond ratings* are quite similar to an individual credit report that you or I may get prior to buying a house or a car. Vogt (2004) describes it this way:

> "A bond rating evaluates a debt issuer's strength or weakness on factors that bear on the issuer's ability and willingness to make principal and interest payments on the debt when due and to comply with other obligations that the issuer assumes under the

debt contract. A rating addresses not only the probability that the issuer will make debt service payments but also the legal protection afforded to investors by laws, regulations, and the debt contract. Such protection or security varies by type of debt and also depends on state and federal laws and regulations" (p. 217).

As shown, the emphasis is on the ability of the entity to repay the amount borrowed with the interest and the protection afforded to the investors (see Vogt 2004 & Aronson and Schwartz 2004 for a description of bonds and ratings).

Some governments are precluded from issuing general obligation debt because of legal restrictions or debt limitations. Other types of financing instruments have been created to allow governments to construct capital facilities. For example, a government might enter into a lease-purchase arrangement with a private contractor to build a water treatment plant. The government makes lease payments to the contractor until the project is paid off. At that point, it is turned over to the government. Another financing option is a *certificate of participation*. A government contacts one or more financial institutions and a pool is formed. Each participant in the pool receives a certificate of participation. The project is financed using the resources in the pool and the resulting facility is leased to the government. Each participant receives a share of the debt service based on its participation in the pool.

A municipality may also secure *short-term notes* or use a *line of credit* (LOC) where "money is made available for the local government to use on an "as needed" basis (Riley and Colby 1983, p. 110).[25] Short-term notes are used during the construction phase of a project because of arbitrage restrictions established by the *Internal Revenue Service* (IRS). Since debt issued by state and local governments is exempt from federal taxes, the IRS requires funding of a capital project to be undertaken as cash is needed. For example, if a government is building a facility that costs $10 million, issuing $10 million in bonds when the project is approved would allow the government to invest the proceeds and earn substantial interest for some period of time. Under the arbitrage rules, a government now has to reimburse the federal government for such arbitrage earnings. Thus, governments finance the projects during the construction period by using short-term notes. City and counties can also *joint finance* projects that will be shared.[26]

Conclusion

While there are some similarities between an operating and capital budget, it is clear that the differences substantiate separating the two. It is important for the reader to understand that investments into capital infrastructure and the use of public resources to fund capital projects play a major role in economic development and growth in states and municipalities. Hence, time and resources devoted to the process should not be taken lightly. Chapters 5 and 6 will further this topic with a discussion of payment options and maximizing use of capital facilities through analytical models and techniques.

Important Terms and Phrases

Bond
Bond Rating
Budget Adoption
Capital Budget
Capital Budget Calendar
Capital Improvement Plan
Certificate of Participation
Fixed Cost
Fungibility
General Obligation Bonds (GO)
Implementation
Internal Revenue Service
Joint Finance

Line of Credit (LOC)
Marginal Cost
Municipal Bond
Needs Assessment
Pay-as-you-go
Pay-as-you-use
Planning
Post Evaluation
Project Evaluation
Revenue Bonds
Recurring Cost
Short Term Note

Chapter 4 Homework Exercises

Directions: Complete each of the assigned questions in Excel. A template for each problem is found in the appendix.

1. As the new chief of Mound Bayou's Fire Department it is your job to write the justifications for the department's proposed FY 2009 capital budget. Specifically, you must prepare justifications for the proposed new fire station near the new Wellman Subdivision. Remember, you are trying to convince the city' elected officials that the construction of a new fire department will allow your department to be more efficient and effective. Further, your justifications should show that you have considered the long range plans of the city's elected officials to expand public services. The items needed to construct the fire department are listed below the table. Note: land that could be used for the station was budgeting for in FY 2008. Although some of the items in the budget are for existing services, the majority of them are for the new station. This is particularly true in FY 2009. Exhibit 4.1 can serve as a point of departure. However, since you are justifying an entire project, your model should follow the example of the Peumansend Creek Regional Jail in Appendix4a at the end of the chapter. Hence, you should have a project summary and a project description in your justification along with the proposed capital budget. While there can be legal reasons to build the station, remember: economic growth, population growth, and other factors contribute to the need to build the station. Use logic and creativity when writing your justifications (use paragraphs).

Fire Department' FY 2009 Proposed Capital Budget

Object Code	Item	Quantity FY 2007	FY 2008 Cost (est.)	FY 2009 Cost (proposed)
3003	Computers	5	$ 5,000.00	$5,000.00
3004	Security System	1		30,000.00
3005	Copy Machine	2	4,000.00	4,000.00
3007	¾ Ton Truck	1		25,000.00
3008	Office Desks	3	1,500.00 (10)	450.00
3009	Pumper	1		95,000.00
3010	Tanker	1		125,000.00
3011	New Fire Station	1		756,000.00
3012	Water Well	1		195,000.00
3013	Land	4 acres	4,500.00 (acre)	9,000.00
TOTAL			$15,000.00	$1,244,450.00

Items Needed for the Fire Station:
Computers   Office Desks   Water Well

Security System	Pumper	Fire Station
Copy Machines	Tanker	Land
¾ Ton Truck		

Note: A Tanker and Pumper are large fire trucks.

2. The city of Robinsonville has several capital projects that the mayor wants to complete over the next 2-3 years (FY 2009-2011). She has asked you, the city manager, to prioritize the eight projects and justify each placement based on some sort of rational methodology. Your ranking will determine where the project will be placed in the final CIP which will be done by another group. Therefore, your job is to review, rank, and justify completing the list of projects on a scale of 1 to 8. The most important project should be listed first (include the projected cost with the project). In addition to considering the information in the text, pay special attention to the list of questions in Table 4.1. Your grade will be determined by how well you justify your project rankings. I have included some background on the city that should be useful in your ranking and justification. Your justifications should be logically creative.

Projects and Costs:
- CBD Sewers: Add 3 miles of sewers in the central business district ($4.2 million).
- NRA: Add 2 miles of sewer lines in the northern residential area ($3 million).
- SRA: Build a new waste treatment lift station in the southern residential area ($1.8 million).
- Beltway Project: Complete the final stage of the beltway around the city (3 miles) ($4.3 million).
- Storm Water Project: Construct 2 storm water management ponds ($1 million).
- Library Renovation ($700,000).
- Garage: Construct a downtown parking garage for city employees and public use ($2.5 million).
- Downtown Artery: Landscaping the main downtown artery ($800,000).

Background Information:
- The population of the city has grown an average of 4% a year for the last 5 years.
- Public service employees have increased an average of 2% a year for the last 10 years.
- Ten new corporations have moved into the city over the last

three years employing 770 new employees.

- The city has 79,000 residents and lies in between two large cities exceeding 1 million residents.
- The land selected for the construction of the ponds is located near a school and a public park.
- The average household income in the city is $60,000 per year.

3. The city of Alexandria is located near a growing metropolitan area with a population exceeding one million residents. Due to urban sprawl, the city is having difficulty providing community service in an efficient manner. As a result, they hire you as a budget analyst to prepare a capital improvement plan for the renovation of the library, construction of a recreational park, golf course and a new route on the public bus system.

First, use the data below to complete the capital improvement plan (see APPC4). Second, using factors associated with urban sprawl as well as the information in the text, justify each project separately. This does not mean that you cannot discuss a project when justifying a different project. Copy and paste the Excel spreadsheet into a word processing program.[27] Place your justifications under the spreadsheet.

- The CIP will run from FY 2009-FY 2013.
- The *Library* renovations will be completed during the first two fiscal years at a cost of $125,000.00 each year.
- The city *Golf Course* will be completed during the last three years of the CIP at a total cost of $560,000.00. Sixty percent of the cost will occur in the first year with the remaining 40% spent equally during the latter two years.
- The construction of the *Park* will take place over the entire duration of the CIP with the following spending patterns. FY 2009 $100,000.00; FY 2010 $85,000.00; FY 2011 $35,000.00; FY 2012 and FY 2013 $25,000.00 each year.
- The extension of the *Bus Route* to the Springfield region will cost $40,000.00 in FY 2009. This cost is for the construction of a bus station near the Springfield Mall. The station will cost $30,000.00 in FY 2010 and 80% of that amount for each year left in the CIP.
- The new *streets and sewers* will cost $560,000.00 in FY 2009, $1.7 million in FY 2008, $2.1 million in FY 2009, $3.5 million in FY 2010, and $4.8 million in FY 2013.

4. You have been hired by the state of Mississippi as a budget analyst to develop a capital improvement plan. The state had an economic windfall with the collec-

tion of revenue from the gaming industry and wants to make good use of some of these funds to improve the states' infrastructure among other public institutions in the state. You have been given a budget of $340 million to develop a five-year CIP. You cannot spend more than your total allotment under any circumstance. Here is some useful information that you should use in developing your FY 2009-2013 CIP. The state assumes that you will not be able to "solve" all of the problems in the state over a five-year period, but they do expect a lot. Justify your spending patterns using a two section format: The projects that you expect to complete should be justified in a section titled: *High Priority Tasks*. Projects that you will not complete should be justified in a section titled: *Lower Priority Tasks* (see APPC4 on the CD). Read all of the information before you begin to work on the justifications.

- The state's primary and secondary educational facilities can essentially be split into two types: Functional and Dysfunctional. Dysfunctional educational facilities are located primarily in the economically depressed Mississippi Delta. There are 45 schools in this area that are identical and each is in need of repair and renovations. Repair and renovation cost average $250,000.00 per school. School renovations should be completed within the first three years (equal amounts spent each year). The Functional schools are completely up to date and require no repair or renovations.
- The state is plagued with a number of two lane highways that cross the state. However, Highway 61, south of Memphis through the Mississippi Delta to Louisiana (240 miles in length) and Highway 82, from the Arkansas border to the Alabama border (85 miles that is currently two-lane) are the main two arteries connecting the state to it neighbors. It will cost $1 million per mile to complete the four-lane highway system. Improvement to the highway system should reap multiple economic benefits. Particularly in the Delta Region.
- The state also has 82 county health departments. Thirty-six of these building are in need of repair. Three additional buildings should be constructed adjacent to existing health departments in Desoto, Jackson and Bolivar counties. It is estimated that it would cost $300,000.00 to build each building. Repair costs are estimated to cost a total of $10 million. Bolivar County has the greatest need followed by Jackson and Desoto County respectively.
- The state Supreme Court building is in need of repair. Given the nature of the repair, at least two fiscal years will be involved with the same amount spent each year. The repairs cost

$5 million.

- For the sake of beautification, the state has also decided to build six new Welcome Centers in the state. These fully functional centers will cost the state $1,000,000.00 each. The Welcome Centers will be located at both ends of the border for Hwy 61, Hwy 82 and Interstate 55. With the new highways under construction, the Welcome Centers should improve the look of the state a lot.

- You can spend up to the following amounts per fiscal year: 2009, $50 million; 2010, $60 million; 2011, $65 million; 2012, $85 million; and 2013, $100 million. However, note that these amounts exceed your total allotment.

References

Aronson, J. Richard and Eli Schwartz. 2004. "Cost-Benefit Analysis and the Capital Budget. In J. Richard Aronson and Eli Schwartz's *Management Policies in Local Government Finance*. 5th Edition. Washington, D.C.: ICMA.

Axelrod, Donald. 1995. *Budgeting for Modern Government*. 2nd Edition. NY: St. Martins.

Bland, Robert and Irene Rubin. 1997. *Budgeting: A Guide for Local Governments*. Washington, D.C.: ICMA.

Bland, Robert L. and Wes Clarke. 1999. "Budgeting for Capital Improvements." In Roy Meyer's (ed) *Handbook of Government Budgeting*. San Francisco, CA: Josey Bass.

Doss, Bradley C. 1993. "Capital Budgeting Practices." In Thomas D. Lynch and Lawrence L. Martin's (eds) *Handbook of Comparative Public Budgeting and Financial Management*. NY: Marcel Dekker.

Gianakis, Gerasimos A. and Clifford P. McCue. 1999. *Local Government Budgeting: A Managerial Approach*. Westport, Connecticut: Praeger.

Kittredge, William P. and Sarah M. Ouart. 2005. *Budget Manual for Georgia Local Government*. Athens, GA: Vinson Institute.

Nice, David. 2002. *Public Budgeting*. Stamford, Connecticut: Wadsworth.

Riley, Susan L. and Peter W. Colby. 1991. *Practical Government Budgeting: A Workbook for Public Managers*. NY: State University of New York Press.

Smith, Robert W. and Thomas D. Lynch. 2004. *Public Budgeting in America*. 5th ed. Upper Saddle River, NJ: Pearson/Prentice Hall.

Vogt, A. John. 1983. "Budgeting Capital Outlays and Improvements." In Jack Rabin, W. Bartley Hildreth, and Gerald J. Miller's *Budget Management: A Reader in Local Government Financial Management*. Athens, GA: The University of Georgia: Carl Vinson Institute of Government.

Vogt, A. John. 1996. "Budgeting Capital Outlays and Improvements." In Jack Rabin, W. Bartley Hildreth, and Gerald J. Miller's *Budgeting: Formulation and Execution*. Athens, GA: The University of Georgia: Carl Vinson Institute of Government.

Vogt, A. John. 2004. *Capital Budgeting and Finance: A Guide for Local Government*. Washington, D.C.: ICMA.

Appendix 4A

City of Alexandria, Virginia FY 2003 Budget
Capital Improvement Program

Peumansend Creek Regional Jail

Subtasks	Priority	Estimated Useful Life of Improvement	Project Manager
Capital Contribution	Essential	40 Years	Office of Management And Budget

Project Summary: The Peumansend Creek Regional Jail opened September 7, 1999 as a facility to house low-risk, non-violent inmates in a minimum security setting. The facility is located at Fort A.P. Hill, an Army base in Caroline County, Virginia approximately 50 miles south of Washington, D.C. In September 1994, City Council approved the Service Agreement establishing the financial and operational commitments of the member juris-dictions regarding the design, construction and operation of the jail. The Virginia local governments whose governing bodies have agreed to participate in the regional jail in-clude the Cities of Alexandria and Richmond and the Counties of Arlington, Caroline, Loudoun and Prince William.

Project Description: During FY 1989, the Northern Virginia Chief Administrative Offi-cers and Sheriff's Task Force approved a feasibility study for constructing a regional minimum security facility to hold sentenced inmates from Alexandria and the Counties of Caroline, Fairfax, Arlington, Prince William and Loudoun. In April 1991, the U.S. Con-gress passed legislation that would provide for the transfer of 150 acres of land at Fort A.P Hill to Caroline County for the regional jail. On March 10, 1992, City Council ap-proved Alexandria's participation in this regional jail. In 1994, the U.S. Congress amended the legislation to extend the date to begin construction of the regional jail from April 1995 to April 1997. Although Fairfax County decided not to participate in the re-gional jail, the City of Richmond subsequently decided to join in this regional effort.

The City entered into an agreement in September 1994 with five other Virginia localities for the construction and operation of a 336 bed regional jail to be located at Fort A.P. Hill in Caroline County. The jail was constructed and is operated by the Peumansend Creek Regional Jail Authority, which was established in 1992. The City is a member of this Authority. The facility was built for approximately $27 million with 50 percent of the funding to be reimbursed by the Commonwealth, and 50 percent from the six localities. Alexandria is allocated 50 beds, or approximately 15 percent of the 336 beds in the facil-ity. The City's share of the capital cost of this facility is estimated at approximately $3.2 million in capital and debt service costs over the 20-year period of debt (1997-2016). The Authority issued revenue bonds in the Spring of 1997.

The capital cost reflected in this project are the City's payments based on the actual bond issuance in March 1997. For FY 2003, the City has budgeted a debt service payment of $182,220.

Project Costs to Date: Prior to the annual debt service payments that began in FY 1998, the City paid a total of $74,018 for its share of planning and one-time capital contribution costs for this regional facility.

PEUMANSEND CREEK REGIONAL JAIL

Estimated Impact on Operating Budget: In FY 2003, a total of $479,533 is included in the operating budget (Other Public Safety and Justice Activities) for the City's share of operating budget cost.

Change is Project From Prior Fiscal Years:

- $182,220 has been budgeted in FY 2003 for the City's annual debt service payment based on the actual bond issuance in March 1997.

Task Title	Unallocated Prior-FY	FY 2003 Current	FY 2004 FY + 1	FY 2005 FY + 2	FY 2006 FY + 3	FY 2007 FY + 4	FY 2008 FY + 5	TOTAL
Contributions	128,792	182,220	177,421	174,953	169,905	164,755	159,503	1,157,549
Construction	0 0	0	0	0	0	0	0	
Total Project	128,792	182,220	177,421	174,953	169,905	164,755	159,503	1,157,549
Less Revenue	0	0	0	0	0	0	0	0
Net City Share	128,792	182,792	177,421	174,953	169,905	164,755	159,503	1,157,549

Source: http://ci.alexandria.va.us/city/budget_reports/budget2003/cip/cipbudgeto3.html.

Appendix 4B

1. As the new director of Mound Bayou's Fire Department, it is your job to improve the department's capital budget process for your office. Your first job is to prepare justifications for the capital budget requests suggested by your predecessor. Below is the department Budget Request (Hint: Be creative in your justifications. Economic growth, population growth, and the age of equipment are examples of reasons for expansion, improvement or replacing equipment). Remember, you are trying to convince the city that these items will allow your department to be more efficient and effective. Further, your justifications should show that you have considered the long range plans of the city's elected officials to expand public services. The items of interest are listed below the table. The number of computers, copy machines and office desks are the same from the previous year as well as the value of the land to acreage ratio. Exhibit 4.1 can serve as a point of departure for you, but remember, there are numerous ways to write justifications, so be professionally creative in your use of space, charts, graphs, etc.

Justifications:

1. Computers

2. Security System

3. Copy Machines

4. ¾ Ton Truck

5. Office Desk

6. Pumper

7. Tanker

8. New Fire Station

9. Water Well

10. Land

Appendix 4C

City of Alexandria
Capital Improvement Plan

	FY 2009	FY 2010	FY 2011	FY 2012	FY 2013	TOTAL
Library						
Golf Course						
Park						
New Bus Route						
Streets and Sewers						
TOTAL						

Appendix 4D

State of Mississippi
Capital Improvement Plan
FYs 2009-2013

	# in Grade	FY 2009	FY 2010	FY 2011	FY 2012	FY 2013	TOTAL
Dysfunctional Schools	45						
HWY 61	240 miles						
HWY 82	85 miles						
Welcome Centers	6						
New Health Depts.	3						
Health Depts Repair	36						
Supreme Court BDLG	1						
TOTAL							

High Priority Tasks:

Lower Priority Tasks:

Chapter 5
Funding State and Local Budgets

Chapter Five Overview

While the previous chapters have more or less centered on the expenditure side of the budget, this chapter concentrates on *revenue*. Revenue is the life-blood of governments and a very important factor for government officials and citizens. At the beginning of FY 2002, more than a dozen states that traditionally had stable budgets projected severe budget deficits. In some cases, these deficits were projected well into the 100s of millions of dollars. Hence, it is quite important that government officials closely examine potential revenue sources and spend quality time conducting accurate revenue forecasts. Due to limited revenue sources it is also important that government engage in *revenue management*. This chapter begins with a general discussion of revenue sources for all levels of government followed with a more detailed examination of state and local revenue sources. This includes the newest form of revenue sources: lotteries and gambling.

Sources of Revenue

The number one source of revenue for state and local governments is *taxes*. Taxes are "compulsory charges made against the public by a government to obtain the money it needs to finance its activities" (Mendosa 1983, p. 63). Taxes come in various forms and differ somewhat from one governmental unit to the next. For example, the federal government depends heavily upon *federal individual income taxes* and *social insurance* receipts while state governments depend a lot on *sales* and *individual state income taxes*. Local governments are more dependent upon *property taxes*. Some taxes are considered *regressive* while others are considered *progressive*.[28] However, taxes are not the only source of revenue for state and local governments. Revenues are also collected from *user fees; intergovernmental transfers; licenses and permit; and excise taxes on motor fuels, alcohol sales and tobacco sales;* and various other charges (fines, forfeitures). Many cities work under the auspices of a charter and this document dictates what sort of taxes will be collected. For example, some cities collect income from earning.[29] However, legislative approval is often needed to add an additional tax. Table 5.1 shows the major categories of revenues for the federal, state and local government along with budget representation estimates.[30] These estimates can differ by state and local governments for any particular year.

As shown, the federal government is heavily dependent upon individual income taxes and social insurance payments. However, social insurance is not used to fund any federal program, it is considered a trust. State and local governments are much more diverse and balanced in their sources of revenue. Most notable with these latter two levels of government is the dependence upon intergovernmental transfers.

Table 5.1 Major Categories of Revenues

	Federal	State	Local
1. Individual Income Taxes	48%		
2. State Income Taxes		17%	
3. Corporate Income Taxes	11%		
4. Sales Taxes		21%	5%
5. Property Taxes			25%
6. Excise Taxes	3%		
7. Social Insurance	33%		
8. Intergovernmental Transfers		22%	34%
9. Insurance Trust Revenues		20%	
10. Charges, Fees and Miscellaneous			21%
11. All Other	5%	20%	15%

Source: Nice, David B. 2002. *Public Budgeting*. Stamford, CT: Wadsworth.

Further, state governments are modestly dependent upon sales and income taxes, and *insurance trust revenues*. Insurance trust revenues are "taxes and fees that finance various insurance trusts to support unemployment compensation programs, state employee pensions, and other programs" (Nice 2002, p. 26). Lastly, local governments depend on property taxes, charges and fees. Taxes are traditionally evaluated using the following dimensions:

A. Yield - How much money can be raised using the tax?
B. Stability – How much does revenue fluctuate based on changes in the economy?
C. Equity - Do similarly situated people pay the same level of tax? Do those who have a greater ability to pay more contribute more?
D. Efficiency – Does the tax distort economic activity? How much does it cost to administer the tax and who covers those costs?

Given the fact that states and local governments have a plethora of revenue sources at their disposal, one can use the following formula to determine the level of revenue needed:

Yield = Rate * Base

A. Yield = Revenue.
B. Rate = The rate is levied against the base (i.e. higher incomes are taxed at a higher rate).
C. Base = Property value, income, subject sales, etc.

In order to change the yield, you simply need to change the definition of the base as well as the rate.

Taxes

Taxes fall into three basic categories: income, consumption, and wealth. In some cases, several categories may be involved in a transaction. Taxes here are split into four general categories: A. Property, B. Income Taxes, C. Sales Taxes, D. Alcohol, Tobacco and Petroleum (see also Gravelle 1999).

A. Property Taxes

A major source of revenue for local governments is *property taxes*. These are taxes levied against real property, personal property and the property of a privately owned utility. Real property consists of land, homes, businesses, and other permanent fixtures. Personal property is property that can be moved from one location to another. It can be inventory, vehicles, and equipment. Privately owned utilities include real and personal property (Mikesell 2003; Kittredge and Ouart 2005; Rubin 2006). The assessed value of these categories is usually determined by a state or local government or by judicial decision. Under normal circumstances, the market will play a role in this value. This process is very complicated to say the least.[31] However, Mendosa (1983) offers the following principles when assigning value to property.

- Uniform procedures should be in place when assigning value to property. Property that are similar should be assessed the same. That is, property that have "equal market value should be assigned approximately equal taxable values" (p. 63).
- Assessed values should be adjusted periodically to keep pace with market value. When market values decrease, the assessed value should likewise decrease and vice versa.

- Officials should make every effort to tax all property. This includes using "aerial photographs, field surveys, comparing utility customer records with personal property tax rolls, and other search and find techniques" (p. 64).

According to Gianakis and McCue (1999) property taxes is one of the most unpopular taxes in the U.S. even though it is considered by most to be progressive. [32] One reason for such a poor ranking is based on the principle of capital gains. That is, as the value of the property increases, so does the amount of the tax unless the rate is reduced. Since the gain in wealth is not realized until the property is sold the tax seems unfair since the property tax is paid each year. The tax can also be used to balance the budget of a local government when other options do not appear to be feasible.[33] Even though a large number of tax bills are escrowed, the bill comes once a year and thus is highly visible to the taxpayer. Infrequent reassessments may also have a negative impact on property during periods of economic downturn. Lastly, taxpayers see the value of their property as subjective and arbitrarily set by the government (Lynch 1995).

Setting the Property Tax Rate

There are quite a few items that are considered when setting the property tax rate. These include items such as the location (city v. rural) of the property and what the property is used for (business v. residential). There are three basic operations used when setting the tax rate: *assessment of property value* (*tax assessor*), establishing the *tax rate* (*millage rate*), and collecting the tax (*tax collector*). The legislative body sets the tax rate while assessment and collection can be done by the same or separate institutions.

-Tax Assessments and Tax Rates

The *tax assessor* office normally identifies and classifies property. Property can be classified as: residential versus business; farm versus non-farm; or farm, residential, commercial or industrial. Farmland is taxed at a much lower rate than non-farm land and businesses tend to be taxed at a much higher rate than residential areas unless they are new to the area (Lynch 1995). Another important characteristic in this process is to determine the role of exemptions. An exemption is the "amount deducted from the assessed value of property for tax purposes" (Riley and Colby 1991). Homestead exemptions are very common. However, there could be exemptions for widowers, senior citizens, handicap residents, etc.

The *market price/value* of the property is also very important when establishing the tax rate. Market price is the price that a seller and buyer are willing to accept without coercion. Normally, this is the price used in the assessment. After the assessor places a value on the property, the tax rate is established. While the government expects other revenue, the tax rate is still influenced by the amount of revenue needed to run the government. If expenditures are not balanced, the property tax rate can increase or the budget can be cut (Raphaelson 2004).

A local government can either decide how much money it needs from property taxes or simply set the property tax rate. In method one, let's assume that the government needs $200,000.00 from individual property taxes and the tax assessor has determined the total assessed value of individual property taxes is $4,000,000.00. So, if you divide the amount of funds needed by the total assessed valued, you will get the *fixed or nominal tax rate*. In this case, the rate would be .05 or 5% ($200,000.00/$4,000,000.00). Therefore, a home assessed at $55,000.00 would yield $2,750.00 in property taxes (.05 x $55,000.00). The tax rate typically changes for business and personal property.

In the second method, property tax rates are set up front and then applied to property. This rate is commonly assessed using a *millage rate* or a "cents on the dollar method. A millage rate is expressed in terms of mills. One mills yields (1/1000 of one dollar) $1.00 of tax liability for every $1,000.00 of assessed value. Again, the rate would vary depending on the type of property assessed. For example, let's consider a business that has a market value of $100,000.00 and an assessed value of $45,000.00. The millage rate is 5% (or 50 mills/dollar). So, you multiply the assessed value by the millage rate and determine the tax ($45,000.00 x .5 = $2,250.00). Another way of looking at this assessment is to use the following calculation: Taxes = 50 mills / 1$ x $45,000.00 = 2,250,000 mills = $2,250.00. [34]

The *most effective tax rate* (METR) can be calculated by dividing the tax assessment by market value ($2,250.00/$100,000.00 = 0.0225 or 2.25%). When calculating multiple units, add all of the tax rates (METRs) together and divide by the total number of properties. All calculations are done after all exemptions are considered (Rabin, Hildreth, and Miller 1996).

An extremely important event in property tax administration involves the date on which the property value is to be fixed. Property changes hands constantly. As a result, failing to fix a date means the government is aiming at a moving target. So, a government specifies that the value of the property will be determined as of a particular date, such as January 1. This is known as the lien date. The government places a lien on the property as of that date. Thus, the government is entitled to the tax. The date on which the actually levy of the tax is made by the legislative body is usually later in the year. For example, the levy date might be April 1. Unlike virtually all other taxes, a property tax is levied to support the activity of the government for the fiscal year. In this example, the fiscal year is July 1-June 30.

Another event that takes place is the reappraisal. Governments have different ways of reappraising property. Some require that an actual appraisal take

place by an appraiser. This might be done every three years or more. Others allow for estimates every two or three years followed by an actual appraisal the
next cycle. Estimates are usually done by analyzing housing sales in the neighborhood during the past two years. The assessor would also look at permits to
see if any improvements were made.

The reappraisal was one of the most unpopular actions that affected a property owner. An increase in the property tax bill resulted from the inflationary
increase in the value of the property without any increase in the rate. For example, a home that had a value of $100,000 and a rate of $20 per thousand would
receive a bill for $2,000. When the property was reappraised, it was valued at
$120,000. Now the bill was $2,400. The most famous instance of taxpayer revolt
was Proposition 13 in California. Its passage required the rate to be reduced so
that the amount paid after appraisal was substantially the same as the amount
paid before. Many states have enacted similar provisions.

Let's assume for a moment that the tax assessments are questionable. That
is: Were the properties assessed based on market price? Are there biases in the
assessment based on the type of property? Are some properties under or over
assessed? In order to answer the first question, the *coefficient of dispersion*
should be checked. This test allows the examiner to determine how close are
assessed values are to each other, relative to the market. Exhibit 5.1 gives us an
example of this test (partially excerpted from Lynch 1995).

Exhibit 5.1 Coefficient of Dispersion Test

Step 1: What are the assessed ratios for a sample of properties
sold? There are three pieces of property that sold for $100,000 and
were assessed at $55k, $64k, and $70k. The assessment ratios are:
55%, 64%, and 70% respectively ($55k/100k = 55%).

	Sales Price	Asse'd Value	Asse't Ratio	Average Deviation	Coef.
Property 1	$100,000.00	$55,000.00	55%	55%-60%=[-5%]	*6.33%*
Property 2	100,000.00	64,000.00	64%	64%-60%=4%	
Property 3	100,000.00	70,000.00	70%	70%-60%=10%	
			63%	19%	

Step2: What is the average assessments ratio for the sample (average)? 55% + 64% + 70% = 189/3 = 63%

Step 3: What is the average deviation of the separate property assessments from the average assessment ratio? ([-5%] + 4% + 10%)
= 19/3 = 6.33%. Note that the first assessment is a negative num-

ber. However, the assessment ratio uses the absolute value of each individual sum (In Excel use the ABS formula: =ABS (cell# - cell#).

Step 4: Compare the average deviation to the median or average assessment ratio (also known as the coefficient of dispersion). 6.33%/63% = 0.10 or 10%. A score higher than .10 or 10% suggests that there are some problems with the assessments. The magnitude of the problem increases as the score increases.

Another test that can be used with the coefficient of dispersion is the *price-related differential*. This test determines if higher priced properties are under assessed. Exhibit 5.2 provides an example of this procedure (The example and subsequent steps in Exhibit 5.2 were excerpted from Smith and Lynch 2004, p. 348).

Exhibit 5.2 Price Related Differential Test

Step 1: Calculate the aggregate assessment-sales ratio, which is weighted by the values of the parcels in the sample. Here is an example:

	Sales Price	Assessed Value	Assessment Ratio
Property 1	$100,000.00	$20,000.00	20%
Property 2	10,000.00	4,000.00	40%
Property 3	10,000.00	4,000.00	40%
Property 4	10,000.00	4,000.00	40%
	$130,000.00	$32,000.00	140%

The aggregate assessment-sales ratio is: ($32,000.00/$130,000.00) = 0.246 or 24.6%

Step 2: Calculate the average of the assessment ratios of the separate parcels. The average assessment ratio of properties is: 140%/4 = 0.350 or 35%.

Step 3: Divide the mean of the assessment ratios by the aggregate assessment-sales ratio to determine the price-related differential. The price-related differential is: 35/ 24.6 = 1.42 or 142%.

Step 4: Interpreting the results. Deviation from 100% is the important figure in this analysis. A price-related differential that is 100% indicates that there in neither over assessment or under assessment.

However, if the differential is more than 100% then there is under assessment of the higher priced properties. If the differential is less than 100% then there is an under assessment of the lower priced properties. In this case, the deviation is 142% indicating the higher priced property is significantly under assessed. Mathematically, the differential indicates that the collective disparity between the sales price and the assessed value of the higher priced properties is greater than the collective disparity between the sale price and assessed value of the lower priced properties.

Tax Collection

The last step in the process is tax collection. In a lot of local governments, tax collection is handled by the Tax Collector or in some instances the Sheriff's office. The Sheriff's office becomes particularly important when property is foreclosed. If property taxes are not paid, the property can be sold in order to collect the taxes. Delinquency rates normally do not exceed 5%. However, it is wise to assume that everyone is not going to pay their taxes when preparing revenue estimates.

Tax assessors assume that the property tax will be paid yielding a one to one ratio. That is, if your taxes are $956 then you will pay $956. However, property tax payments frequently come in schedules based on months. For example, let's say that your payment is due by November 30. The bill might have a payment schedule for October, November, December, and January. The property owner could save money by paying the bill early (October date) or pay the actual tax amount by paying by November 30. By delaying payment, the property owner can be penalized with a 1% penalty in December, 2% in January and then become delinquent in February with a flat 3-5% penalty. Although it is not a good accounting practice, you can budget for the penalties. Arguments for doing so should be based on strong historical trend analysis.

B. Income Taxes

For a lot of states, *income taxes* make up a large proportion of taxes collected. In 2002, 43 states collected state income taxes.[35] These taxes tend to follow the same format as federal income taxes. That is, income is defined as all income rather than just wages. An income tax is considered to be a *progressive tax*: the greater the income, the higher the tax rate. Individual income taxes make up about 13% of all revenue collected in a state (Nice 2002; Rubin 2006).

Local governments can also levy and collect income taxes (*payroll taxes*). Some local governments limit the tax to earned income, such as salary and wages, rents and royalties; and lottery and other gambling winnings. In other instances, the tax is only applied to wages and salaries earned and are deducted directly from individual earnings. The tax rate is usually 1-2% of earned wages. Generally speaking, these taxes are considered to be *regressive taxes* because all individuals pay the same rate regardless of their salaries or wages. Thus, the rate for the CEO is the same as the rate for the mail clerk. Hence, the impact is more significant for the lower income individual. Payroll taxes also have an impact on commuters who do not live in the jurisdiction where they work, since they are also required to pay the tax. Commuters essentially pay a tax for services that they receive associated with their place of employment, such as police, fire, and road maintenance. This is particularly important for cities that have large employment centers, but whose employees live in suburbs.

Since income and payroll taxes are taxpayer assessed, they have a low administrative overhead. The tax is collected by the employer and sent to the state or local government. Some state governments also allow local governments to collect a *corporate income tax*. However, this tax can be detrimental to promoting the business industry unless other local governments also have the tax (Bland 2005). Payroll taxes are not as stable as property taxes and are very susceptible to the business cycle. The majority of local governments do not collect payroll taxes. However, this aspect is very regional in nature.[36]

Let's consider the example in Exhibit 5.3. There are four employees listed in City X's legal affairs office. Note that two of the employees are listed by name while the other two are not. If you have several employees who make the same salary, it is easier to put them into one category listed by their title rather than listing them separately.

- Federal income tax rates: $0-$11,999.99 in salary = 10% rate; $12,000.00-$46,699.99 = 15%; $46,700.00-$112,850.99 = 27%

- State income tax rates: $0-2,000.00 = 3% rate; >$2,000.00 = 4.5%

- Local payroll tax: A flat 1.75%

Exhibit 5.3 Income Tax Payments

Employee	FTE	Salary	Fed. Income Tax	State Income Tax	Payroll Tax
Jesse Harris	1	$95,000.00	$19,446.00	$4,245.00	$1,662.50
Andre Kemp	1	90,000.00	18,096.00	4,020.00	1,575.00
Exec. Asst.	2	100,000.00	14,592.00	4,440.00	1,750.00
	3	$285,000.00	$34,056.00	$12,885.00	$4,987.50

In this example, there are two executive assistants who make the exact same salary. Therefore, the amount of taxes owed would be the same after any exemptions. This method is much more efficient and effective than listing each employee.

Income taxes are normally graduated. As salary increases, so does the *tax rate*. For example, the following tax rates were used with the example in Exhibit 5.3 (all of the calculations are rounded to two digits to the right of the decimal).

While this process may seem complicated, it is really quite easy. The one thing that you should remember is that employees who make lower salaries pay fewer taxes and as their salaries increase, so does the amount of the tax. However, do not make the mistake of taking the entire salary and applying one tax rate. Jesse Harris' federal income tax was calculated in a three-step process. First, take the first $11,999.00 of his salary and apply a 10% tax rate to that amount. Second, apply a 15% tax rate to the next $34,699.00 ($46,699.00-$12,000.00) of his salary, and finally apply a 27% tax rate to the last $48,300.00 ($95,000.00-$46,700.00) of his salary. If you calculate the math, it would essentially look like this:

Salary Range	Calculations	Taxes Owed
$0-11,999.99	= $11,999.99 x 10% =	$1,199.99
$12,000.00-$46,699.99	= $34,699.99 x 15% =	$5,205.00
$46,700.00-$95,000.00	= $48,300.00 x 27% =	$13,041.00
		$19,445.99

In order to calculate state income taxes you would follow the same format as the federal model. Since the payroll tax is a flat rate, it can be computed by simply multiplying the rate times the total salary for each employee.

Let's say that an employee has a salary of $75,000.00 and I want to use Excel to calculate the salary. I could use this formula to calculate the social security tax (=11999.99*10%+(46699.99-12000)*15%+(C8-46700)*27%). Depending on the size of the salary, you may not need all of this formula. For example, if the employee made $46,500.00 you would not need the latter part of the formula (C8-46700)*27%).

C. Sale and Use Taxes

One of the largest sources of income in a state is the *sales tax*. Sales taxes are funds collected at the retail transaction stage. They are collected when goods and services are sold. One advantage for the government is that retailers bear the burden of handling most of the paperwork. The government is concerned with timely and accurate payments from the retailer. Once the taxes are collected by the state, they redistribute the funds to the appropriate local government. Many local governments also have the discretion to levy sales taxes. In many states, only counties are able to levy a sales tax. In others, a municipality may levy a tax if the county chooses not to. In still others, both the county and municipality may levy the tax. Local governments should consider all other options prior to making this decision because it could have a negative impact on revenue collections.[37] To lessen the burden on retailers, local government sales taxes are piggy-backed to state sales taxes and remitted in total to the state.

Sales taxes are *regressive taxes* because citizens pay the same sales tax rate regardless of their income level. They also are not as stable as property because of fluctuating business cycles. Citizens will stop buying "luxury items" and reduce discretionary purchases when the economy slows down. Each state sets its own sales tax rate. States and localities also have some discretion as to what sales taxes will be applied to. For example, sales taxes are not applied to the sale of un-prepared food in Kentucky. Other products that may be exempt from sales taxes are medicines and clothing. An additional item for a state to consider is collecting the tax from the retailer. The Department of Revenue in the state of Tennessee has officers who are charged with collecting delinquent sales tax payment from retailers who choose not to send in the payments.

A *use tax* differs slightly from a sales tax. A use tax is imposed by a state to compensate for the sales tax lost when an item is purchased outside of the state, but is used within the state. For example, let's say that you buy a car in a state that has no sales tax, but you live across the border in a state that does have a sales tax. When you bring your car home and register it in your state, the state taxing authority will bill you for the sales tax it would have collected had you bought the car within the state. Otherwise, you are not able to "use" the car in the state where you live (Kittredge and Ouart 2005).

D. Alcohol, Tobacco and Motor Fuel Taxes

Alcohol, tobacco, and motor fuel taxes are also collected at the time of sale. These are also called *excise taxes* because a rate is applied to a specific product on a per unit basis. In many cases, such as alcohol and tobacco, the purpose of the tax is to curtail the use of the product. Excise taxes are also applied to luxury items such a luxury boats and cars and hotel rooms. In some cases, these funds are also returned to the locality where they were collected. Further, they may be *earmarked* for a specific purpose. For example, motor fuel taxes are commonly used for building and maintaining roads and highways. The advantage to this tax is that it is benefit-based. The citizens that pay the tax reap the benefit of improved highways and roads. Unfortunately, these funds may be needed in other areas, but there is no chance of diversion given the rigid nature of the funds (Mikesell 1999, 2003).

E. User Charges and Impact Fees

A *user charge* is a fee charged to individuals who voluntarily use a publicly provided service. For example, large municipalities may implement a toll charge to pay for the construction of a new road. If you do not use the new road, then you do not pay the charge. The purpose of a user charge is to relieve the financial burden placed on the general revenue system. In most cases, user charges are geared toward the population that is benefiting from public service. User charges are useless if they are not enforceable and the charge must cover the cost of the service without disrupting other revenue sources.

A more common example of a user fee is the funds collected for police and fire protection or a school district. Charges for this service will often appear on a utility or cable television bill. The address on the utility bill essentially alerts government officials that a new customer has moved into the jurisdiction.[38] Likewise, small towns often operate one or more utilities where they can charge fees. This includes water, gas, and electrical utilities. These government businesses have little or no competition (*monopoly*). Mendosa (1983) points out that "utility charges are calculated by applying a predetermined rate to a measured volume of service received by a utility consumer. Thus, the amount of revenues due from the utility charges is known before the payments are actually received" (p. 66).

Impact fees are charges that are passed on to developers in order to off set the cost to community resources and the infrastructure. According to Lynch (1995) these fees are more popular in high-growth areas and larger cities. Development frequently causes wear and tear on the roads in these areas, requires additional water resources, sewage and so forth. Further, the increase in the population that results from development impacts the local parks, community centers, and libraries.

Setting a User Fee Rate

While it may be clear to government officials that they should implement a user fee, it might not be clear how much that amount should be. One method to determine the amount is to use *cost-volume profit* (CVP) or *break-even analysis*. This tool assesses how price, volume, and variable and fixed costs interface. At some point, revenue and cost equal (Bierhanzl and Downing 2004; Smith and Lynch 2004).

Let's consider an example. A local government has decided to charge individuals driving a motor vehicle a fee to use a newly constructed four-lane road that will save the user 100 miles of travel. Government officials expect that 75,000 vehicles will pass through the road on a yearly basis, the traceable fixed costs (for example, permanent salaries, insurance equipment, and utilities) are projected at $400,000, and the allocated fixed costs (for example toll overhead and general government overhead) are $80,000. The variable costs (for cleanup, supplies, and part time workers) are projected at $3 per car. A subsidy of $100,000 is budgeted from the city's general fund.

The CVP equation is: $P = VC + \dfrac{[(TFC + AFC) - S]}{Q}$

P = The correct user fee charge per vehicle
VC = Variable Cost per car
TFC = Traceable Fixed Costs
AFC = Allocated Fixed Costs
S = Subsidy
Q = Total number of vehicles

$P = 3 + \dfrac{[(400,000.00 + 80,000.00) - 100,000.00]}{75,000}$

$P = 3 + \dfrac{380,000.00}{75,000}$ $P = 3 + 5.07$ P = 8.06 or $8.07 per car

Let's go a step further and add another caveat to this scenario. For 12 weeks in the summer, city official perceive that the amount of traffic on the highway will increase by 100,000 cars per week. In the past, the city has used its current police force to manage any increases in traffic. However, they have concluded that they cannot continue with this practice. As a result, they are interested in hiring more police officers to two of the shifts 7 days a week for the twelve-week period. So, how many policemen will be needed to provide 16 hour coverage for the 3 month period or 90 days?

The first thing that we must do is calculate the number of hours that could be gained by each additional employee over the 3-month period. If each employee works 40 hours per week for 12 weeks, the number of paid hours (P) is 480. Let's also provide the following benefits over the period: 1.) 2 sick days, 2.) 1 paid holiday, and 3.) 4 paid days off. Assuming that the five paid days are taken, the following would apply: 5 x 8 hours = 40 hours (A). Hence, the effective hours per employee (E) is:

Effective Hours Per Employee   = P – A
                                     = 480 – 40
                                     = 440 Effective Hours

The formula for calculating a single shift is:

Staffing Factor = $\dfrac{\text{Hours per year of operation}}{E}$

$$= \frac{8 \text{ hours per day x 90 days}}{440}$$

$$= \frac{720}{440}$$

$$= 1.64 \text{ (single shift)}$$
$$= 3.28 \text{ (double shift } 1.64 \text{ x 2)}$$

If you want to double the shift, you simply need to double the number of hours to 16 per day. This would bring the total to 3.28 officers per day (see also Ammons 2002). Unlike other numbers (such as income or average age), it is more difficult to round people. For example, if we use the data in the above example and traditional rounding methods, we would round 1.64 to 2 employees and 3.28 to 3 employees. However, if the formula is indeed valid we would have too many employees or not enough. So, what do you do in these circumstances? Research by Ammons (2002) suggests that you round to the nearest whole number (ie. 1 full time employee) or a part time employee. In the above example, 1.64 would be rounded to 1.5 persons and 3.28 would be rounded to 3.5 persons.

F. Intergovernmental Transfers

A large percentage of a state's revenue comes in the form of *federal grants*. The amount of a grant varies and is quite dependent on federal activities. During the 1960s and 70s federal grants to states increased as the federal government sought to expand the role of the states. By the 1980s grants leveled out and then rose again in the late 1980s. Grants come in two major forms: categorical and block. *Categorical grants* make up the largest type of grants that a state receives. A categorical grant is used for a specific program and has very strict guidelines for the activities to be carried out within a specific time period. Medicaid and food stamps are included in this category. Categorical grants exploded during Johnson's Great Society programs in the 1960s. Formula and project grants fall within the umbrella of categorical grants. *Formula grants* use a distribution formula to determine the amount to be allocated to the state or locality. Population, geography, income and education are variables that are used in formula grants. A *block grant* is used for broad policy areas. It can be used in a variety of programs and activities by state and local governments. States prefer this type of grant due to fewer restrictions on the funds (Riley and Colby 1991; Axelrod 1995).

Local governments receive grants directly from the federal government or passed through from the state government. Local governments also receive grants from the state. In many cases, the grants from the state are a form of revenue sharing. For example, the state will share income and sales tax collections with local government on some formula basis. School districts receive major funding from the state, along with additional funding from the federal government. Transportation authorities receive significant funding from the federal government to purchase capital equipment.

G. Licenses, Permits, and Franchise Fees

Another source of revenue for local governments comes from licenses and permits. A *license* or *permit* is defined as "special rights or privileges granted to an individual or business by a governmental unit in return for the payment of designated fees" (Mendosa 1983, p. 65). Licenses are provided to businesses and individuals to conduct an array of different activities. These include, operating a street side kiosk to operating a restaurant. Permits allow individuals and businesses to build structures and to authorize other regulated actions. The cost of the license fee differs by activity. For example, the cost of a hunting license is different from that of a license to operate a restaurant. Without a license, an individual or business is forbidden to engage in the activity legally. The owner of a license does not receive any specific government service by having the license. Under normal circumstances, everyone who applies for a license receives it if they are qualified. However, a person does receive services from a permit. For example, the issuance of a building permit will result in a number of inspections by the government. The purpose is to ensure that the building or improvement meets the building code requirements established by the government.

One positive aspect of a license and permit is that they are easy to track. Because each license and permit is numbered; government officials can monitor, measure and control the process. It also allows the government to audit the revenue source with little effort. When problems occur, they can be easily pinpointed. For example, if building permits are decreasing, officials can determine whether the drop is the result of a dip in the economy or some other factor.

A *franchise fee* is closely related to a license fee, but there are some subtle differences. Franchises are provided on a limited basis. A franchise presupposes that the business will serve the entire community, operate with a certain quality and rate, and outline the responsibility of the owner and the government. It also may involve the use of the government's rights-of-way. In certain parts of the country cable companies operate on a franchise fee basis. Other examples could include telephone services. These fees can generate large amounts of funds.

H. Gaming

States and local governments began dabbling in games of chance in the mid

1960s, but in the last 15 years they have become very popular as an alternative source of revenue as a result of opposition to tax increase. Since New Hampshire adopted the lottery in 1964, forty-three states and the District of Columbia have legalized some form of gaming. These institutions come in the form of state lotteries, bingo, riverboat gambling, casinos, and slot machines. Despite the social and moral concerns that residents have with gaming, they tend to support these measures because they raise funds voluntarily versus compulsory taxes. As a result, states have been able to generate millions of dollars in revenue. However, there is a fair amount of overhead associated with the gaming industry. In each case, state and local governments have established bureaucratic structures to regulate the industry. Some states, however, see minimum economic benefits from casino operations. This is the case in states where casinos are owned and operated by American Indians on reservations. They are exempt from taxes and other fees.[39] However, these states do reap benefits in other ways. Many Indian casinos contribute payments-in-lieu-of-taxes to the government. Others provide substantial support to schools within the reservation, thus reducing state support.

I. Other Revenues

Occasionally governments will receive funds from sources that do not fit into any of the above-mentioned categories. For example, gifts, donations, and sales of equipment and assets fit into this category. There are no tax levies and there is no method to distributing the funds. Cities and states can also collect funds from investments and leasing of property to the private sector or other governments. Governments that operate jails may charge smaller governments that do not have such facilities for the housing of prisoners.

Governments also receive monies from fines, forfeits, and penalties. These funds usually come from the actions of police and the courts. Since these activities are well documented and are standardized, it is fairly easy to keep track of them (Mendosa 1983).

Revenue Management

Gianakis and McCue (1999) define revenue management as "the assessment and maintenance of a local government's capacity to generate sufficient funds from all available sources to support policy decisions regarding service levels" (p. 102). Revenue management attempts to establish revenue performance standards, compare actual with expected performance, record revenue performance, initiate corrective change, and constructs a support system that facilitates that model. There are three general components to proactive revenue management: *revenue development, revenue analysis* and *revenue support systems*. Revenue development is mainly concerned with developing a tax structure that considers short and long term funding. A lot of revenue management techniques are time limited and tend to reflect election cycles and short term political needs rather than long term strategic planning. Revenue analysis systematically examines each revenue source with an eye to achieving the optimal benefit from the source. This includes issues such as equity, yields, and the cost of administration. Lastly, revenue support systems examine the day-to-day management of revenue (Gianakis and McCue 1999).

Let's consider a simple example. The city of Columbia was considering passing a law increasing the millage rate on business property for FY 2008 in order to balance the proposed budget. If passed, the law would increase the amount of property taxes by $598,000.00. However, when the law was examined, it was found that it would have a negative impact on the tax structure for small businesses. The city has 35 businesses, but one business (Business X) employs 65% of the private workforce. As a result of the increase, Business X would see a 3% increase in taxes owed while the remaining 34 businesses would owe the balance. So, is it feasible to pass on 97% of the cost to the remaining small businesses despite the fact that they represent only 35% of the private workforce? Businesses can pass on tax increases to customers or the land owner, but this can also have a negative domino affect on the cost of doing business. In this example, the equity issues raised by the law did not seem to affect the city council since small businesses were the fastest growing industry in the city.[40] While the decision on paper would have a positive impact on the city's budget, the council members did not consider the long-term effect of the law on the city's small business sector.

Situations like this one bring value to revenue management. It is crucial that a budget manager communicate to elected officials the value of revenue management. In order to properly implement a revenue management system, it is important that the organization's culture is understood. That includes a good understanding of the social, political and economics dynamics associated with a city or state.

Revenue management is a proactive approach concerned with "establishing revenue performance standards, documenting revenue performance, comparing actual with expected performance, initiating corrective action and creating a support structure that facilitates the approach" (Gianakis and McCue 1999 p. 103). This means that elected officials and agency heads need to:

- Develop a commonly accepted method for funding services in the short and long term.
- Identify where the city currently stands in relation to its revenue capacity.
- Explore other options for achieving vision.
- Institute a program for measuring progress.

There are a number of items that must be considered when evaluating revenue structures and determining the revenue management strategy. Consider the questions in Exhibit 5.4 when thinking about the previous example. Essentially, as a budget officer, you are asking yourself how any particular factor will affect the tax structure and vice versa. For example, if we consider the current example, the budget director would want to know: will the increase in the rate generate the needed funds, who is going to be affected by the property tax increase, how that change will affect their ability to pay and still make a profit, will that cost be passed on to other individuals, will it hurt our tax structure and so on. As an elected official, you want to know if your chances of reelection will be impacted, will you get support from other elected officials, will the tax adversely impact your constituents and so on.

Exhibit 5.4 Developing a Revenue Management Plan

Political Questions
1. What are the dominant political attitudes (party/council unity)?
2. What is the dominant political culture (mixed or unified)?
3. Is raising taxes feasible right now (election year)?

Tax Questions
4. Can user fees or special districts solve the tax deficit?
5. Should funds be earmarked from the current budget?
6. Can taxes be raised legally?

Demographic Questions
7. Is a particular group benefiting from the tax increase?
8. Will increasing taxes have an adverse economic impact on a particular sector (business, personal, education, etc)?
9. What is the level of education in the city? [41]
10. What is the age of residents?[42]
11. What type of industries exists and are we facilitating their growth?

Administrative Questions
12. Is there a cost associated with the decision?
13. If yes, what kind (payer cost, convenience cost, administrative cost)?

These and other questions address political, efficiency, effectiveness and equity issues. However, equity and equality are not synonymous. Decision makers can also: A.) Divide the number of users by the total cost and spread the burden evenly without concern for impact. B.) Apply the *ability to pay* rule where those who can afford to pay more are taxed at a higher rate, and C.) Apply the *benefits received principle* where those that receive the benefit bear the cost associated with the benefit.

Conclusion

The chapter shows that there are a number of different ways in which state and local governments finance the administration of government. Some of the methods discussed are political in nature while others apply across the board to everyone. Effective revenue management models must consider a plethora of important political, cultural, economic, demographic and administrative questions. Despite the fact that no one really wants to pay more taxes, financial decisions are more palatable when the decisions that led to the tax structure are well thought out and developed based on good questions and answers.

Important Terms and Phrases

Ability to Pay Rule
Assessed Value
Aggregate Assessment-Sales Ratio
Allocated Fixed Cost
Benefits Received Principle
Block Grants
Break Even Analysis
Categorical Grants
Coefficient of Dispersion
Cost-Volume Profit (CVP)
Earmarked Funds
Econometric Model
Excise Taxes
Federal Grants
Federal Income Taxes
Fines
Forfeitures
Formula Grants
Franchise Fees
Impact Fees
Insurance Trust Revenues
Input-Output Model
Intergovernmental Transfer
License
Market Price/Value
Microsimulation Model
Millage Rate

Monopoly
Multiple Regression Model
Payroll Taxes
Permit
Price-Related Differential
Progressive Taxes
Property Taxes
Public Utilities
Regressive Taxes
Revenue
Revenue Analysis
Revenue Development
Revenue Support Systems
Revenue Management
Sales Taxes
Simplistic Model
State Income Taxes
Taxes
Tax Assessment
Tax Assessor
Tax Collector
Tax Rate
Traceable Fixed Cost
User Fees
Use Tax
Variable Fixed Cost

Chapter 5 Homework Exercises

Directions: Questions 1-5 and 8 should be completed in Excel. You can complete question 6 and 7 in a word processing program. Round all of your data in the same fashion as it is done in the text. Unless noted other wise, dollar amounts should be rounded to two digits to the right of the decimal. See the appendix for Excel templates.

1a. You are interning at the Tax Assessor's Office for the City of Johnsonville and your supervisor, Mrs. Betty Jean Jones, has asked you to prepare a property tax estimate for a newly built subdivision after she conducted her assessment of the property. Apply a 15% millage rate on the assessed value of each house and the park. The land that the house sits on is included in the market value of the property. Also, what is the total assessed value of all of the properties and the total estimated tax?

- The new subdivision has 100 units and one recreation center. The prices given are based on assessed value.
- There are 10 two-bedroom houses on 5 acres of land valued at $60,000.00 each.
- There are 20 two-bedroom houses on 20 acres of land valued at $70,000.00 each.
- There are 50 three-bedroom houses with a two-car garage on 75 acres of land. The houses are valued at $110,000.00 each.
- The last remaining houses are four-bedroom units with a two-car garage on 20 acres of land. They are valued at $150,000.00.
- Lastly, the subdivision has a park with a swimming pool, tennis court, and a basketball court. The park is valued at $25,000.00.

b. The City of Paytonburg needs $1,500,000.00 in individual property taxes and the tax assessor indicated that the total assessed value of individual property is $20,000,000.00. What should the fixed or nominal tax rate be set at to collect the $1,500,000.00 in property taxes?

Tax rate =

_____.

c. The City of Gilliam has set the millage rate at 3.5% for all businesses. The spreadsheet in Appendix C5 has a partial listing of the city's businesses. Calculate the amount of taxes that can be expected along with the most effective tax rate (METR) for each business and an average tax rate using the partial list of businesses provided.

2. Calculate the coefficient of dispersion using the following information. Should the assessor reapportion the assessed property values (use average assessment)? Explain.

a. There are five pieces of property that sold for $150,000.00 each and were assessed at $105,000.00, $120,000.00, $100,000.00, $110,000.00 and $75,000.00.

b. There are ten pieces of property that sold for $95,000.00 each and were assessed at $89,500.00, $90,900.00, $95,000.00, $95,400.00, $92,000.00, $93,000.00, $90,100.00, $90,900.00, $89,250.00, and $95,459.00.

3. Using the price related differential test, calculate the aggregate assessment-sales ratio using the following data. Are the higher priced properties over assessed or are the lower priced properties under assessed?

Sales Price	Assessed Value	Assessment Ratio
$200,000.00	$170,000.00	85%
150,000.00	100,000.00	66%
25,000.00	15,000.00	60%
30,000.00	20,000.00	66%
25,000.00	15,000.00	60%
35,000.00	28,000.00	80%
$465,000.00	$348,000.00	417%

4. Calculate the revenue collected from federal income taxes, state income taxes, and the local pay roll tax for FY 2008 and prepare a revenue estimate for the City of Sparta's Public School System for FY 2009 based on the following information. Assume that no other deductions came from the employee's salary other than what is listed in the spreadsheet. Hint: New employees are not eligible for raises, which are based on performance from the previous fiscal year.

FY 2008 Facts:
- The school system currently has 34 full time employees. There is one superintendent, two principals, three janitors, ten kitchen staff, and eighteen teachers.
- The superintendent has a salary of $75,000.00.
- Each principal has a salary of $65,000.00.
- Four of the teachers (Teacher A) had salaries of $40,000.00; six teachers (Teacher B) had salaries of $35,000.00; and six teachers (Teacher C) had salaries of $30,000.00.

- There are two additional teachers, at the Teacher A level that coach the basketball and football teams. The football coach receives an additional $5,000.00 in salary and the basketball coach receives an additional $7,000.00 in salary each year.
- Mrs. Jones manages the kitchen. Her FY 2008 salary was $35,000.00.
- The remaining kitchen staff made $25,000.00 each in FY 2008.
- The three janitors made $20,000.00 each in FY 2008.
- Use these federal income tax rates: $0-$11,999.99 in salary = 10% tax rate; $12,000.00-$46,699.99 = 15%; $46,700.00-$112,850.99 = 27%. The tax rates were the same in FY 2008 & FY 2009.
- The state income tax rate is 3% for the first $3,000.00 of employee salary and 5.5% on everything above that amount. The rate is the same in both years.
- The local payroll tax is 1.75% in FY 2008 and 1.85% in FY 2009

FY 2009 Facts:
- In FY 2008, the school system hired 2 more teachers at the Teacher D level. They will begin work in FY 2009 at a salary of $30,000.00.
- In FY 2009, each school employee received a 5% raise except the principals and superintendent. They received a 2% raise. Note, new employees do not receive a raise.

5. Using the information that is listed below, prepare a revenue estimate and revenue projection for the City of Winstonville in FY 2008 and FY 2009 respectively. All of the changes to the FY 2009 budget are based on FY 2008 estimates. Hint: Complete each of the FY 2008 estimates prior to beginning the FY 2009 projections. Round all data to the nearest dollar amount since these are estimates.

- User fees in FY 2008 are expected to increase 5%. In FY 2009 the fee will increase 5% due to an increase in the number of street meters.
- Franchise fees and permits are expected to increase 2% in FY 2008 and 1% in FY 2009 because of new development near the mall.
- Property tax collections have been quite stable. A modest 2% increase is expected in FY 2008 and a 3% increase in FY

2009. News alert: The new Sherwood subdivision will be completed in FY 2008. So, property tax receipts should increase an addition 1% in FY 2009 for a total of 4% in FY 2008.

- Sales tax collections are also expected to increase 4% FY 2008 based on the expanded business sector. It is expected to increase 11% in FY 2009.
- Utility fees/charges are expected to decrease 5% in FY 2008 and 5% in FY 2009.
- Storm water management is expected to increase by 5% each year.
- Impact fees remain unchanged.
- Intergovernmental transfers are expected to increase 4% in FY 2008 and 2% in FY 2009.

6a. The City of Arlington has constructed a swimming pool in FY 2008 and you have been asked to calculate the user charge based on an estimate of 10,000 swimmers. Since the pool is inside a building it will remain open all year. Household income in Arlington is $100,000.00 per year. After you calculate the user fee, explain the impact of the fee on the population. Use the cost-volume profit formula, the information in the directions, and the items listed below to construct your user charge. This problem can be completed in a word processing program.

- Employee salaries, insurance, fringe benefits, equipment maintenance, and utilities are projected at $65,000.00.
- The city received a one-time gift of $60,000.00 to subsidize the first year of operation.
- Allocated fixed costs are projected at $25,000.00.
- Variable costs are projected at $3.00 per swimmer.
- Using the same figures estimate the user charge for the second year as well. However, assume that the number of swimmers increases by 2,000 and the local government will take $45,000.00 from the general fund to subsidize the pool. What can the government do to maintain the current user fee?

b. Using question 6a as a point of departure, the city has to determine how many additional life guards it needs to operate the pool during the summer when children are out of school. Due to the sheer volume of children and city codes, the city cannot ask the existing employees to work additional shifts. Hence, they are interested in hiring lifeguards for *three* of the shifts. Each lifeguard will work a four-hour shift seven days a week for the twelve-week period. They cannot work more than one shift per day. The new lifeguards will get three paid days off over the 12 week period. So, how many life guards are needed to provide 12 hours of additional coverage for the 84-day period? This problem can be completed in a word processing program.

7. The City of Cambridge has appointed you to work on the FY 2009 budget. Your job is to modify the FY 2008 budget according to these guidelines. Print a hard copy of the completed assignment for your instructor and save the new file under a new file name. Assume that FY 2008 revenue collections are identical to those collected in FY 2009 unless the information indicates something different. Hint: Funds should be placed in funds that have jurisdiction. The fund balance for FY 2009 is the exact amount as it was FY 2008.

Revenue
- Revenue created as a result of changes in these areas goes into the General Fund.
  a. Property taxes increased 3.5%.
  b. Business licenses increased 4.7%.
  c. Vehicle stickers decreased 1.3%.
  d. Insurance taxes increased 2% in the general fund only.
- The total amount of user charges increased 10% in FY 2009. The new revenue from the user charges went into the Water & Sewer Fund and the Natural Gas Fund. Each Fund received half of the new revenues.
- The remaining funds maintained their FY 2008 revenue funding levels.

Expenditures
- General Fund Modifications
  a. Half of the new revenues (dollar amount change in Total Revenue from FY 2008 to FY 2009) in the General Fund went to Public Safety.
  b. General Government received 3% of the new revenues in the General Fund.
  c. Public Works received 17% of the new revenues in the General Fund.
  d. Sanitation and Capital Expenditures each received 15% of the new funds in the General Fund.

- Water and Sewer and Gas System Operations received increases as a result of increased revenues in their departments.
- The remaining departments and funds went unchanged. That is, expenditures were the same as they were in FY 2008.

8. The city of Jonestown is contemplating the construction of a football arena near the down town main artery and the city administrator has requested that you (finance officer) develop a tax plan to fund the construction of the structure. The proposed structure will cost the city $35,000,000.00 to construct and could bring in over a $1,000,000.00 a year in revenue. Your job is two fold. First, prepare a funding structure with the percentage and dollar contribution of each entity. Second, develop a set of economic questions that are likely to arise in the city council meeting concerning your plan. You should also provide answers to these questions. When formulating your questions, remember that there are political issues that are likely to arise.

References

Ammons, David N. 2002. *Tools for Decision Makers: A Practical Guide for Local Government*. Washington, D.C.: CQ Press.

Axelrod, Donald. 1995. *Budgeting for Modern Government*. 2nd Edition. New York: St. Martins.

Bierhanzl, Edward J. and Paul B. Downing. 2004. "User Charges and Special Districts." In *Management Policies in Local Government Finance*. Eds. J. Richard Aronson and Eli Schwartz, Washington, D.C.: ICMA.

Bland, Robert. 2005. *A Revenue Guide for Local Government*. 2nd Ed. Washington, D.C.: ICMA.

Bland, Robert and Irene Rubin. 1997. *Budgeting: A Guide for Local Governments*. Washington, D.C.: ICMA.

Bland, Robert L. and Wes Clarke. 1999. "Budgeting for Capital Improvements." In Roy Meyer's (ed) *Handbook of Government Budgeting*. California: Josey Bass.

Bretschneider, Stuart and Wilpen L. Gorr. 1999. "Practical Methods for Projecting Revenues." In Roy Meyer's (ed) *Handbook of Government Budgeting*. San Francisco, CA: Josey Bass.

Clynch, Edward J., Douglas G. Feig, and James B. Kaatz. 2001. "Local Government Casino Gaming Tax Receipts in Mississippi: An Impact Appraisal." Paper presented at the Southeastern Conference for Public Administration Conference, Baton Rouge, Louisiana.

Doss, Bradley C. 1993. "Capital Budgeting Practices." In Thomas D. Lynch and Lawrence L. Martin's (eds) *Handbook of Comparative Public Budgeting and Financial Management*. New York: Marcel Dekker.

Downing, Paul. B. 1983. "User Charges and Service Fees." In Jack Rabin, W. Bartley Hildreth and Gerald J. Miller's (eds) *Budget Management: A Reader in Local Government Financial Management*. University of Georgia: Carl Vinson Institute of Government.

Fleeter, Howard and L. Lee Walker. 1997. "Revenue Forecasting." In *Case Studies in Public Budgeting and Financial Management*. Eds. Aman Khan and W. Bartley Hildreth. Dubuque, IA: Kendall Hunt Publishing.

Gianakis, Gerasimos A. and Clifford P. McCue. 1999. *Local Government Budgeting: A Managerial Approach*. Praeger: Westport, Connecticut.

Gruber, Jonathan. 2005. *Public Finance and Public Policy*. NY, NY: Worth Publishers.

Kittredge, William P. and Sarah M. Ouart. 2005. *Budget Manual for Georgia Local Government*. Athens, GA: Vinson Institute.

Lee Jr., Robert D. and Ronald W. Johnson. 1998. *Public Budgeting Systems*. Maryland: Aspen Publishers.

Liner, Charles D. 1983. "Projecting Local Government Revenue." In Jack Rabin, W. Bartley Hildreth and Gerald J. Miller's (eds) *Budget Management: A Reader in Local Government Financial Management*. University of Georgia: Carl Vinson Institute of Government.

Lynch, Thomas D. 1995. *Public Budgeting in America*. New Jersey: Prentice Hall.

Mendosa, Arthur A. 1983. "Revenue Sources." In Jack Rabin, W. Bartley Hildreth and Gerald J. Miller's (eds) *Budget Management: A Reader in Local Government Financial Management*. University of Georgia: Carl Vinson Institute of Government.

Mikesell, John. 1999. *Fiscal Administration: Analysis and Applications for the Public Sector*. Florida: Harcourt Brace.

Mikesell, John. 2003. *Fiscal Administration: Analysis and Applications for the Public Sector*. 6th Edition. CA: Thomson Wadsworth.

Mikesell, John. 2004. "General Sales, Income, and Other Nonproperty Taxes." In *Management Policies in Local Government Finance*. Eds. J. Richard Aronson and Eli Schwartz, Washington, D.C.: ICMA.

Nice, David. 2002. *Public Budgeting*. Wadsworth: Stamford, Connecticut.

Rabin, Jack, W. Bartley Hildreth and Gerald J. Miller. 1996. *Budgeting: Formulation and Execution*. University of Georgia: Carl Vinson Institute of Government.

Raphaelson, Arnold H. 2004. "The Property Tax." In *Management Policies in Local Government Finance*. Eds. J. Richard Aronson and Eli Schwartz, Washington, D.C.: ICMA.

Riley, Susan L. and Peter W. Colby. 1991. *Practical Government Budgeting: A Workbook for Public Managers*. New York: State University of New York Press.

Rubin, Irene S. 2006. *The Politics of Public Budgeting: Getting and Spending, Borrowing and Balancing*. 5th ed. Washington, D.C.: CQ Press.

Smith, Robert W. and Thomas D. Lynch. 2004. *Public Budgeting in America*. 5th ed. Upper Saddle River, NJ: Pearson/Prentice Hall.

Vogt, A. John. 1983. "Budgeting Capital Outlays and Improvements." In Jack Rabin, W. Bartley Hildreth, and Gerald J. Miller's (eds) *Budget Management: A Reader in*

Local Government Financial Management. The University of Georgia: Carl Vinson Institute of Government.

Appendix 5A

Question 1A
Property Tax Estimate
Sherwood Subdivision
City of Johnsonville
FY 2009

Items	#of Units	Total Assessed Value	Millage Rate	TOTAL Tax Est.
Two BR on 5 Acres	10		15%	
Two BR on 20 Acres	20		15%	
Three BR on 75 Acres	50		15%	
Four BR on 20 Acres	20		15%	
Park	1		15%	
TOTAL	101			

Question 1B   Tax Rate=
City of Paytonburg

Question 1C   Tax Assessment/Market Value
Millage Rate
City of Gilliam
FY 2009

Business	Market Value	Assessed Value	Millage Rate	Tax Est.	METR
Blackwell's Clothing	$600,000.00	$400,000.00	3.5%		
Payton's Tax Service	450,000.00	350,000.00	3.5%		
Stacie's Lawn Care	265,000.00	152,000.00	3.5%		
Blakemore's Finishing School	500,000.00	250,000.00	3.5%		
Tiffany's Day Care	150,000.00	75,000.00	3.5%		
Yiesha's Hair Care	470,000.00	298,000.00	3.5%		
Yohance's Boys Club	250,000.00	175,000.00	3.5%		
TOTAL	$2,685,000.00	$1,700,000.00			

Appendix 5B

	Sales Price	Assessed Value	*STEP 2* Assessment Ratio	*STEP 3* Average Dev.	*STEP 4* Coefficient
Property 1	$150,000.00	$105,000.00			
Property 2	$150,000.00	120,000.00			
Property 3	$150,000.00	100,000.00			
Property 4	$150,000.00	110,000.00			
Property 5	$150,000.00	75,000.00			
	$750,000.00	$510,000.00			

	Sales Price	Assessed Value	*STEP 2* Assessment Ratio	*STEP 3* Average Dev.	*STEP 4* Coefficient
Property 1	$95,000.00	$89,500.00			
Property 2	$95,000.00	90,900.00			
Property 3	$95,000.00	$95,000.00			
Property 4	$95,000.00	95,400.00			
Property 5	$95,000.00	92,000.00			
Property 6	$95,000.00	93,000.00			
Property 7	$95,000.00	90,100.00			
Property 8	$95,000.00	90,900.00			
Property 9	$95,000.00	89,250.00			
Property 10	$95,000.00	95,459.00			
	950,000.00	921,509.00			

Appendix 5C

Aggregate Assessment Ratio

	Sales Price	Assessed Value	Assessment Ratio
Property 1	$200,000.00	$170,000.00	85%
Property 2	150,000.00	100,000.00	66%
Property 3	25,000.00	15,000.00	60%
Property 4	30,000.00	20,000.00	66%
Property 5	25,000.00	15,000.00	60%
Property 6	35,000.00	28,000.00	80%
	$465,000.00	$348,000.00	417%

STEP 1

STEP 2

STEP 3

Appendix 5D

City of Sparta
Public School Sys.
FY 2008
Projected Revenue

Position Description	# in Grade	FY 2008 Salary	Fed.Inc.Tax	State Inc. Tax	Payroll Tax	Total Taxes
Superintendent	1					
Principal	2					
Teacher A	4					
Teacher B	6					
Teacher C	6					
Janitor	3					
Kitchen Manager	1					
Kitchen Staff	9					
Football Coach	1					
Basketball Coach	1					
TOTAL	34					

City of Sparta
Public School Sys.
FY 2009
Revenue Estimate

Position Description	# in Grade	FY 2009 Salary	Fed. Lnc. Tax	State Inc. Tax	Payroll Tax	Total Taxes
Superintendent	1					
Principal	2					
Teacher A	4					
Teacher B	6					
Teacher C	6					
Teacher D	2					
Janitor	3					
Kitchen Manager	1					
Kitchen Staff	9					
Football Coach	1					
Basketball Coach	1					
TOTAL	36					

Appendix 5E

City of Winstonville
Revenue Estimate
FY 2007-FY2009

Items	FY 2007 (act.)	FY 2008 (est.)	FY 2009 (proj)
Property Taxes	$540,000.00		
User Fees	35,000.00		
Frachise Fees	5,000.00		
Permits	2,500.00		
Utility Fees	102,000.00		
Intergover. Transfers	220,000.00		
Sales Taxes	95,000.00		
Impact Fees	6,000.00		
Storm Water Mgt.	8,500.00		
TOTAL	$1,014,000.00		

Appendix 5F

City of Cambridge
Budget Summary
FY 2008

REVENUE SOURCE	General Fund	Cemetery Fund	City Tax Aid	911 Fund	Central Garage	Water &Sewer	Sanitation	Natural Gas	Capital Exp.	GRAND TOTAL
Property Taxes	$1,483,000.00	$0.00	$0.00	$0.00	$0.00	$0.00	$0.00	$0.00	$0.00	$1,483,000.00
Insurance Taxes	885,000.00	0	0	0	0	41,500.00	0	0	0	$926,500.00
Vehicle Stickers	420,000.00	0	0	0	0	0	0	0	0	$420,000.00
Business Licenses	350,000.00	0	0	0	0	0	0	0	0	$350,000.00
User Charges	0	27,500.00	0	0	116,250.00	3,421,500.00	1,884,000.00	5,375,000.00	0	$10,824,250.00
Special Assessments	0	0	215,000.00	94,000.00	0	195,000.00	50,000.00	285,000.00	0	$839,000.00
Other & Misc.	662,779.00	1,000.00	4,000.00	7,500.00	0	0	0	0	0	$675,279.00
Fund Transfers	0	47,800.00	0	0	0	0	0	0	1,037,200.00	$1,085,000.00
TOTAL Revenues	$3,800,779.00	$76,300.00	$219,000.00	$101,500.00	$116,250.00	$3,658,000.00	$1,934,000.00	$5,660,000.00	$1,037,200.00	$16,603,029.00
Fund Balance	$650,000.00	$7,500.00	$40,000.00	$170,000.00	$0.00	$0.00	$50,600.00	$0.00	$0.00	$918,100.00
TOTAL Available Funds	$4,450,779.00	$83,800.00	$259,000.00	$271,500.00	$116,250.00	$3,658,000.00	$1,984,600.00	$5,660,000.00	$1,037,200.00	$17,521,129.00

EXPENDITURES	General Fund	Cemetery Fund	City Tax Aid	911 Fund	Central Garage	Water &Sewer	Sanitation	Natural Gas	Capital Exp.	GRAND TOTAL
General Government	$1,309,454.00	$0.00	$0.00	$0.00	$0.00	$0.00	$0.00	$0.00	$0.00	$1,309,454.00
Public Safety	2,781,100.00	0	0	271,500.00	0	0	0	0	0	$3,052,600.00
Public Works	360,225.00	0	165,000.00	0	0	0	0	0	0	$525,225.00
Central Garage	0	0	0	0	116,250.00	0	0	0	0	$116,250.00
Sanitation	0	0	0	0	0	0	1,984,600.00	0	0	$1,984,600.00
Water &Sewer Oper.	0	0	0	0	0	3,658,000.00	0	0	0	$3,658,000.00
Cemetery Operations	0	83,800.00	0	0	0	0	0	0	0	$83,800.00
Gas System Oper.	0	0	0	0	0	0	0	5,660,000.00	0	$5,660,000.00
Capital Expenditures	0.00	0.00	94,000.00	0.00	0.00	0.00	0.00	0.00	1,037,200.00	$1,131,200.00
TOTAL Expenditures	$4,450,779.00	$83,800.00	$259,000.00	$271,500.00	$116,250.00	$3,658,000.00	$1,984,600.00	$5,660,000.00	$1,037,200.00	$17,521,129.00

Chapter 6
Budgeting Techniques and Analytical Models

Chapter Six Overview

By definition, budgeting requires some level of technical analysis and the ability to understand how forecasting can play an integral role in these analytical models. This fact has become more realistic today as an increasing number of state and local governments deal with a variety of problems ranging from budget deficits to urban sprawl. In a lot of cases, governments provide services that cannot be performed or are too large to be provided by the private sector or through normal market forces. As a result, it is imperative that budget analysts apply various analytical techniques and models to their analysis in order to determine the most efficient and effective approach.

This chapter discusses several practical techniques and analytical models that are useful in assisting state and local budget analyst in dealing with spending issues from an array of different perspectives. The chapter begins with a method of understanding policy problem and analysis. Next, there is a discussion of various forecasting techniques. Last, some specific techniques are discussed. These include: discounting, cost benefit analysis, cost-effectiveness analysis, internal rates of returns, payback method, productivity analysis, and multiple regression analysis.

Understanding the Methods and Techniques of Analysis

Once a decision has been made to solve a public problem or expand services, policy experts must ensure that the problem is fully understood along with the alternatives to solving the problem. Weimer and Vining (1989) provide a succinct model to understanding the problem and examining the options to solving the problem. Bureaucrats and budget analysts can follow these steps in providing policy makers with viable policy options.

Problem Analysis
1. Understanding the Problem
   a. Receiving the Problem: Assessing the Symptoms

b.   Framing the Problem: Analyzing Market and Governmental Failures
c.   Modeling the Problem: Identifying Policy Variables
2. Choosing and Explaining Relevant Goals and Constraints
3. Choosing a Solution Method

Solution Analysis
4. Choosing Evaluation Criteria
5. Specifying Policy Alternatives
6. Evaluating: Predicting Impacts of Alternatives and Valuing them based on a Criteria
7. Recommending Actions

Forecasting Revenues

Good revenue estimations or forecasts are considered by most to be more of an art than a science. In addition to good judgment, economic savvy and a variety of methodologies go into the process. Any particular methodology will lead to a different estimate. To say the least, an analyst should understand the revenue system and have a good understanding of all the factors that have impacted past revenue collections. The budget office or the comptroller's office will normally handle revenue estimates (Axelrod 1995; Wang 2006). Most state and local governments will begin revenue projections about six months before the beginning of budget implementation. The advantage to starting early is that it allows an analyst time to revise their estimates as they get closer to the actual day of implementation and determine whether revenue collections will exceed or fall short of expectations (Fleeter and Walker 1997). To say the very least, a state or local government should forecast revenues and expenditures over a couple of years regardless of the level of economic and political stability in the jurisdiction. Hence, forecasting is an integral part of any model assessing expenditure or revenue patterns over time. *Forecasting* is an attempt to predict future revenue collection based on present administrative, structural conditions, demographic and economic factors. For example, the federal government has predicted that the social security fund will disappear in the next twenty years based primarily on the number of persons currently contributing to the fund and those taking money out of the fund.

Depending on the size ($) of the budget in a jurisdiction, forecasters should begin the process anywhere from 6 to 18 months prior to the beginning of the fiscal year. A good time frame is useful because it saves a lot of time and effort on the part of agency directors who are charged with preparing their budget. It is not efficient or effective to budget for funds that may or may not exist. Hence, budget forecasts should be modified as new information is added to the equation. The Office of Management and Budget (OMB) and the Congressional

Budget Office (CBO) along with Presidential advisors estimate the federal budget while state and local budget offices handle the responsibility at lower levels (Lee and Johnson 1998; Mikesell 1999; Nice 2001).

Key Factors to Consider When Forecasting Revenues

- *Revenues should be projected separately.* Because each revenue source is distinct and has its own set of nuances it is rational to estimate them separately. By so doing, it limits the number of errors and may bring greater balance to the overall estimates due to over and under estimates for individual tax expectations.

- *Focus efforts on the large revenue sources.* As indicated in Table 5.1, the property tax is the largest source of income for a local government. Hence, it is important that great care be taken in this preparing this estimate. Small revenue sources do not have a great impact on the budget.

- *Historical data is the key to success.* Revenue projections do not tend to change dramatically over time. As a result, data and financial records should be closely examined. Once this data is examined, projections can be made after adjustments are made for other factors in the environment such as demographic shifts and economic development. Further, it is important that the analyst pay attention to items that may not reoccur. For example, the government may receive a grant for five years that is not renewable.

- *Underestimate rather than overestimate budgets.* Although budgets are based on solid economic factors, the ramification of budget deficits can be very political in nature. State and local elected officials do not want to explain budget deficits to voters because the repercussions could be felt in the next election cycle. Therefore, estimates should be somewhat conservative.

- *Good Judgment.* While a state or local government's tax base may seem stable, it is important that estimators keep an eye on other nearby jurisdictions that may have an impact on their revenue estimates. Further, estimators may receive estimates

from other sources that are not inline with their estimates. Ultimately, it is up to the judgment of the estimator to decide
what to consider in the estimate.

Forecasting Models

Riley and Colby (1991) discuss five models that local governments can use
when estimating revenue. Deciding which model to use can be determined by a
number of factors. Particularly, the size of the city's budget and resources available to conduct the estimate are important. The first model is called a *simplistic
model*. This model is based on historical data. An analyst would simply use
trend analysis and extrapolate the data for the current fiscal year. In addition,
expected changes in the use of services that might be relevant to revenue collections are also considered. For example, a factory that closes with several hun-
dred residents may have a disparate impact on revenue collections. The second
model is a *multiple regression model*. A multiple regression model uses factors
such as unemployment, population shifts, and changes in the economy to predict
revenue. An *econometric model* synchronizes revenue estimates with a review
of interdependent variables, such as the consumer price index, interest rates, cost
benefit analysis, net present value (NPV), internal rate of return (IRR), and construction activity. The fourth model is called a *mircrosimulation model*. This
model uses various forms of data such as a sample of IRS returns to predict future trends. The last model is an *input-output model*. This model uses purchase
and sales data to ascertain where the revenue is produced.

Most local governments use the simplistic model because it is very clear-cut
and uses data and financial resources that are readily available. Liner (1983)
argues that multivariate regression is not an appropriate tool for local government revenue projections. However, he does make a case for time series analysis
since it makes use of internal data that is readily available and can be computed
using simple equipment such as a calculator. A three to five year period is typically used in the model (Bretschneider and Gorr 1999). Special attention should
be paid to calculating property tax estimates. Liner (1983) suggests that revenue
should be split into component parts and then the analyst has to decide whether
to analyze actual revenues or the base of the revenue sources. Property tax revenue has assessed value (base), the tax rate, and the collection rate (actual). Further, it may be necessary to separate, real versus personal property. It may be
useful if the analyst can prepare graphs or charts showing the revenue trend over
time. The amount of time designated to this process will clearly be dictated by
the size and level of importance for the revenue source.

State governments are more likely to use one of the more sophisticated
models because their budgets are larger and a lot more complicated. Axelrod
(1995) argues, "the critical phase in revenue estimation is calculating the effect

of the economic assumptions on the tax base for each tax" (p. 78). For example, income taxes come from three major sources of income: wages and salaries, corporations, and other non-wage income such as rents, dividends and interests. Analysts can then use the set tax rates to estimate revenue. Lastly, they can adjust the estimate for various exemptions, deductions, refunds or expected delinquencies.

"For sales, excise, and other consumption taxes, it is necessary to estimate, tax by tax, the effect of economic activity on wholesale and retail sales. After deducting exemptions, analysts come up with a new tax base to which they apply the tax rates. Property taxes are determined by the assessed value of property and the appropriate tax rates and adjusted to reflect exemptions, deductions, and statutory tax limits" (Axelrod 1995, p. 78).

Selecting the Best Forecasting Model

Mikesell (2003) discusses six points that are useful as a guide to forecasting. First, the user should completely understand the revenue source. This includes administration and collection measures. Further, forecasters should ensure that the variables included in the model are as close to perfect as possible. Unreliable data for the dependent variable in particular compromises the validity of the estimate (Liner 1996). Second, the data should be plotted in a graph to show the movement of the revenue. Forecasters can use this information to determine the affects of other variables on the revenue. If possible, corrective measures can be taken to improve the administration or collection mechanisms.

The third point is honesty in reporting. Elected officials often have their own agendas and may seek to manipulate the process with low or high forecasts in an attempt to increase or decrease expenditures. Mikesell's (2003) fourth suggestion considers "what" the forecaster is trying to do with the revenue source. For example, if an annual forecast is needed, then a regression model would suffice. If a long-term forecast is needed, then a trend extrapolation model would work. Fifth, each revenue source should be estimated separately. There are too many factors that are indigenous to a particular revenue source that would inflate or deflate the total revenue source. It is easier to compensate for errors in separate revenue models. Lastly, revenue sources should be monitored throughout the year and compared with the projections. With that stated, the forecaster should be aware that a change in revenue projections for one month may or may not make a drastic difference for the rest of the year. Regardless to what is found, the forecaster should use the information to improve the model (see also Riley and Colby 1991 and Liner 1996).

Generally speaking, state and local governments initiate budget projections about six months prior to the beginning of the next fiscal year or budget cycle. The size of the budget and the number of factors affecting the budget are likely indicators of how much lead time is needed (Bretschneider and Gorr 1999).

Types of Forecasts

- *Status Quo Model*: This model assumes that the future will look a lot like the present. For example, if a state spent $75,000,000.00 on capital expenditures last year, then it will cost approximately that amount this year. This model works well in stable governments. The major advantage of the model is that it is simple and easy to administer. The major disadvantage is that any shift in economic conditions will compromise the validity of the model (Nice 2001).

- *Extrapolation Model*: This model uses current trends (time-series data) in revenue and expenditures to explain future revenue and expenditure trends. Extrapolations can use constant increments, constant percent changes, simple growth models using the average annual compounding formula, or linear or nonlinear time trends in which revenue for the budget year is estimated as an arithmetic function of time ($R = a + bt$). For example, if property tax receipts have increased an average of 2% over the last five years, the model would assume that they would increase 2% during the forecasted year as well. While more accurate than the status quo model, it does have the same disadvantages. For example, it makes no attempt develop a model examining cause and effect relationship between the revenue source and a particular economic factor (Bretschneider and Gorr 1999; Mikesell 1999; Nice 2001).

- *Judgmental or Brainstorming Model*: In some instances, budget managers have substantive experience and knowledge of the nuances of a jurisdiction. They essentially use all of their contacts that also have longevity and the exact information that they need to project the budget. Initially, all sorts of data and information are generated. Then, these data and information are analyzed and scored for usefulness. Third, the best information and data are synthesized. Lastly, the best information and ideas are considered in the model. The obvious disadvantage to this model is dependence on the experts. While human judgment is important, it is enhanced tremendously with known facts that are quantifiable (Gianakis and McCue 1999).

- *Delphi Model*: In this model, experts discuss forecasts under the auspices of a moderator who handles only the logistical part of the discussion. Each participant is asked the same question by the moderator with the intent or hope that a consensus can be reached. The advantage of the model is that participants are not pressured to accept the position of other participants. This model also serves to allow minority views to be espoused (Gianakis and McCue 1999: Nice 2001).

- *Time-Series Model*: A time-series model can be simple or very complex. The model essentially attempts to break down and explain all of the component parts to the budget into four components: a long-term trend, seasonal variation, cyclical variation and irregular variation. The model addresses questions such as: When are the most property taxes, user fees, and sales taxes collected? When are public utilities the most heavily utilized? (Liner 1996; Gianakis and McCue 1999; Mikesell 1999, 2003; Nice 2001).

- *Multiple Regression Model*: A regression model is a more complex time series model that estimates revenue using several independent variables such as the unemployment rate and income levels. The advantage of this model is that it is relatively simple to estimate each revenue source separately (Bretschneider and Gorr 1999: Gianakis and McCue 1999; Mikesell 2003).

- *Econometric Models*: These models estimate revenue "within a simultaneous system of interdependent equations that express theoretical and empirical relationships between economic and fiscal variables" (Mikesell 1999, p. 486). The advantage to this model is that it allows the user to examine revenue sources that are not independent on other revenue sources.

Cost-Benefit Analysis and Cost-Effectiveness Analysis

These techniques "attempt to relate the costs of programs to performance and both quantify costs in monetary terms, but they differ in the way they measure the outcomes of programs" (Lee and Johnson 1998, p. 179). *Cost-benefit analysis* (CBA) compares the cost of a program with the benefits of the program. The alternative that yields the greatest net benefit at the least amount is normally chosen. In addition to a dollar amount being placed on the variables in the analysis, benefits are also assessed from a quantitative perspective. Both of these techniques are quite dependent on data, so the analyst should ensure that he/she has the most reliable data available.

The main objective of the technique is to improve internal and allocative efficiency in public spending. Spending today does not equate to spending tomorrow. As a result, it is necessary for budget analysts to be aware of items such as: present value, discount rates, recurring costs, and compounded interests when putting together cost-benefit models. [43]

There are some problems associated with cost-benefit models. One problem is with *free riders*. That is, some citizens enjoy the benefits of public service without paying for them. A second problem is the uneven distribution of benefits. Nice (2002) uses the example of a car licensing fee in Washington that offered the greatest reduction in the cost of the fee to those who owned the most expensive cars. From a political perspective, this proposal was not viewed at beneficial. A third example is political manipulation. In order to make a project look more attractive, the costs of the program can be lowered arbitrarily while the benefits can be increased (Axelrod 1995). Further, it is sometimes difficult to identify all of the costs and benefits associated with a program. There may be some spillover affects as well as other externalities that are hard to predict (Ammons 2002). There are also some benefits that are not necessarily considered when providing public services. For example, research shows that crime tends to decrease in neighborhoods when a police officer parks a squad car in the driveway at his/her private residence. Apparently, criminals avoid neighborhoods where policemen reside (Gianakis and McCue 1999).

Calculating cost-benefit analysis can be very complex since all of the factors involved in the process must be quantifiable and measurable over time. "Benefits are measured by the market price of the project outputs or the price consumers are willing to pay. Costs are measured by the monetary outlays necessary to undertake the investment" (Lynch 1995, p. 160).

Let's look at an example of a municipality that wants to decrease the amount of non-violent crime in a particular part of the city. They look at three possible alternatives to improving the problem: 1.) Increase the amount of time patrolmen spend in the neighborhood. 2.) Place a police substation in the neighborhood. 3.) Add a bicycle/foot patrolman in the department whose jurisdiction would include that neighborhood.

Alternative 1: Increase Patrol Time

Cost: The first option is to increase the amount of patrol time in the neighborhood in question, while reducing the amount of time in other neighborhoods, using existing officers. Overall, patrol time will increase by 15%. There should be minimum, if any, increases in cost since we will use existing law enforcement personnel.

Benefit: Based on previous patterns, crime should decrease by 5% for every two hours added to the day patrol and decrease by 4% for every four hours added to the patrol in the evening and night. However, data suggest that shifting officers from one neighborhood to another is likely to shift crime from one neighborhood to another over time.

Alternative 2: Add a Substation

Cost: The city has several options: A. Rent space. The most desirable area costs $750.00 per month plus utilities. B. Purchase and refurbish one of the older buildings in the neighborhood. While the average building in the neighborhood is relatively cheap as a result of the crime level ($72,000.00), the cost to refurbish the site can range from $7,000.00-$15,000.00 based on the condition of the building. C. Build a new substation. The building, land and furnishing will cost the city $175,000.00 and take at least seven months to complete. D. Purchase a building that is ready for occupation. Buildings that are ready for occupation tend to sell 10-15% higher than the average building. For example, a 700 square foot building that is completely ready for occupation will cost about $85,000.00. Two additional officers will be hired at a total cost of $116,000.00 per year after training.

Benefit: Based on previous crime patterns, we expect the crime rate to decrease by 50% within the first month of operation. Whether we lease, buy or build a substation will not affect this rate. However, the speed in which the officer's occupy the space obviously will impact how quickly their presence will impact the crime rate.

Alternative 3: Add a Bicycle/Foot Patrolmen to the Area

Cost: The city would hire one new police officer at a cost of $58,000.00 per year after training. One fully equipped bicycle would cost $589.00.

Benefit: One additional foot patrol would increase visibility in the neighborhood by 100%. Crime decreased by 10% when the first foot patrol was hired last year. We expect that rate to increase an additional 15% since both officers will work simultaneously. Fur-

ther, a citizen satisfaction survey indicated that citizens felt 75%
safer as a result of the increased interaction with police officers
that were on foot.

Now that we have three options, which one is the most efficient and effective? Let's look at each of the three alternatives. Alternative 1 is by far the most
cost efficient, but is the worse in terms of benefits given the impact of moving
an officer from one location to another location. Alternative 2 is the most expensive and has the greatest amount of benefits. Alternative 3 falls squarely in the
middle of Alternatives 1 and 2 in terms of costs and benefits. In this example,
Alternative 3 is probably the best option. If your arguments are based on fiscal
years, you may find it easier to use tables.

Cost-effectiveness analysis (CEA) assumes that there are benefits and concentrates on spending the least amount of funds to achieve the objective. Another way to look at cost-effectiveness is to examine all viable policy options
and determine which option is the most cost efficient. Gianakis and McCue
(1999) point out that this model provides for technological efficiency, but not
allocative efficiency "because no effort is made to determine whether the cost
supports the pursuit of the goal" (p. 89). Cost-effectiveness models are useful in
both operating and capital budgets.

For example, a cost-effectiveness model would examine the amount of
time saved by allowing potential voters to register to vote by mail rather than
going to an official location to do so. A second example would consider the cost
of building a new post office to handle an increase in population or expanding
the old building. The quantitative techniques used in cost-effectiveness models
are similar to those used in cost-benefits models (Axelrod 1995).

Financial Decision Making Tools

Discounting To Present Value/Discount Rates

Discounting to the present value is a very useful tool for public administrators because it considers the value of the dollar today relative to some other period in time. Analysts will find discounting useful when comparing two items
that occur during different periods with similar financing methods. For example:
leasing versus purchasing items or contracting out versus providing the service
from within the government. Lee and Johnson (1998) indicate that discounting
serves two main purposes. First, funds are diverted from the private sector to the
public sector. If these funds reap at least a dollar for dollar ratio, then it is feasible from an economic perspective to provide the service from within the government. Second, citizens prefer to reap the benefits of spending now rather than
in the future. Hence, citizens are aware that the spending power of a dollar is

greater today than it is in the future and are not inclined to endorse programs or invest money unless the interest is likely to reap greater future benefits (Wang 2006).

If we had a choice, we would like our money to increase in value over time, rather than decrease. Discounting works similar to compounded interest collected on a savings account in reverse. For example, if we were contemplating putting $10,000.00 in a saving account at a 6% interest rate, we would want to make sure that the spending power of the principal and interest ($10,600.00) will equal or exceed its current value in one year. If principal and interest does not equal or exceed the current value, then it would not be economically feasible to put money into the account. The 6% interest rate measures our willingness to trade $10,000.00 today (PV) for $10,600.00 in twelve months (FV). Interest rates calculate *future values*, while discount rates calculate *present value*.

Future Value (FV) = Present Value (PV) X (One + Interest Rate (IR))

FV = $10,000.00 X (1 + .06)

FV = $10,600.00

Present value is calculated using the same data as future value. However, the term discount rate is used rather than interest rate because the value that of what we will receive in the future is smaller today because we subtract an amount to compensate us for the delay in receiving the benefit. Hence, we are putting a value on time (Miller 1996; Ammons 2002; Aronson and Schwartz 2004).

Discount to the Present Value = Future Value / (1 + IR)

Example 6.1

Deldrick City has a project that will take four years to implement from the day that construction begins. The city expects to save $5,000.00 a year once the project is implemented. Since funds will be spent prior to the completion of the project, time becomes a cost. Hence, it is feasible to use discounting. Using the PV formula and a 5% discount rate, the expected value of a $5,000.00 forecasted benefit for the project at the end of four years is $4,113.50. So, city officials can decide if the project is worth the investment based on this figure. That is, is it worth the effort to complete the project to save $4,113.50 a year?

Year 1 PV = $5,000.00 / (1 + .05) = $4,761.90
Year 2 PV = $4,761.90 / (1 + .05) = $4,535.14
Year 3 PV = $4,535.14 / (1 + .05) = $4,319.18
Year 4 PV = $4,319.18 / (1 + .05) = $4,113.50

A simple or short way to calculate the value of the savings in the fourth year is to use the formula given below. By cubing the discount factor, you can calculate the present value the same way as you did with the long method. However, you can expect the sum to vary based on rounding error. You can decrease this error by not rounding the sum to two digits to the right of the decimal as you did in the long method. In this example, 1.05 raised to the fourth power is 1.21550625, which would give us a PV of $4,113.51. This is only one cent off of the long method. In Excel, you can use the formula = $(1+5\%)^4$ to calculate the answer.

$$PV \text{ (of } \$x \text{ over 4 years @ 5\%)} = \frac{\text{Future Value}}{(1 + .05)^4} = \frac{\$5,000}{1.21550625} = \$4,113.51$$

Example 6.2

The City of Brassell has been offered $150,000.00 for a building that is leased to Barnett Real Estate. The real estate company pays $1,200.00 per month on a 5-year lease with the option to buy the building at the end of the lease for $80,000.00. The city has to decide if it is better to sell the building now, or continue to lease it. Using a 5% discount rate, for a property that had annual benefits for n years, we can use the following formula to calculate the present value. Note: n = number of years.

$$PV = Annual\ Value\ X\ \frac{[(1 + Discount\ Rate)^n - 1]}{Discount\ Rate\ (1 + DR)^n}$$

A. Leasing/Purchase Option

- Annual Benefit   = $14,400.00   ($1,200.00 X 12 months)

- One Time Benefit   = $80,000.00

- PV Annual Benefit   = $14,400.00   X $\frac{(1.276-1)}{.05\ (1.276)}$

                         = $14,400.00   X $\frac{(.276)}{.064}$

                         = $14,400.00   X 4.31

                         = $62,064.00

- PV One Time Benefit   = $80,000.00 / $(1.05)^5$

$$= \$62,695.92$$

Total Benefit $= \$62,064.00 + \$62,695.92$
$= \$124,759.92$

B. Sale Option
* $150,000.00

C. Comparing Options

It would seem feasible to sell the property given the small but positive disparity between the two options ($150,000.00 - $125,047.92 = $24,952.08). If the difference was smaller, other items such as the current status of the lease holder, future plans of the city, and expenditure and revenue priorities should be closely scrutinized. More than anything, PV allows decision makers the opportunity to examine the current lease and assess what it is really worth (([5 X $14,400.00] + $80,000.00) = $152,000.00).

Example 6.3

The City of Burnside has determined that it is losing money in the billing department due to its inferior computer network. So, prior to spending $150,000.00 on new computers, city officials decided to use discounting to determine if it is worth the money to buy a new computer system. Specifically, is the expected $47,500.00 saved each year worth it in another five years when the cost of buying the computers is considered?

Depending on the item in question, it might be useful for a city to also secure bids and contract the project out to the lowest bidder if it is cost efficient. When leasing or contracting out a service/project is an option, the analyst should pay close attention to the net present value (NPV). The NPV should be large (positive number) enough to justify the city providing the service. If the net present value is small, the city might want to seriously consider the lowest bidder.

Table 6.1 shows the results of the analysis using a 9% discount rate over a 6 year period. When the amount invested is subtracted from the total present value of annual saving the net present value is $63,081.14. This amount is over and beyond the cost of purchasing the computers. Hence, it would be a good investment for the city. However, what if the NPV was smaller given the potential size of a city's budget? What if the savings were smaller and the discount rate was larger or smaller? What if the computers had a life span of seven years rather than six years? What if we had a private company offering the service at a lower amount? The NPV is ultimately affected by the data that is put into the equation. Hence, an analyst should be fully cognizant and understand this principle. Lastly, if the NPV is a negative number, it is a bad investment.

NPV (Present Value) =   Annual Savings
                              (1+r)

Table 6.1 Discounting Cash Flow Technique

Year	Savings	NPV*	9% D.R.
1	$47,500.00	$43,577.98	.917
2	47,500.00	39,979.80	.842
3	47,500.00	36,678.72	.772
4	47,500.00	33,650.20	.708
5	47,500.00	30,871.74	.650
6	47,500.00	28,322.70	.596

Total Present Value of Annual Savings   = $213,081.14

Amount Invested   = $150,000.00
Net Present Value (NPV)   = $63,081.14

* Figures are rounded.

Note: See also Kramer, Fred A. 1976. "The Discounting to Present Value Technique as a Decision Tool." *Special Bulletin.*

In order to get the figures in Table 6.1, use the present value formula. After the first iteration, the sum becomes the new value. Over a six-year period, the city would save $213,081.14.

NPV (Net Present Value) = Annual Savings = $47,500.00 = $43,577.98*
                               (1+r)   (1 + .09)

$43,577.98/$47,500.00 = .917 $43,577.98/1.09 = $39,979.80
$39,979.80/$47,500.00 = .842 $39,979.80/1.09 = $36,678.72

*Figures are rounded.

Note: The formula that was used in Example 6.2 can also be applied to the problem discussed in Example 6.3. It is particularly useful in this setting because we are expecting annual benefits over several years.

Rate of Return

The *rate of return* (RI) is a private sector technique that solves for the rate of return on investments. In some instances, government officials have to decide if it is economically feasible to provide a service or contract the service out to the private sector. RI is calculated by dividing the net yearly/annual savings by the average investment in the project. There is an underlying assumption in this technique that government entities depreciate assets on an annual basis.

We can use the example in Table 6.1 to explain and apply this technique. As shown previously, the city had yearly/annual savings of $47,500.00 by investing $150,000.00 into a new computer system. So, the first thing that we do is calculate annual depreciation using the following formula:

I (Initial Investment) / EL (Expected Asset Life) = AD (Annual Depreciation)

$150,000.00 / 6 years = $25,000.00

Next, we calculate the average investment (AI). We know that the computers will be worth $150k during the first year (FI) and $25k during the sixth year (LI) or the last year of the project. So, if we add the value of the computers in the first year to their value in last year and divide it by two, the average investment is $87,500.00. By the way, the last year value and the annual depreciation are the same.

First Year Value (FI) + Last Year Value (LI) /2 = Average Investment (AI)

$150,000.00 + $25,000.00 / 2 = $87,500.00

After doing the math we see that the rate of return on the average investment is 53.7% using the formula:

Annual Savings (AS) /Average Investment (AI) = Rate of Return (RI)

$47,500.00 / $87,500.00 = .543 or 54.3%

City officials now have to decide if a rate of return of 54.3% is large enough to justify the project. While there is not an exact cut off for an acceptable rate of return, one can follow a basic rule, a larger rate of return is more acceptable than a smaller rate of return. In this case, 54.3% is not as good as 75%, but better than 40%.

Payback Method

The payback method is a tool that allows decision makers to examine the time needed to recover an investment through net annual savings. In simple terms, how much time is needed to recover the cost of the investment? In the private sector, the question is: how much time is needed to make a profit?

Let's use the City of Burnside in Example 6.3 where the city expected to save $47,500.00 annually by purchasing $150,000.00 in new computers for the Billing Department. The annual operating cost to the city is $25,000.00. The first thing that we must do is calculate the net annual cash flow saving.

Net Annual Cash Flow Savings (NSAV) = Annual Saving (AS) – Operating Cost (OC)

$22,500.00 = $47,500.00 - $25,000.00

Since we know the total dollar amount needed to complete the investment, we simply need to determine the expected life of the computers. Generally speaking, high end technology hardware and software is expected to have a life span of five years in the public sector. So, we can determine the payback period by dividing the annual investment (Ai) by the net annual cash flow saving (NSAV).

Ai / NSAV = PP

$150,000.00 / $22,500.00 = 6.6 years

In this example, it is clear that 6.6 years is barely larger than the 6-year expected life of the computers. Therefore, it would suggest that the computers are not a great investment. However, all is not necessarily lost. The city can also use this information to formulate other scenarios and ways to save money or reduce operating expenditures. For example, what would happen if the city received a lower bid on the computers or the life expectancy of the computers is extended one more year? The basic goal is to ensure that the expected life of the investment is greater than the pay back period.

This model can be modified a bit to calculate the remaining life (RL) of an asset and actual savings (aS). Using the above example, we can calculate RL using this formula:

EL – PP = RL

6 – 6.6 = -.6 years

In this example, the computers fall .6 years short of the period needed to pay for them. Again, this would support the previous finding that this would not be a great investment. It also supports the proposition that the city should ensure that they are getting the best possible estimates/bids on the computers. Actual savings can be determined using the formula:

RL X AS = aS

In the above example (-.6 X $47,500.00), we would have a net sum of zero since we are not saving any money. RL and AS must be positive numbers in order to reap savings (Round the remaining life years to one digit to the right of the decimal prior to calculating annual savings). Realistically, you want the item of expenditure to last longer than the period needed to pay for it (See Chapman 1996 for a nice snapshot of these three methods).

Productivity Analysis

The term *productivity* can be measured in a number of different ways, but the most common method compares the ratio of the quantity to the quantity of input used in the production of that output. The key question is: Can the work be completed more efficiently and effectively with the addition of more resources? Contrary to popular belief, governments do in fact make an attempt to do more with less. Using better work procedures, better equipment, and improving employee attitude toward the job can work toward achieving this end. Assessing productivity can be achieved through an examination of outputs and outcomes. However, it is better to examine the benefits to individuals and society (outcomes) rather than the product of the project (outputs). Performance audits make it easy to obtain outputs, but outcomes require value judgments to determine if society is better off. There are a number of factors that can affect the relationship between outcomes and outputs, so it is difficult to have a meaningful analysis of outcomes. Review the section in chapter 1 on program and performance budgets to see how expenditures are tied to outcomes and outputs. Further, an increase in production may suggest a decrease in cost, but a reduction in cost does not necessarily mean an increase in production. Programs may appear to be more efficient by cutting the budget without much regard for productivity.

One of the most commonly cited reasons for increased productivity are increased workload. Some employees are simply bored and unchallenged while others do not have enough to do. Others find their work too complex and thus do not perform. When the work is simplified, they tend to perform better. As a result, unit costs can be lowered. Improved training procedures, new equipment, better use of job evaluations, improved employee relations, and opportunities for mobility have also been shown to improve productivity.

Essentially, programs and projects must be evaluated on their own merits. Evaluators must understand the mechanics of the work performed and human behavior in order to provide good recommendations (Follett 1918; Lynch 1995).

Multiple Regression Analysis

Regression analysis is used quite a bit as a forecasting method by most states and large local governments. Users of this technique should be familiar with statistical packages such as SPSS or SAS to conduct this sort of analysis. Regression analysis is particularly useful in budgeting when examining revenue and expenditure models. It allows the user to determine the affect of each independent variable on the dependent variable while controlling the other independent variables.

A simple regression model uses a straight line where $Y = a + bX$ to describe the relationship. In this model, Y is the dependent variable, a is the distance between the point where the regression line intercepts the Y axis and the origin, the slope b is the regression coefficient and measures the change in Y given one unit change in X (Lynch 1995; Mikesell 2003).

Again, the technique works on the basic assumption that a change in a dependent variable (Y) is correlated with a change in an independent variable (X). This change can be negative or positive. Regression analysis uses interval or ratio data. However, nominal or ordinal data can be converted to numbers and then the numbers are used as proxies (also called dummy variables). For example, let's think about region. The words south and north do not mean anything to a computer program. So, if we convert the terms to 0 and 1, where 0=south and 1=north, we can then use the numerical data in our analysis. However, the user has to remember not to make false claims with the data. For example, a mean score of 145 for south and 239 for north means absolutely nothing. Let's take a look at an example to clarify the concepts listed above.

In this example, Mrs. Dorcas Young is the Secretary of Health and she is trying to make an argument that the federal government needs to continue supporting the Medicaid and SCHIP programs in their efforts to decrease the number of uninsured children in the United States. The following directional hypothesis summarizes her argument:

H_1: *Enrolling children in SCHIP and Medicaid will decrease the percent of uninsured children.*

The basic premise of her model is that variables (independent) such at the percentage of children who: graduate from high school, live below the poverty level, live in a certain region of the country, etc have an affect on the percentage of uninsured children. Each of the variables used in the model are in rates or percentages with the exception of region. Region is a dichotomous dummy variable.

$$Y = b_0 + b_1 x_1 + b_2 x_2 + b_3 x_3 + b_4 x_4 + b_5 x_5 + b_6 x_6 + b_7 x_7 + e$$
where:

Y = Percentage of Uninsured Children

Demographic Variables (annual)
x_1 = Poverty Rate
x_2 = High School Graduation Rate,
x_3 = Unemployment Rate,
x_4 = Percent of Population that is Caucasian,
x_5 = Geographical Region (South and Southwest=0, Other States=1),

Public Health Variables (annual)
x_6 = Children Medicaid Enrollee Rate, and
x_7 = Children SCHIP Enrollee Rate.

What does the model reveal? Table 6.4 shows that each of the independent variables has some affect on the dependent variable. The most important item for Mrs. Young is to show that the Medicaid and SCHIP program variables are significant. The coefficients for each of these variables are significant at the .01 level of analysis and in the correct direction (-.0236 and –0.591 respectively). That is, as the percentage of Medicaid and SCHIP enrollees increase the percentage of uninsured children decreases. The negative sign next to the coefficient indicates a decrease. A positive coefficient would indicate an increase in the coefficient. For example, the model shows that the percentage of uninsured children increases as the poverty rate increases.

Other things that are useful in this table are the F score and Adjusted R^2. The R^2 coefficient ranges from 0-100. The coefficient basically defines the level of predictability for the model. In this example, the adjusted R^2 is .969. So, that would mean that the effects of all of the independent variables explains 96.9% of the variance in uninsured rates.

Table 6.4 OLS Children's Health Care Regression Model (Pooled Data)

Demographic Variables
-High School Graduates   -0.192 (.023) ***
-Children in Poverty   0.175 (.028) ***

Economic Variables
-Unemployment Rate -0.423 (.138) **

Medicaid and SCHIP Variables
-White Population   -0.076 (.006) ***
-Region   16520 (9507.7) *

-Medicaid Enrollees -0.236 (.038) ***
-SCHIP Enrollees   -0.591 (-.591) ***

-Total Population 0.203 (.012) ***
F=771.23*** R^2=.970

-Intercept -14019 (7539.7)
Adjusted R^2 =.969   N=301

Note: The table reports unstandardized coefficients with the standard errors in the parenthesis. It also includes a dummy variable for all but one year in the fixed effects model.

***Significant at the .01 level.   **Significant at the .05 level.
*Significant at the .10 level.

Reading and Understanding Reports

Reports that are filled with statistics and models are useful when they are understood by the user. Hence, it is important that the bottom line be clearly stated with references to the difficult sections. For example, when conducting a cost benefit analysis, it would be prudent to describe the many features of the model during the conceptualization stage. In addition, provide the consumer with alternatives paradigms that describe how a change in one factor may bring about a change in the outcome. For example, how would a half percent increase in the discount rate affect the value of an option?

Conclusion

As mentioned at the beginning of the chapter, there are a number of techniques that are useful to budget analysts and politicians in understanding how to forecast the amount of revenues needed for the budget. In addition, there are tools that allow analysts the ability to determine if policy decisions, upon implementation, are good or bad. While there are no hard and fast rules in estimating revenues, the chapter does show that there are some basic principles that should be adhered to regardless to the size of the government. Basically, good projections come from analysts who stick to the basic principles while paying close attention to population shifts, economic fluctuations, industry movement, etc. Sophisticated models are only as good as the analysts using them. These as well as other tools are quite useful and can save governments thousands of dollars over multiple fiscal years.

Important Terms and Phrases

Annual Benefit	Initial Investment
Annual Depreciation	Input-Output Models
Annual Savings	Judgmental Model
Annual Value	Last Year Value
Average Investment	Marginal Cost
Brainstorming Model	Micro Simulation Model
Congressional Budget Office (CBO)	Multiple Regression Model
Cost-Benefit Analysis (CBA)	Net Present Value (NPV)
Cost-Effectiveness Analysis (CEA)	Net Annual Cash Flow Saving (NSAV)
Delphi Model	Office of Management and Budget (OMB)
Discounting/Discount Rates	One Time Benefit
Econometric Model	Operating Cost
Expected Asset Life	Payback Method
Extrapolation Model	Present Value
First Year Value	Productivity
Fixed Cost	Rate of Return (RR)
Forecasting	Recurring Cost
Free Rider	Remaining Life (RC)
Future Value	Status Quo Model
Interest Rate	Time-Series Model

Chapter 6 Homework Exercises

Directions: Complete questions 1 in a word processing program and questions 2-6 in Excel. Do not round any numbers until the final step. You can complete the remaining questions in Excel and paste the answers into a word processing program.

1. Mayor Casey's Task Force conducted an employee survey and found that city employee's greatest need is child day care. The city is unsure if it should provide the service or hire a company to provide the service. Your job is to create a three-year proposal for the city (Williamsburg City Day Care) and a private contractor (Burhart's Child Care). Your proposal should be in the form of a *cost benefits analysis*. After which, you should make a recommendation to Mayor Casey's Task Force. While there is not necessarily an incorrect answer, your answer should reflect a degree of creativity when quantifying items that appear to be qualitative in nature. Mayor Casey should clearly see the benefits and cost of each program and have few questions regarding the programs. It might be useful to review a performance budget when completing this question because it ties performance to dollars. Since both are quantifiable it may serve as a good technique to make correlations.

Useful Information: The city has 10,000 employees with 285 children aged 1 month-3, and 198 children aged 4-6. The ratio for teachers to children cannot exceed 1-5. Tuition costs per child tend to decrease for every 50 children greater than 100 children. Consider making your arguments using categories such as personnel, supplies, equipment, etc.

Hint: It might be useful if you visit a child day care center or speak with a child day care provider in order to get a feel for the sort of issues that you should consider. You might also consider these issues: insurance, constructing buildings, meals, supplies, equipment, start up costs versus yearly costs, and employees.

2. The City of Youngstown has decided to build a downtown parking garage to house city employee's vehicles. Since the city has to demolish several buildings on the site, the project will take five years to complete. The city expects to save $25,000.00 a year once the project is completed. Using a 7% discount rate, determine the present value (PV) of the $25,000.00 savings at the end of the five year period.

3. The Hutchinson County Board is contemplating selling a building that is currently leased to Dr. Tarria Whitley, a local veterinarian, for $95,000.00. Whitley leases the building for $900.00 per month and is currently on a six year annually renewed lease with the option to buy the property at the close of the lease for

$45,000.00. Using the present value formula and a 6% discount rate, calculate the total benefit of the leasing option and compare it with the option to sell the property.

4a. Chief Derrick Bernard of the local police department has submitted a proposal to the budget director of Robertsonville requesting the purchase of ten new police cars. He estimates the department will save $22,500.00 a year by having the new cars. The cars will cost the city $200,000.00. Unfortunately, the life span of a police car is only four years at best. Using an 8% discount rate, calculate the net present value of the proposal. Explain the results.

b. Using the above example, calculate the NPV using the following data: Discount Rate = 5%, Cost of Cars = $185,000.00, Annual Savings = $94,000.00, Life span of car = 5 years. Explain the results.

5. Using the data in Question 4a and b, calculate annual depreciation, average investment, and the rate of return for the police department's proposal. Explain the results in each problem.

6. The Parks and Recreation department has suggested renovating the municipal golf course at a cost of $1,000,000.00 with an annual operating cost of $225,000.00 and an annual savings of $395,000.00. The expected life of the golf course is 7 years before the city will have to make a major investment in improving the course. Calculate the payback period, remaining asset life, and the actual savings. Explain the results.

References

Ammons, David N. 2002. *Tools for Decision Makers: A Practical Guide for Local Government*. Washington, D.C.: CQ Press.

Axelrod, Donald. 1995. *Budgeting for Modern Government*. 2nd ed. N.Y.: St. Martins Press.

Bretschneider, Stuart and Wilpen L. Gorr. 1999. "Practical Methods for Projecting Revenues." In Roy Meyer's (ed) *Handbook of Government Budgeting*. San Francisco, CA: Josey Bass.

Chapman, Ronald. 1996. "Capital Financing: A New Look at an Old Idea." In *Budgeting Formulation and Execution*. Eds. Jack Rabin, W. Bartley Hildreth, and Gerald J. Miller. Athens, GA: Carl Vinson Institute of Government, University of Georgia.

Follett, Mary P. 1918. *The New State: Group Organization, the Solution of Popular Government*. New York: Longmans, Green.

Gianakis, Gerasimos A. and Clifford P. McCue. 1999. *Local Government Budgeting: A Managerial Approach*. Westport, CT: Praeger.

Gruber, Jonathan. 2005. *Public Finance and Public Policy*. NY, NY: Worth Publishers.

Lee, Robert D. and Ronald W. Johnson. 1998. *Public Budgeting Systems*. 6th ed. Gaithersburg, MD: Aspen Publishers.

Liner, Charles D. 1996. "Projecting Local Government Revenue." In *Budget Management: A Reader in Local Government Financial Management*. Eds. Jack Rabin, W. Bartley Hildreth, and Gerald J. Miller. Athens, GA: Carl Vinson Institute of Government, University of Georgia.

Lynch, Thomas D. 1995. *Public Budgeting in America*. 4th ed. Englewood Cliffs, NJ: Prentice Hall.

Mendosa, Arthur A. 1983. "Budgeting." In *Budget Management: A Reader in Local Government Financial Management*. Eds. Jack Rabin, W. Bartley Hildreth, and Gerald J. Miller. Athens, GA: Carl Vinson Institute of Government, University of Georgia.

Mikesell, John. 1999. *Fiscal Administration: Analysis and Applications for the Public Sector*. 5th ed. Ft. Worth, TX: Harcourt Brace Publishers.

Mikesell, John. 2003. *Fiscal Administration: Analysis and Applications for the Public Sector*. 6th ed. Belmont, CA: Thomson Wadsworth.

Miller, Gerald J. 1996. "Cost-Benefit Analysis." In *Budgeting Formulation and Execu-*

tion. Eds. Jack Rabin, W. Bartley Hildreth, and Gerald J. Miller. Athens, GA: Carl Vinson Institute of Government, University of Georgia.

Nice, David. 2002. *Public Budgeting*. Stamford, CT.: Wadsworth.

Wang, XiaoHu. 2006. *Financial Management in the Public Sector: Tools, Applications, and Cases*. M.E. Sharpe: Armonk, NY.

Weimer, David L. and Aidan R. Vining. 1989. *Policy Analysis: Concepts and Practice*. Prentice Hall: Englewood Cliffs, NJ.

Chapter Six

Appendix 6A

STATE	Medenr00	Med$00	Povr00	Emr00	Edr00	wpopr00	Region
Alabama	387482	360677851	14.4	4.6	77.5	0.701	1
Alaska	72558	193363632	8.2	6.6	90.4	0.676	0
Arizona	436164	820720436	12.0	3.9	85.1	0.638	1
Arkansas	289370	507976998	17.8	4.4	81.7	0.786	1
California	3849152	4398626127	12.8	4.9	81.2	0.467	0
Colorado	221109	464519875	8.1	2.7	89.7	0.745	0
Connecticut	230067	381310766	6.6	2.3	88.2	0.775	0
Delaware	66316	160128110	9.1	4.0	86.1	0.724	0
Florida	1245949	1805732773	10.6	3.6	84.0	0.654	1
Georgia	780146	1046483726	11.2	3.7	82.6	0.627	1
Hawaii			9.9	4.3	87.4	0.229	0
Idaho	101006	158633186	12.9	5	86.2	0.88	0
Illinois	1042649	1574317911	11.5	4.4	85.5	0.678	0
Indiana	478900	691657260	8.7	3.2	84.6	0.858	0
Iowa	172243	341861892	7.2	2.6	89.7	0.926	0
Kansas	162695	252931557	9.6	3.7	88.1	0.831	0
Kentucky	401986	833846546	11.9	4.1	78.7	0.892	1
Louisiana	513346	617009282	17.3	5.5	80.8	0.625	1
Maine	103265	377971366	8.4	3.5	89.3	0.964	0
Maryland	427123	1042673053	7.6	3.9	85.7	0.621	0
Mass.	499912	920258655	10.1	2.6	85.1	0.819	0
Michigan	809521	849708349	10.0	3.6	86.2	0.786	0
Minnesota	330045	733999328	6.0	3.3	90.8	0.882	0
Mississippi	350486	446169873	12.9	5.7	80.3	0.607	1
Missouri	572899	775559500	8.0	3.5	86.6	0.838	0
Montana	53453	119547672	15.7	4.9	89.6	0.896	0
Nebraska	151741	244268393	9.0	3.0	90.4	0.873	0
Nevada	94746	158416801	8.5	4.1	82.8	0.652	0
NH	67541	139031925	5.2	2.8	88.1	0.951	0
New Jersey	491360	951601659	8.0	3.8	87.3	0.66	0
NM	270588	451843766	16.8	4.9	82.2	0.447	1
New York	1525759	4090912236	13.4	4.6	82.5	0.62	0
NC	688420	1166042723	12.1	3.6	79.2	0.702	1
ND	33364	60331323	1.0	3.0	85.5	0.917	0
Ohio	822277	1290884389	10.0	4.1	87.0	0.84	0
Oklahoma	384761	449823191	15.4	3.0	86.1	0.74	1
Oregon	263455	448524053	11.2	4.9	88.1	0.835	0
Penn	861341	1614221034	8.9	4.2	85.7	0.84	0
RI	92938	196387796	9.1	4.1	81.3	0.819	0
SC	453295	699694916	10.6	3.9	83.0	0.661	1
SD	62572	109816549	9.6	2.3	91.8	0.881	0
Tennessee	709954	1095440216	14.7	3.9	79.9	0.792	1
Texas	1706960	2617756752	14.7	4.2	79.2	0.524	1
Utah	131408	237785842	9.6	3.2	90.7	0.853	0
Vermont	69596	147457822	11.3	2.9	90.0	0.961	0
Virginia	398334	580688265	7.7	2.2	86.6	0.702	0
Washington	568245	702050781	10.1	5.2	91.8	0.789	0
WV	196345	282842513	14.0	5.5	77.1	0.946	0
Wisconsin	331047	539546969	9.6	3.5	86.7	0.873	0
Wyoming	32193	51326629	11.0	3.9	90.0	0.889	0

Chapter 7
Financial Management

Chapter Seven Overview

Although the focus of this book is not on financial management, the subject matter is crucial to politicians as well as bureaucrats given the stream of time that we live in. The chapter begins by discussing financial solvency and then moves on to five specific topics. These topics include: cash management, risk management, procurement, cutback management, and debt management. These and similar topics have become increasingly more important due to poor cash management, insufficient tax bases, an increase in the use of technology, an increase in the number of retirees, population growth in some areas while other cities suffer from population depletion and slow industrial and economic activity. The overall objective of this chapter is to introduce students to basic concepts and techniques that can be used to effectively manage governments during economic prosperity as well as economic downturns.

Financial Condition

Under the right set of circumstances it may be necessary for a local government to use financial practices that it may not commonly employ. With that in mind two important practices are discussed in this section. First, financial practices that may compromise the financial position of the local government are examined. Second, practices that can sustain an operating deficit are discussed.

Financially Solvent or Not?

Financial solvency or financial condition can be defined as the ability of a local government to finance its services on continuous basis. Specifically, "financial condition refers to a government's ability to (1) maintain existing service levels, (2) withstand local and regional economic disruptions, and (3) meet the demands of natural growth, decline, and change" (Nollenberger, et al 2003, p. 2).

Maintaining existing services includes maintaining current services funded by existing revenue, funding programs that are funded by outside sources, maintaining capital facilities, and providing for future liabilities that may be currently unfunded (pensions, debt, lease purchase agreements or post employment benefits).

Economic disruption can occur in a number of different ways. This includes but is not limited to: recessions, high unemployment, tax delinquencies, and lower investments as a result of lower interest rates. Good planning can lessen the impact of these factors.

Growth and decline in a municipality is fairly common. However, stability can also create financial pressure. Population shifts and changes in the population can destabilize a budget. For example, the population of an area could maintain numerical stability, but not economical stability. For example, what would happen if 20% of a cities middle income population was replaced with a low income population? Would that shift affect social services and compromise the government's financial health? More than likely it would affect the entire system. However, existing tax payers may be less inclined to support these new programs. As a result, decision makers have to decide if the current tax and revenue structure can sustain expanding the new or current program. Can reserve funds or other mechanisms pay for the service? If a government cannot meet this sort of challenge it is not financially sound.

Measuring financial condition is not as easy as it appears. There are a number of factors that hinder the process. According to Nollenberger, et al (2003), "the nature of a public entity, the state of municipal financial analysis, and the character of municipal accounting practices" may hinder measuring financial condition.

First, let's examine the nature of a public entity. Success is measured in the private sector in dollars. However, success in the public sector is not concerned with making a profit, but with efficiency and effectiveness of programs and services. This includes issues of health and welfare, political satisfactions and other subjective measures. As a result of subjective measures, determining financial solvency is more difficult.

Second, municipal financial analysis focuses on cash and budgetary solvency with less attention to long run and service level solvency with few exceptions. The one exception to this is with regards to investments. Hence, more attention to long run and service solvency has to improve in order to overcome this obstacle. Another issue with respect to financial analysis is the lack of normative standards. For example, what is an acceptable level of debt? What is a healthy reserve fund balance? Benchmarks established by credit rating agencies should be used in conjunction with subjective factors such as the diversity of a municipality's tax base.

Accounting practices is the final component that should be examined when considering financial solvency. As mentioned in chapter 1, governments use fund accounting. Fund accounting stresses legal compliance and balancing the flow of money rather than examining program cost accounting and the measurement of long term financial health. Budgets do not tend to show the detailed cost of services provided, postponed costs, the unfunded pension liabilities, or employee benefit liabilities. Nor do they show "the reductions in purchasing power caused by inflation or the decreasing flexibility in the use of funds that result from increasing state and federal mandates. Financial statements and budgets do not show the erosion of streets, buildings, and other fixed assets. Finally, these reports are prepared for a one year period and do not show in a multiyear perspective the emergence of favorable or unfavorable conditions" (Nollenberger, et al 2003, p. 3).

Nollenberger, et al (2003) developed a *Financial Trend Monitoring System* (FTMS) paradigm with eleven financial conditions factors that should affect management practices and legislative policies related to financial solvency. The paradigm is split into two dimensions: financial factors and environmental factors. Table 7.1 shows the two dimensions along with the defining organizational setting of each. This is not an exhausted list of organizational settings.

Table 7.1 Factors Affecting Financial Condition

Financial Factors:
A. Revenues: growth, flexibility, elasticity, dependability, diversity, and administration.
B. Expenditures: growth, priorities, mandated costs, productivity, and effectiveness.
C. Operating Position: operating results, fund balances, reserves, and liquidity
D. Debt Structure: short term debt, long term debt, debt schedules, and overlapping debt.
E. Unfunded Liabilities: pension obligations, pension assets, and post employment benefits.
F. Condition of Capital Plant: maintenance effort, capital outlay.

Environmental Factors:
A. Community Needs and Resources: population, density, age, income, property value and distribution, home ownership, vacancy rates, business activity, crime and employment rates.
B. Intergovernmental Constraints: intergovernmental mandates and restrictions on revenue.
C. Disaster Risk: potential for natural disasters and local preparedness.
D. Political Culture: attitudes toward taxes, services, and political processes.
E. External Economic Conditions: national and regional inflation, employment and market conditions.

In order to use the system, analysts simply have to address the issues as they are laid out. Nollenberger, et al (2003) lays out three basic evaluation questions for each area:

Financial Factors: Is your government currently paying the full cost of operating, or is it postponing costs to a future period when revenues may not be available to pay these costs?

Environmental Factors: Do the environmental factors provide enough resources to pay for the demands they make?

Organizational Setting: Do your management practices and legislative policies enable your government to respond appropriately to changes in the environment?

Essentially, the analyst examines each of the aforementioned characteristics using arrows. For example, population and density are found in the community needs and resources list of environmental factors. So, if you are assessing a municipality, determine if the population is increasing ↑ or decreasing ↓ as indicated with an arrow. The same procedure is used for density and the other characteristics. Notice that the system does not require the user to insert an amount. You are simply concerned with the direction of the characteristic at this juncture. The direction of the arrow will determine whether further investigation is needed. In some cases, more analysis is needed regardless to the direction of the arrow.[44] If additional analysis is needed, the user should use graph, tables, and other visual tools to show the trends.[45]

After which, the results should be evaluated. As mentioned, trend analysis is the primary tool that the system uses. Trend analysis will allow the user to: identify unfavorable trends, determine when the unfavorable trend began, consider mitigating circumstances, identify the causes underlying the unfavorable trend, compare the indicator trends to one another, compare the economic condition of the local government to national or regional trends, determine whether further analysis should be done, compare the trends to the benchmarks used by crediting firms, take other factors into consideration, and add his/her professional judgment. Last, policy statements should be developed to plan a strategy to manage the areas of concern (Nollenberger, et al 2003).

Exhibit 7.1 provides a partial example of a financial solvency statement for the City of Paige. The exhibit has several pertinent items. First, it shows the major financial indicators for the city over the last five fiscal years. In the revenue section, we can see the direction of each revenue stream over time. However, note that it is necessary to explain why user fees decreased over time despite the fact the growth is still positive. Also, it is not necessary to chart every single revenue source in a chart. Elected officials tend to be more concerned with major sources of revenues. However, you can use your discretion when using tables and graphs. In addition to revenues and expenditures, you should also create a table and chart for the other financial categories in your budget. These should include items such as operating expenditures, debt structure and the capital plant.

Revenue Explanations: Each revenue source has increased incrementally over-time. However, user fees have clearly leveled off as a result as more residents are using internal roads rather than the toll roads. This is more than likely the direct result of widening Stateline Road to three lanes.

Exhibit 7.1 Financial Solvency Model for the City of Paige

A. Revenue	FY05	FY 06	FY07	FY08	FY09	Dir.
Property Taxes	$5,890,423	$6,234,129	$6,398,490	$6,589,123	$6,657,239	↑
Sales Taxes	$1,239,459	$1,298,098	$1,359,128	$1,459,872	$1,590,213	↑
Franchise Fees	$239,125	$245,908	$251,908	$275,234	$289,990	↑
User Fees	$245,129	$254,890	$278,568	$278,578	$279,001	↑
TOTAL	$7,624,136	$8,033,025	$8,288,094	$8,602,807	$8,816,443	

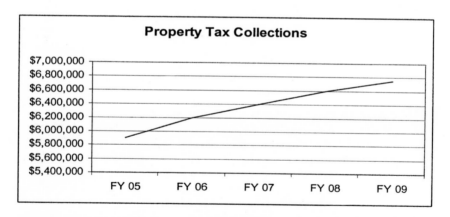

Expenditure Explanations: Expenditures for the city are consistent with reve-nue allocations over time. The data in the tables shows growth in each subcate-gory and the graph indicates overall growth. Hence, expenditures are stable with little volatility.

*B. Expenditures**	FY05	FY 06	FY07	FY08	FY09
Personnel	$5,336,895	$5,703,448	$5,967,428	$6,021,965	$6,171,510 ↑
Utilities	$152,483	$160,661	$165,762	$172,056	$176,329 ↑
Supplies	$304,965	$321,321	$331,524	$344,112	$352,658 ↑
Equipment	$686,172	$642,642	$580,167	$774,253	$793,480 ↑
Capital Fund	$1,143,620	$1,204,954	$1,243,214	$1,290,421	$1,322,466 ↑
TOTAL	$7,624,135	$8,033,026	$8,288,095	$8,602,807	$8,816,443

* Figures are rounded to the nearest dollar amount.

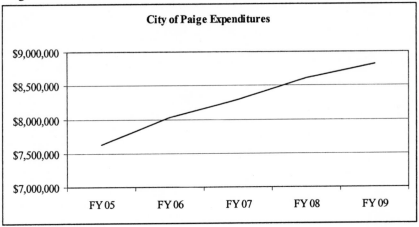

Detecting an Operating Deficit

Generally speaking, a deficit in one year may or may not cause much consternation. The government may use reserves to cover the deficit. However, frequent short falls should raise a red flag. If a city ignores the causes of the deficit or continues to maintain the same level of services and expenditures at the current pace without a commensurate increase in revenues, more serious issues will have to be addressed. The following paragraphs briefly discuss several items that suggest that the government may have an operating deficit.

In some instances, governments may have a *budget surplus*. This allows them the flexibility to put money into a *budget reserve* to be used when *budget shortfalls* occur. Reserves are also useful because they can reduce the need to increase taxes. However, if the budget reserve continues to drop over several years, it could be an indicator that expenditures are exceeding revenues (Nollenberger 2003).

Short-term borrowing can be another indicator of operating deficits. *Short-term borrowing* is debt that is incurred and expected to be paid within a single fiscal year and is usually done for cash flow purposes, particularly if the government's major funding source is property taxes. Property taxes are usually paid every six months. As a result, a government might need to borrow to pay bills. If revenues or fund balances are not high enough, *tax anticipation notes* (TAN) can be issued to cover operating needs. The debt service will be paid when the next property tax collection takes place. In some cases, a city can pay off the debt and then reborrow the funds or pay only the interest on the loan. This is called *rolling over* short- term debt. Unfortunately, this is a clear indicator that a problem exists and can lead to debt obligations, perhaps causing higher interest rates on future borrowing, negatively affect the city's credit rating, or force the city to reduce service and raise revenues (see Lauth 1997).

City administrators can also borrow from other funds. Internal borrowing occurs when one fund borrows from another fund rather than from external sources. Not all *internal transfers* are loans. Some funds have lower expenditures and consistently operate with surpluses. As a result, internal transfers may be made as a matter of policy. For example, states that operate liquor stores will transfer excess "profits" to the general fund. The term "borrow" clearly suggests the intent to return funds to the original source within a designated period of time. Frequent borrowing can create a liability that the city cannot manage and subsequently impact services.

A city can also sell assets to bring in *one-time revenues*. If one-time revenues are used to fund current operating expenditures, rather than for one-time expenditures, the city is sustaining a deficit. *Saleable assets* include items such as buildings, land, as well as equipment. Selling city assets may affect services, in that services may have to be reduced the following year unless more revenue can be generated. Furthermore, if the assets that are sold are not excess, the city may incur additional costs to procure replacements in the future.

Accounting gimmicks can also be used to balance a budget. For example, if the last day in a pay period falls on the last day of the fiscal year, the staff may wait the extra day to record that expense. As a result, expenses for the current year appear smaller. Typically, three accounting gimmicks are used to manipulate the budget: 1.) postponing current cost to future periods, 2.) accruing revenues from a future fiscal year to the current fiscal year, and 3.) extending the length of the current fiscal year, For example, extending the period from 12 to 13 months, so that revenues collected in the 13th month can be counted in the current fiscal year (Nollenberger 2003).

Deferment of a payment is the last practice that is indicative of an operating deficit. This occurs when a city receives invoices in the current fiscal year but delays the payment until the next fiscal year. For example, a city only pays invoices when it has the cash available to make the payment. Deferment of payment of the city's obligation to the pension fund is a major indicator of financial stress.[46]

Another indicator of financial stress is deferment of maintenance expenditures for things like streets, public buildings, equipment, and bridges. If these items are not maintained, it has a negative domino affect on everything else. Service is likely to diminish, efficiency will drop, and replacement costs are likely to increase (Mikesell 2003; Nollenberger 2003).

The techniques and gimmicks that have been discussed are used to try to solve budget deficiencies. However, they are detected when the government undergoes the audit at the end of the year. A major reason for auditing a government is to disclose such practices. For example, delaying payment of the payroll may address the budget problem but the expenditure will be recorded on the financial statements prepared in accordance with GAAP. The same is true for the pension obligation—it will be recorded as an expenditure and a fund liability. Paying pensions on a pay-as-you-go basis on the budget basis will not resolve a shortfall on the GAAP basis since the true pension liability will be reported on the GAAP statements. The same is true for accruing future revenues in the current fiscal year—GAAP reporting will reveal this practice. This is why it is important for state and local governments to have their financial statements audited.

The above items essentially reinforces the point that agency heads and directors should pay close attention to activities within their agency, revenue and expenditure trends, and other conditions that could impact their budget and cause a deficit.

-External Cash Management Practices

Determining how much money is needed at one particular point in time can be an arduous task for a local government. Basically, expenditures must equal revenues collected by the end of the fiscal year. Two problems can arise when revenues are collected and expenditures are made. First, there could be a *cash flow problem*. A cash flow problem occurs when the amount of revenue available is not sufficient to cover immediate expenditures. Barring any unforeseen occurrences, cities do not tend to have cash flow problems because they know when tax collections are due. Hence, they can time their expenditures with revenue receipts. At the other end of the spectrum, a city may have an *idle cash problem*. This problem occurs when a city has more money on hand than its immediate financial obligations and does not take any measures to invest the surplus funds. Good *cash management* occurs when a city meets all of its financial obligations and invests the balance.

The concept of cash management is another concept that is not as simple as it may appear. In order to engage in cash management, a government needs to know how much money is available at any given time and how much is needed to pay obligations. Further, estimates of future revenues may also be needed. This may require daily, weekly, or monthly forecast. This information can be used to construct a *cash budget*. There are four steps to calculating a monthly cash budget: 1.) Estimate cash receipts for the month, 2.) Estimate cash disbursements that will take place during the month, 3.) Subtract cash receipts from cash disbursements to determine excess or deficit (*net cash flow*), and 4.) Add this balance to the prior month's balance to find the projected total cash balance.[47]

Khan (1997) and Larson (2004) discusses six ways to achieve effective cash management: managing liquidity, accelerating collections, maximizing investment earnings, reduce borrowing, managing disbursements efficiently and providing accurate and timely reporting, and depositing checks in a timely fashion (see also Hughes 1997).

- *Managing Liquidity*: There should always be enough funds on hand to meet obligations.
- *Accelerating Collections*: Monies owed should be collected in the most efficient and effective manner available.
- *Maximizing Investment Earnings*: Available cash should be invested until they are needed. However, the government should minimize exposure to risk.
- *Reduce Borrowing*: Careful cash management can help prevent the need for internal borrowing from other funds or issuing tax anticipation notes to cover budget shortfalls.
- *Manage Disbursements Efficiently*: Determine the most effective manner to disburse funds by reducing guess-work and reducing the opportunity of fraud. Determine if a centralized or decentralized disbursement system works best.
- *Depositing Checks*: Checks should be deposited as soon as possible. This can reduce the amount of time that is needed to collect the payment and clear the banking system (*float*).

Once the government has determined that funds are available for investment, analyst can use the *Economic Ordering Quantity Formula* (EOQ) to determine the cash position of the government (Khan 1996; Larson 2004; Smith and Lynch 2004; Thai 2004). "In this approach, an analyst weighs carrying cost, which foregone earned interest represents, against the total cost of the transaction. This model recognizes that the government incurs an opportunity cost for holding rather than investing idle cash. And each bank transaction (for example, transferring from securities to cash) involves an administrative cost to the government. If the government is to save idle cash and earn more than its administrative cost for investing, then it must recognize that more transactions drive up the cost of investing. To make money on investments, more transactions require a higher cash amount to invest" (Smith and Lynch 2004, p. 255-256; see also Khan 1997). Smaller governments tend to hold a certain number of days' expenditures as cash rather than use sophisticated methods. Exhibit 7.2 provides a formula to calculate optimal transfer size, number of transfers, average cash balance, and initial cash balance.

Exhibit 7.2 Economic Ordering Quantity Formula

$P = b\,(T/c) + vT + i\,(c/2)$

    P = Total cost of cash management
    b = Fixed cost per transaction of transferring funds from marketable securities to cash or vice versa
    T = Total amount of cash payments or expenditures over the period
    c = Size of the transfer, which is the maximum amount of cash
    v = Variable cost per dollar of funds transferred
    i = Interest rate on marketable securities

The formula used to solve for the *optimal transfer size and initial cash balance* is:

$$c = \sqrt{2bT/i}$$

The *average cash balance* is:

$$c = \sqrt{2bT/i}\ /2$$

The *total number of transfers* is computed by dividing the cash payments (T) by C.

Transfers = T/C

    Let's look at an example. The city of Letbetter has total cash payments of $8 million (T) for a 6-month period. The payment over this period is steady. The cost per transaction is $75 (b), the interest rate is 4% for the period (i), and the cost per dollar of funds transferred is .06% (v). Therefore:

$$c = \sqrt{2bT/i} = \sqrt{2(75)(8,000,000)/.04} = \$173,205.08$$

    So, the optimal initial cash balance and transfer size is $173,205.08, and the average cash balance is $86,602.54 ($173,205.08/2). If you divide $8,000,000 by $173,205.08 you will find that the number of transfers equals 46 (46.19). The total cost of cash management for the 6-month period:
= $75 ($8,000,000.00 / $173,205.08) + .0006 ($8,000,000 / 1) + .04

($173,205.08 / 2)

= $3,464.10 + $4,800.00 + $3,464.10

= $11,728.20

^ Note that the interest rate (i) and the cost per dollar of funds transferred (v) is converted in the formula (4% = .04 and .06% = .0006).

Managing Cash Internally

Regardless of the size of a government agency, day-to-day functions require funds to be spent by cash or check. As a result, it is important for managers to manage cash internally by instituting controls on spending and records in order to limit mismanagement of funds, fraud and abuse. Managing cash internally improves bookkeeping, improves internal controls, and auditing. Even though it is impossible to completely eliminate problems, these pointers will improve the process.[48]

- Use checks as much as possible to pay for services. Checks should always be associated with an invoice or voucher. Cash is harder to trace and invites theft and fraud. Petty cash is the only exception to this rule.
- Never write checks payable to cash. This impedes the auditing process. Again, a voucher or invoice should be included with all transactions.
- The person writing the checks should not be used to reconcile the accounts. It is more difficult to cover up a potential crime when a second person is involved in the process.
- Checks should be used in numerical order and signed only by authorized staff. Checks should never be presigned for later use. These three things make it easier to track checks and allow minimum time for checks to be negotiated.
- Maintain firm control over blank and voided checks.
- Use separate bank accounts for each fund in order to maintain merging of funds. This also facilitates the auditing process.
- Sporadically audit petty cash. This should not be an elaborate and costly procedure.
- All checks should be tied to vouchers or invoices. This not only prevents fraud, but overpayment, double payment, and no payment.

- Make sure that the correct check number is placed on vouchers and invoices.
- Cash and checks should be deposited at least once a day. It should be done more often if a large sum of money is involved. This lessens the likelihood of theft, robbery and allows the investment of idle cash.
- Use computer technology to facilitate fund transfers as well as any other financial transactions. This includes accepting credit card payments.
- Negotiate with banks for better rates as well as services.
- Take advantages of discounts for prompt payment.

Risk Management

Risk is a very active term that is used formally or informally in government at all levels. Like most things, there is a cost associated with risk, *cost of risk* (cost of loss and cost of uncertainty). As a result, it is necessary for city officials to be proactive in managing risk. This might entail using a small army of staff who perform risk related functions to one or two persons who may have additional responsibilities. More often than not, risk managers tend to be found in or work very closely with the finance office. What are the responsibilities of risk managers? Given the continued complexity and dynamic nature of government it is difficult to construct an exhaustive list of responsibilities under the label risk manager. Nonetheless, the following list highlights some of these functions (Miller and Hildreth 1996; Lee and Johnson 1998; Young and Reiss 2004; Smith and Lynch 2004; Keown, Martin, Petty, and Scott 2005).

- Risk Financing, including the purchase of insurance.
- Management of insurable risks.
- Maintain records of losses, loss costs, premiums, and related costs.
- Occupational health and safety programs.
- Workers' compensation management.
- Compliance with regulatory and legal requirements.
- Catastrophe planning.
- Contract review.
- Security.
- Coordinate all activities involving risk.
- Public policy research.
- Some involvement in employee benefits.
- Some involvement in the management of financial risk and accidental losses.

From a budgetary perspective there are two important issues related to risk: purchase insurance to cover the risk or self fund the risk. If you opt to purchase insurance, then you have fewer problems. The amount of the insurance is a known amount, but you also have to cover any deductibles that might be needed. If you self-fund the risk (self-insurance is an oxymoron—by definition, insurance means you transferred the risk to someone else), there may be all kinds of problems. Many governments self-fund health care for employees and liability. However, several questions are raised. How will the government finance it? Use a internal charge for each funding source? Use general fund money? Fund it on a pay-as-you-go basis? These are the kinds of issues that are involved in self financing.

Framing Risk Management

According to Young and Reiss (2004), risk management incorporates five fundamental elements: 1.) Mission Identification, 2.) Risk and Uncertainty Assessment, 3.) Risk Control, 4.) Risk Financing, and 5.) Program Administration. Exhibit 7.3 provides a framework that describes the major components of risk management (See the Appendix for an example of a risk management assessment plan).

Exhibit 7.3 A Framework For Risk Management

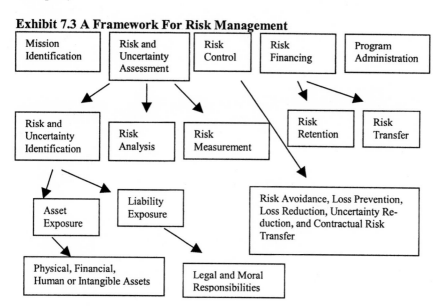

1. Mission Identification: Mission identification provides the goals and objectives associated with risk management as they relate to the overall purpose of the bureaucratic and political structure. It is very important in this step that analysts ensure that the plan advances the goals of the organization and those of political leaders.

2. Risk and Uncertainty Assessment: This is a three-pronged process that includes *risk and uncertainty identification, risk analysis,* and *risk measurement.* Identification of risk and uncertainty is "a systematic process of discovering an organization's risks and exposures to risk" (Young and Reiss 2004, p. 481). Given the dynamic nature of government, identifying risk is an ongoing process. There are two basic types of risks: *asset exposure* and *liability exposure.*

Physical structures, funds (stocks, bonds, money, etc), personnel, or intangible assets (community reputation, bond rating, credit score, etc) fall into the asset exposure category. Liability exposure focuses on legal liability, moral, and ethical responsibilities. There are numerous forms of liability exposure. This includes things such as premise liability (injuries on government property), contractor liability (work performed by entities employed by the government), employee liability, product or service liability (fire fighting services), environmental liability (leaks in land fills or water treatment facility), employment practices liability (sexual harassment and discrimination), police and law enforcement liability (wrongful arrest, excessive force). There are many other types of exposures that may relate to specific types of government agencies and departments. Although legal exposure may be easier to identify than moral liability, they are equally important. For example, placing a water treatment facility in a poor neighborhood because the residents are the least likely to resist the move rather than choosing the best location based on other well grounded factors (Young and Reiss 2004).

Risk analysis helps analysts to determine how dangerous conditions lead to actual losses. Large governments may have a number of sophisticated techniques and devices at their disposal to determine risk, but smaller governments with fewer resources are more often than not left to use other less costly means. This includes things such as: examining the causes of previous loss, soliciting feedback from similar cities about their losses, seek advice from risk control staff about common vulnerabilities, conduct informational sessions with staff at every level, consult the government's risk manager or insurance broker, identify and examine incidents that could have been disastrous (Young and Reiss 2004).

Risk measurement focuses on the impact of risk on the cities resources and on its capacity to maintain services. Since some ventures are more risky than others, it is wise to focus on or prioritize activities that may have the greatest impact on the organization as a whole. Measurement can vary based on the size of the government. Larger governments, with greater resources, "may conduct a quantitative analysis of their loss history to determine the frequency, severity, and financial or operational impact of different types of losses. Smaller local governments may have to rely on intuitive estimates of the effects of what they believe to be their greatest exposures. In such cases, "measurement" may be limited to categorizing risks according to frequency (how often losses occur) and severity (the financial and other impact of losses whey they do occur) (Young and Reiss 2004, p. 484; see also Miller and Hildreth 1996).

3. Risk Control: *Risk Control* emphasizes "avoiding, preventing, reducing, transferring, or neutralizing risks and uncertainties (Young and Reiss 2004, p. 484). This can include items such as wearing safety goggles to complex evacuation plans. Risk avoidance, loss prevention, loss reduction, uncertainty reduction, and contractual risk transfer are the major categories in risk control.

Risk avoidance is simply avoiding some activity that can cause a risk of loss. This is difficult to carry out since the government must provide services even during difficult circumstances. For example, a government may close one lane of a highway because of bridge construction in order to avoid possible liability issues (Miller and Hildreth 1996).

Loss prevention controls are intended to prevent losses from occurring such as work place safety techniques and procedures that limit the opportunities to commit fraudulent acts and theft. *Loss reduction* controls limit the amount and magnitude of losses that do occur from accidents. This would include things such as the wearing of protective gear inside hazardous waste areas or having an adequate number of fire extinguishers in the right places.

Uncertainty reduction procedures are designed to direct attention to the areas where risks are most likely to occur. Examining an agencies loss history to see where resources should be concentrated can expedite this process. Another option is to contract the risk producing activity to an outside entity. This is called *contractual risk transfer*. The third party entity would assume any responsible for losses resulting from loss. "Responsibility is generally assumed through a combination of contractual indemnification, hold-harmless agreements, and insurance requirements" (Young and Reiss 2004, p. 484). For example, a city may contract with an outside vendor to collect waste.

Whether to choose one method or another depends solely upon the government. There are a number of possible risk methods. In some cases, the government must employ risk control techniques while others are optional. When risk control methods are optional, cities should fully research their functions and use limited resources in the most productive manner.

4. Risk Financing: *Risk financing* has two components: 1.) securing reimbursement for losses that occur and, 2.) provide resources to programs that decrease uncertainty and risk or improve positive outcomes. Examples include: "qualifying with the state as a self-insured entity, buying insurance, establishing a letter of credit, and participating in a public risk pool" (Young and Reiss 2004,

p. 484). Another example is establishing a safety program for an agency.

There are two categories of risk financing, risk retention and risk transfer. *Risk retention* occurs when a government assumes all or part of the risk or loss. *Risk transfer* occurs when another organization, like an insurance company, assumes the risk and pays for the loss when it occurs for a premium. Governments can use an amalgamation of risk financing techniques (Miller and Hildreth 1996; Young and Reiss 2004).

5. Program Administration: Program administration is concerned with a variety of technical and general management actions, such as purchasing insurance, creating hedging arrangements, administering claims, and implementing loss control programs and safety instruction. In order to be the most effective, staff should have technical as well as management capabilities (Miller and Hildreth 1996; Young and Reiss 2004).

Procurement

Similar to the private sector, the government must spend revenues to purchase (*procurement*) equipment in order to maintain the infrastructure as well as provide services in the most efficient and effective manner (Lee and Johnson 1998). Thai (2003) defines procurement as "buying, purchasing, renting, leasing, or otherwise acquiring any supplies, services or construction, and it also encompasses the development of requirement and specifications, the selection of vendors, the solicitation of sources, the preparation and award of contracts, and all phases of contract administration" (p. 421).

Why is it important to discuss procurement? First, the government must provide services in an efficient and effective manner. Second, the government must secure equipment at the most reasonable price available. Third, the government must ensure that the procurement process is free of fraud and abuse. Lastly, given the size of government, procurement also helps the government to achieve some of its broader economic goals.

The remainder of this section discusses the procurement of equipment at the most reasonable price using a life-cycle cost technique. There are two things that are important in the procurement process when a life-cycle cost application is used: cost and quality. Cost entails the bid price of the item, the life-time maintenance cost of the asset, the energy cost, and the final disposal cost or repurchase price of the item (Ammons 2002). Quality refers to the degree to which the government needs are met with the purchase. Responsible bidders should be required to submit documents indicating the expected energy consumption, anticipated life span of the equipment, and expected use over a one-year period (McManus 1997; Gianakis and McCue 1999: Nollenberger 2003). All of this information is vital in order for this process to be effective.

The basic formula for a life-cycle cost model is:

Life-Cycle Cost =   Acquisition Cost + Lifetime Maintenance Cost + Lifetime
                         Energy Cost – trade in allowance – expected resale value

The example in Exhibit 7.4 shows the results of applying the life-cycle cost model to the purchase of two trucks with similar horsepower and amenities. If you focus your decision to purchase on the price of the truck, you would buy the truck from the second bidder because it is six thousand dollars cheaper than the other truck. However, when you look at the other items, particularly energy cost and diesel mileage along with maintenance cost, you note that the disparities between the two trucks changes dramatically.[49] In fact, the cost difference of the two trucks over a six-year period is almost $15,150.00.[50] So, which truck should the government purchase? It is pretty clear that the truck from the first bidder should be accepted. However, the government should ensure that the information that is used in the model is accurate and based on tried and tested measures from responsible bidders. Further, the government should be certain that it will keep the truck for a six-year period. If any of these values change, the difference between the two bids will change as well (Nollenberger 2003).

Exhibit 7.4 Life-Cycle Costing

Life-Cycle Cost	Truck from Bid 1	Truck from Bid 2
Bid Cost	$45,000.00	$39,000.00
Expected Use	100,000 miles	100,000 miles
Life Expectancy	6 years	6 years
Efficiency Rating	85%	75%
Energy Cost	$17,936.03	$26,900.00*
($2.69 per gallon)	(15 mpg)	(10 mpg)
Maintenance Cost	$8,814/6yrs	$21,000.00/6yrs^
Life-Cycle Cost	$71,750.03	$86,900.00

Life-Cycle Cost Difference $15,149.97 ($86,900.00 - $71,750.03 = $15,149.97)

*(100,000 miles / 15mpg) x $2.69 = $17,936.03; and 100,000 miles / 10mpg x $2.69 = $26,900.00
^ $1,469.00 per year for Bid 1 and $3,500.00 per year for Bid 2.

Source: Lee, Roderick C. 1996. "Life-Cycle Costing." In *Budgeting: Formulation and Execution*. Eds. Jack Rabin, W. Bartley Hildreth, and Gerald J. Miller. Athens, GA: Carl Vinson Institute of Government, University of Georgia.

There are a number of other items that can be used in a life-cycle cost model such as trade in value of an existing piece of equipment, acquisition cost, failure cost, labor cost, and expected resale value. For obvious reason, more information allows decision makers to make more informed decisions.

Cutback Management

Without question, cities are more likely to see fewer resources than surpluses. As a result it is necessary to engage in what is called *cutback management*. In simple terms, this is implementing cost cutting reductions in resources while attempting to maintain services at their current level. Under the worst conditions, cutback management can lead to the demise of programs as well as a reduction in services. Quite naturally, this process can and does have an adverse impact on all sectors of the economy.

Causes of Cutbacks

According to Levine (1996) cutbacks result primarily from five things: problem depletion, erosion of the economic base, inflation, taxpayer revolt, and limits to growth. *Problem depletion* occurs when a public sector problem is solved, eliminated, controlled or the pressure to solve the problem subsides. This can be long or short-term problems/crises such as program consolidation, program termination or school closing (Levine 2004). For example, the city of Memphis, Tennessee recently closed several schools due to low enrollment rates and consolidate the students into one school. On one hand, this caused many political headaches despite the fact that it saved the city money. On the other hand, it created more busing expenditures.

A second cause of cutbacks is *erosions in the tax base*. There is an array of items that can cause the tax base to erode in a city. This includes things such as: the relocation of citizens to suburbs, an aging population, the movement of industry to other locations, aging or deterioration of the housing stocks resulting in lower valuations, and the growth of dependent populations. Levine (2002) offers further explanation of this phenomenon in his discussion of *environmental atrophy*. He points out that those who cannot afford to move to the suburbs are left to make up for the loss in the tax base and as a result are worse off. The third cause is *inflation*. Inflation is an increase in the amount of money and credit relative to available goods resulting in a substantial and continuing rise in the price level. The funds needed to operate a government efficiently and effectively has continued to rise dramatically over time. Some suggests that it has doubled in the last ten years. Unless the government raises taxes or other revenue generating tools they are forced to cut back services.

Taxpayer revolt is the fourth reason that Levine (1996) argues causes cutbacks. "These explanations usually include reference to the difficulty of tracing the well-being of individual taxpayers to specific government services, the desire of voters to alleviate the impact of inflation on their personal disposable incomes, the backlash of taxpayers against the salary increases of unionized public workers and the services offered to the poor and minorities, and the cumbersomeness of financing local services through the mechanism of the property tax" (p. 131). The last cause of cutbacks is limits to growth. The Midwest saw many of their cities become "rustbelts" because of the out migration of businesses to the west and south. Many cities are landlocked. They have no ability to attract new residents or businesses. There is a severe imbalance between imports and exports in the United States. This is particularly true when we look at depletable resources and energy sources such as fossil fuels. There is currently no end in sight for this problem. Generally speaking, history suggests that economic growth will slow down in the foreseeable future.

Cutbacks in government are particularly difficult because it will inevitably impact all aspects of service. Levine (1996) argues that change in services is most palatable when those affected have something to gain. Unfortunately, the impact of cutbacks consistently means that the outcome will have a negative impact on the consumer and as a result cooperation will be at a minimum. There are also a plethora of traditions, procedures and agreements in place that will constrain the ability of the government to make the cuts. This includes things such as affirmative action and collective bargaining agreements, veteran's preferences and civil service procedures. Third, cutbacks affect the morale of public servants. They are not inclined to work harder during these periods to make up for a decrease in staff or revenue. Last, cutbacks affect the overall behavior of administrators and staff because everyone is forced to deal with having fewer resources (Levine 1996).

Cutback Strategies

There are five general strategies that can be used to cutback resources. The first strategy is to resist or *smooth* the cuts. Generally speaking, budget managers engage in what is called *budget maximizing*. That is, they attempt to get the maximum budget as possible. As a result they will almost instinctively resist the cuts. In some cases, managers will cut the most pertinent services first to show policy makers that they need their entire budget allotment. When this and other strategies do not work, managers will reluctantly try to limit the impact of the cuts without reducing services, selling assets, instituting layoffs and defaulting on contractual obligations.

The second option is to make a one time drastic cut with the hope of recuperating later or small cuts over several fiscal years in order to minimize the impact. The problem with making a large cut is that the funds may never return to their current levels. The problem with small cuts is that the agency may function at the same level suggesting that the cuts were warranted. As a result, the funds are less likely to return at the same level in the near future. Public outcry over either one of these is also likely to impact decisions. In fact, some agency heads may use this tactic in order to advertise their resistance. Like most tactics, it can come with political repercussions because politicians are not ignorant of the behavior.

One commonly used technique is to make across the board cuts. While this may help to improve morale among the employees it is not a good management strategy because all agencies are not equivalent and do not contribute equally to the goals and objectives of government. In some cases, agencies and programs may be cut after they are prioritized based on the goals of the government. However, these debates essentially facilitate things such as the budget maximizing strategy and political turf battles.

The fourth strategy looks at the *efficiency* versus *equity* question. Efficiency is "meant to mean the sorting, sifting, and assignment of cuts to those people and units in the organization so that for a given budget decrement, cuts are allocated to minimize the long-term loss in total benefits to the organization as a whole, irrespective of their distribution" (Levine 2004, p. 514). Equity "is meant to mean the distribution of cuts across the organization with an equal probability of hurting all units and employees irrespective of impacts on the long-term capacity of the organization" (Levine 2004, p. 514). This quandary results from the cost of providing services to the various groups and the makeup of personnel. The poor, elderly and minorities are the most dependent upon the government and tend to be the most costly to serve. Hence, blind cost cutting based on restricted productivity measures can be very damaging to them. This quandary is further exasperated due to the recent rise in minority employment and the prevalence of laying-off the last one hired first. Nonetheless, history suggests that the politically weak are disproportionately adversely impacted by budget cuts (Levine 1996; 2004).

The fifth and final cutback mechanism is *attrition*. That is, employees leave the public work force and create a void. Administrators can and often do leave the position open for a period of time in order to save resources. In some cases, it may be possible to shift those responsibilities to other employees or outsource the tasks at a cheaper rate. However, the implications of shifting the responsibilities to other employees can be financially detrimental to the agency in the long run. If an organization can run smoothly without the position it would clearly suggest that the position was not needed and thus should be removed from the organization chart. This is probably the most commonly used method. It is very hard for a government to layoff employees. There are both civil service laws as well as collective bargaining agreements that have to be followed. By the time you try to go through this process, one or more years may pass. Thus, it is easier to just use attrition to cutback resources.

Druker and Robinson (1993) point out several additional strategies that have been employed at the state and local levels. These include: freezing vacancies, implementing an early retirement plan, offering voluntary leave, implementing mandatory furloughs and layoffs, reducing hours, job sharing, increasing the workweek, deferring pay increases, reducing the cost of benefits, shutting down operations, implementing user fees, cutting salaries, lagging payrolls, and reorganizing the work force (see also Lauth 1997). Marlowe and Nyhan (1997) made these additional suggestions based on work examining the Palm Beach County Government: reduce travel and office equipment, privatize functions, reassign costs, defer capital spending, implement franchise fees, defer library projects, reduce the level of service, and defer replacing equipment.

Debt Management and Investment

Why do governments incur debt? States and local governments can incur *debt* when "(1) covering deficits (annual expenditures greater than annual revenues)[51], (2) financing capital-project construction, and (3) covering short periods within a fiscal year in which bills exceed cash on hand" (Mikesell 2003, 543). As shown in Exhibit 7.5, the amount of state and local debt has grown from FY 1994 to FY 2004. The data also indicates that the total amount of debt outstanding and long-term debt increased by almost $900 million over the period. Also, the amount of full faith and credit bonds more than doubled and long-term debt for education nearly tripled.[52] Hence, it is apparent that governments are moving towards greater debt rather than less debt. As a result, it is important that governments have a debt management policy to facilitate debt.

Exhibit 7.5 State and Local Debt, FY 1993-1994 and 2003-2004

Type of Debt	1993-94	2003-04
Debt Outstanding	$1,074,660,212	$1,951,374,559
Short-Term	26,666,271	38,374,375
Long-Term	1,047,993,941	1,913,286,184
Full Faith and Credit	345,517,973	751,034,857
Nonguaranteed	702,475,968	1,162,251,327
Long-Term Debt by Purpose:		
Public Debt for Private Purposes	301,634,651	448,359,211
Education	143,466,341	406,693,192
Utilities	164,898,088	243,792,258
Other	437,994,857	814,441,523
Long-Term Debt Issued	207,806,935	346,812,785
Long-Term Debt Retired	$166,552,039	$241,111,048

Source: U.S. Census Department,
http://ftp2.census.gov/govs/estimate/04slsstab1a.xls.

-Debt Management Policy

The Government Finance Officers Association (GFOA) lists a debt management policy as a "recommended practice." Specifically, they recommend that state and municipal governments adopt a comprehensive written debt management policy. Further, they recommend that these policies be reviewed and revised annually to reflect changes in debt policy (www.gfoa.org).

A debt management policy provides benefits to citizens and bureaucrats. First, it assures bondholders that debt burdens and operational debt expenditures will be maintained at controllable levels with a plan to meet capital infrastructure needs. Second, it provides staff with a framework to work from and assures the legislative body that any proposals brought forward by staff meets the policy mandates set out by the legislative body. Third, it assures continuity in financial operations whether there is a change in the legislative body or management personnel. Last, Moody's Investor Services points out that a strong debt management policy is a practice that a city can use to strengthen its credit position. Since debt has a potential long term impact on future budgets it is important that it is issued with great care. If something goes awry in the process, the ramification for tax paying citizens can be a source of great consternation. The basic rule of debt policy is to never issue debt for a project that has a life span shorter than the debt payback period. Knowing when to issue debt is an important question. This is particularly true for long term debt. However, long term debt could very well be appropriate for long-life capital structures such as public buildings. Economic development by definition often requires financing large scale expenditures prior to an expansion in revenue. If future revenue will cover the cost of the project an argument can be made to fund the project using long term debt.

However, some governments with large fund balances and a growing general fund opt to use the pay-as-you-go method to funding capital projects out of the operating budget. As discussed earlier, there are several advantages to using this method. However, there are inefficiency and inequity issues that could arise. Mikesell (2003) points out four factors. First, given population shifts, individuals paying for the project may not be present to receive benefits when the project is completed. Second, the high cost of the project in a single year may discourage construction even if it is reasonable. Third, it might cause instability in the tax rate. It might be artificially high during the construction phase and artificially low when the project comes to fruition. Last, it "produces annual debt service charges that are fixed by contract. Therefore, when the area tax base grows. the tax rate required for debt service for a project will decline over time" (p. 555).

Appendix 7D contains the debt management policy for the city of Lawrence, Kansas. As shown, the policy contains some additional items not discussed in the earlier paragraphs. This includes: the structure of debt financing (possible source of funding); debt administration and financing; refunding of debt; conduit financing; arbitrage liability management; and credit ratings. It is important that governments consider all of these items when creating a debt management policy.

Additional Budget Options

Cutback and debt management has also caused governments to look more closely at utilizing zero-based budgeting and performance budgeting techniques. *Zero-based budgeting* (ZBB) is a future oriented budgeting strategy that requires analysis of current and future expenditures, "allows for tradeoffs between programs and units below their present funding levels, allows a ranking of decision packages by political bargaining and negotiation so that attention is concentrated on those packages or activities most likely to be affects by cuts. As a result, ZBB allows both analysis and politics to enter into cutback decision making and therefore can incorporate an expression of the *intensity of need* for resources by participating managers and clients while also accommodating estimates how cuts will affect the activity levels of their units" (Levine 2004, p. 515-516). With that said, ZBB is not without faults, analysis and political disagreements can come at a high price. While elements of ZBB are currently utilized, it is not widely used today.

Performance based budgeting (PBB) concentrates on agency-activity objectives and outcomes rather than the purchase of resources. In simple terms, the budget is tied to accomplishing objectives. As a result, agencies that fail to reach their stated outcomes can be targeted for cuts. Again, if the budget maximizing strategy is at work, this would suggest that agency heads are requesting the maximum amount of funds that they can get and only use performance measures that they know they can accomplish (Mikesell 2003).

Conclusion

While there are many other tools that can be used to assist city administrators and analysts in improving the financial position of the city, the chapter provides a sample of several administrative and management techniques that can be useful when applied at the right moment. Other important topics not covered would include items such as bond management and economic development. It is important that administrators realize that economies do not tend to turn around over night. This is particularly true in situations where management practices are in disarray. However, the chapter shows that minor changes can have a major impact on budget decisions and the morale of staff and supervisors.

Important Terms and Phrases

Asset Exposure
Attrition
Average Cash Balance
Average Final Compensation
Budget Maximizing
Budget Reserve
Budget Shortfall
Budget Surplus
Cash Budget
Cash Flow Problem
Cash Management
Contractual Risk Transfer
Cost of Risk
Cutback Management
Debt Capacity
Debt Instrument
Debt Management
Deferment of Payments
Disability
Dividends
Economic Ordering Quantity Formula (EOQ)
Efficiency
Environmental Atrophy
Erosion in the Tax Base
Equity
Equity Securities
Idle Cash Problem
Inflation
Initial Cash Balance
Interest Rates
Internal Transfers
Investing
Liability Exposure
Life-Cycle Cost

Long Term Borrowing
Loss Prevention
Loss Reduction
Net Cash Flow
Operating Deficit
One Time Revenues
Optimal Cash Balance
Optimal Transfer Size
Performance Based Budgeting
Portability
Procurement
Problem Depletion
Risk Analysis
Risk Avoidance
Risk Control
Risk Financing
Risk Management
Risk Measurement
Risk Retention
Risk Transfer
Rolling Over
Saleable Assets
Smoothing
Short-term Borrowing
Stocks
Tax Anticipation Notes (TAN)
Tax Payer Revolt
Transfer
Transfer Size
Uncertainty Reduction
Variable Cost
Vesting
Zero-Based Budgeting

Chapter 7 Homework Exercises

Directions: Please read all of the questions as well as the accompanying materials prior to answering the questions. Answer question 1 and 3 in Excel. Question 2 and 4 can be answered in a word processing program.

1. Daniel Wessel, the budget manager for the city of Henderson, has requested that you assist him with the management of the cities' funds. Specifically, he wants you to calculate the two scenarios listed below based on the following information. This problem can be completed in a spreadsheet or in a word processing package. See Appc7.

>   a. The city has total cash payments of $10 million (T) for a 6-month period. Assume that the payment over this period is steady. The cost per transaction is $65 (b), the interest rate is 3% for the period (i), and the cost per dollar of funds transferred is .05% (v).

- Calculate the optimal initial cash balance and transfer size
- Average cash balance
- The number of transfers
- The total cost of cash management

>   b. The city has total cash payments of $13 million (T) for a 6-month period. Assume that the payment over this period is steady. The cost per transaction is $55 (b), the interest rate is 4% for the period (i), and the cost per dollar of funds transferred is .04% (v).

- Calculate the optimal initial cash balance and transfer size
- Average cash balance
- The number of transfers
- The total cost of cash management

2. Using the sample risk assessment form that is located in the appendix to chapter 7, your job is to conduct a risk assessment of a public service project that is occurring, will occur, or has recently taken place in your city or at your university. You are completing this question from the perspective of a city employee. You are free to modify this assessment to fit your circumstances. In addition, you should include the risk assessment policy that the city or university that you choose operates under when you turn in your assignment if it is available. You should come to class prepared to discuss your risk assessment plan. If needed, you are free to consult with public officials when completing this assignment. Lastly, explain the overall results of your assessment. Is the project worth the risks?

Suggestions: Construction projects, road construction, large renovation projects, clear cutting land, household waste or hazard waste disposal issues, providing security at a public facility, investment of public funds, or any changes in the infrastructure are suitable topics for this question. Other items can be more thematic or policy in nature. For example, what are the risks involved in raising property taxes when 95% of the property owners are in the low middle income bracket and operate small businesses? Will this result in an increase in the number of delinquent property tax payments and thus reduce the amount of revenue to the city as well as potential loss of property and bankruptcy? Other broad categories can include any type of service that the city provides.

3. Using Exhibit 7.3 as a model along with the additional items in the example, prepare a life-cycle cost analysis for the procurement of a front end loader for the city of Warwick based on data from three companies. Also, the city is trading in the old front-end loader. Note that the Trade in and Resale Value should be subtracted from the amount of the life-cycle cost. All calculations should be rounded to the nearest dollar amount. Solve for the energy cost prior to calculating the life-cycle cost. When you finish your calculations, indicated which of the bids should be accepted. Briefly explain your response. See Appc7.

	Duncan's Heavy Equipment Company 1	Haley International Company 2	Heath's Front End Loaders Company 3
Bid Price	$67,980.00	$69,000.00	$72,000.00
Trade in Value	$3,100.00	$2,900.00	$3,500.00
Expected Use	65,000 miles	65,000 miles	65,000 miles
Life Expectancy	5 years	5 years	5 years
Efficiency Rating	82%	80%	89%
Energy cost	_____	_____	_____
	(12 mpg)	(11 mpg)	(14 mpg)
Resale Value	$6,000.00	$5,200.00	$6,500.00
Maintenance Cost	$24,000.00	$22,000.00	$20,000.00
Life-Cycle Cost	$	$	$
Life Cycle-Cost Difference	_____	**	

*Currently, diesel cost $2.74 per gallon.   ** Subtract the two lowest bids

4. Using one set of the factors (environmental or financial) used to determine financial solvency discussed in the chapter, analyze the financial condition of a

municipality or county in your local area (identify the factors that you are using as well as the city). You are interested in the condition of the city, not an agency within the city. Your trend analysis must use at least 5 years of data. Hence, you will need the city budgets for at least five years and be familiar with financial or environmental trends in the city. It is not possible to examine each characteristic, so limit your table/graph, etc construction to four key financial or economic factors. First, create a table with each factor indicating the direction of the trend. Second, create four graphs, tables, etc examining the factors that require more analysis. Third, write a brief evaluation of the factors and develop a policy statement based on your findings. If you are not familiar with table or graph construction, review chapter 8 prior to completing this question.

References

Aman, Khan. 1996. "Cash Management: Basic Principles and Guidelines." In *Budgeting: Formulation and Execution*. Eds. Jack Rabin, W. Bartley Hildreth, and Gerald J. Miller. Athens, GA: Carl Vinson Institute of Government, University of Georgia.

Ammons, David N. 2002. *Tools for Decision Makers: A Practical Guide for Local Government*. Washington, D.C.: CQ Press.

Bland, Robert L. and Irene S. Rubin. 1997. *Budgeting: A Guide for Local Governments*. Washington, D.C.: ICMA.

Druker, Marvin, and Betty Robinson. 1993. "State's Responses to Budget Shortfalls: Cutback Management Techniques." In the *Handbook of Comparative Public Budgeting and Financial Management*. Eds. Thomas D. Lynch and Lawrence Martin. New York: Marcel Dekker.

Hildreth, W. Bartley, and Laurie W. Adams. 1997. "The Politics of Pension Investment Returns." In *Case Studies in Public Budgeting and Financial Management*. Eds. Aman Khan and W. Bartley Hildreth. Dubuque, IA: Kendall Hunt Publishing.

Hildreth, W. Bartley, and Gerald J. Miller. 1996. "Pension Policy, Management, and Analysis." In *Budgeting: Formulation and Execution*. Eds. Jack Rabin, W. Bartley Hildreth, and Gerald J. Miller. Athens, GA: Carl Vinson Institute of Government, University of Georgia.

Hughes, Jesse. W. 1997. "Comparative Analysis of Key Governmental Financial Indicators." In *Case Studies in Public Budgeting and Financial Management*. Eds. Aman Khan and W. Bartley Hildreth. Dubuque, IA: Kendall Hunt Publishing.

Keown, Arthur. J., John D. Martin, J. William Petty, and David F. Scott Jr. 2005. *Financial Management: Principles and Applications*. 10th ed. Upper Saddle River, NJ: Pearson Prentice Hall.

Khan, Aman. 1997. Learning From Experience: Cash Management Practices of a Local Government. In *Case Studies in Public Budgeting and Financial Management*. Eds. Aman Khan and W. Bartley Hildreth. Dubuque, IA: Kendall Hunt Publishing.

Larson, M. Corrine. 1996. "Cash and Investment Management." In *Management Policies in Local Government Finance*. Eds. J. Richard Aronson and Eli Schwartz, Washington, D.C.: ICMA.

Lauth, Thomas P. 1997. "Reductions in the FY 1992 Georgia Budget: Responses to a Revenue Shortfall." In *Case Studies in Public Budgeting and Financial Management*. Eds. Aman Khan and W. Bartley Hildreth. Dubuque, IA: Kendall

Hunt.

Lee, Robert D. and Ronald W. Johnson. 1998. *Public Budgeting Systems.* 6th ed. Gaithersburg, MD: Aspen Publishers.

Lee, Roderick C. 1996. "Life-Cycle Costing." In *Budgeting: Formulation and Execution.* Eds. Jack Rabin, W. Bartley Hildreth, and Gerald J. Miller. Athens, GA: Carl Vinson Institute of Government, University of Georgia.

Levine, Charles H. 1996. "Cutback Management in and Era of Scarcity: Hard Questions for Hard Times." In *Budgeting: Formulation and Execution.* Eds. Jack Rabin, W. Bartley Hildreth, and Gerald J. Miller. Athens, GA: Carl Vinson Institute of Government, University of Georgia.

Levine, Charles H. 2004. "Organizational Decline and Cutback Management." In *Government Budgeting: Theory, Process, Politics.* 3rd Edition. Ed. Albert C. Hyde. Toronto, Canada: Wadsworth.

Marlowe Jr., Herbert A. and Ronald C. Nyhan. 1997. "Innovations in Public Budgeting: Applying Organizational Development Processes to Downsizing." In *Case Studies in Public Budgeting and Financial Management.* Eds. Aman Khan and W. Bartley Hildreth. Dubuque, IA: Kendall Hunt.

Miller, Gerald J. and W. Bartley Hildreth. 1996. "Advantages of a Risk Management Program." In *Budgeting: Formulation and Execution.* Eds. Jack Rabin, W. Bartley Hildreth, and Gerald J. Miller. Athens, GA: Carl Vinson Institute of Government, University of Georgia.

Mikesell, John. 2003. *Fiscal Administration: Analysis and Applications for the Public Sector.* 6th ed. Belmont, CA: Thomson Wadsworth.

Nollenberger, Karl, Sanford M. Groves and Maureen G. Valente. 2003. *Evaluating Financial Condition: A Handbook for Local Government.* Washington, D.C.: ICMA.

Petersen, John W. 2004. "Public Employee Pension Funds." In *Management Policies in Local Government Finance.* Eds. J. Richard Aronson and Eli Schwartz, Washington, D.C.: ICMA.

Rubin, Irene S. 2006. *The Politics of Public Budgeting: Getting and Spending, Borrowing and Balancing.* 5th ed. Washington, D.C.: CQ Press.

Smith, Robert W. and Thomas D. Lynch. 2004. *Public Budgeting in America.* 5th ed. Upper Saddle Rive, NJ: Pearson/Prentice Hall.

Thai, Khi V. 2004. "Procurement." In *Management Policies in Local Government Finance.* Eds. J. Richard Aronson and Eli Schwartz, Washington, D.C.: ICMA.

Young, Peter C. and Claire Lee Reiss. 2004. "Risk Management." In *Management Policies in Local Government Finance*. Eds. J. Richard Aronson and Eli Schwartz, Washington, D.C.: ICMA.

Appendix 7A

Risk Assessment Questionnaire

Project Title: _____

Project Location: _____

Project Supervisor: _____

Brief Description of the Work or Policy: _____

_____

_____

_____

Each of the questions used in this assessment are scored using a risk factor rubric from 0-5. A zero indicates no risk and a five indicates high risk. Your description of risk should detail how the organization is managing the risk. Limit your description of the risk to no more than half of a page. Use as much space as you need to describe the risk. Read the notes at the bottom of this assessment prior to addressing the question.

1. Human Resource Risk

a. Description of Risk:

b. Overall Risk Factor: 0   1   2   3   4   5

2. Environmental Risk

a. Description of Risk:

b. Overall Risk Factor: 0   1   2   3   4   5

3. Information and Technology Risk

a. Description of Risk:

b. Overall Risk Factor: 0   1   2   3   4   5

4. Regulatory Risk

a. Description of Risk:

b. Overall Risk Factor: 0   1   2   3   4   5

5. Internal Control Environmental Risk

a. Description of Risk:

b. Overall Risk Factor: 0   1   2   3   4   5

6. Asset/Revenue Management Risk:

a. Description of Risk:

b. Overall Risk Factor: 0   1   2   3   4   5

7. Consumer Impact:

a. Description of Risk:

b. Overall Risk Factor: 0   1   2   3   4   5

8. Equipment Risk:

a. Description of Risk:

b. Overall Risk Factor: 0   1   2   3   4   5

9. General Field Work Hazards

a. Description of Risk:

b. Overall Risk Factor: 0   1   2   3   4   5

Risk Summary:

a. Average Risk Score: 0   1   2   3   4   5

b. Total Risk Score _____

Description of Substantive Points and Methods to Managing the Risk

_____

_____

Risk Questionnaire Notes

The questions that are listed below offer you a snap shot of the sort of issues that will come up during your query. Feel free to add any additional information that you find.

1. *Human Resource Risk*: Do employees work? Do employees work near water? Do employees work in an isolated area? Have all employees been properly trained (safety)? What is the possibility of employee fatigue, accidents, or allergic reactions occurring? Are there any non city/university employees working? If yes, are they insured by their company?

2. *Environmental Risk*: Will weather conditions impact completion of the project? Will terrain or field boundaries affect the project? Is animal or plant life affected by the project? Is hazardous waste a byproduct of the construction? Is there a chance that the environment may be polluted with hazardous waste? Will the ground water, lakes, or nearby streams be impacted by the project? Is there a procedure to facilitate hazardous waste cleanup or disposal?

3. *Information and Technology Risk*: Generally speaking, this section examines computers, computer technology and information. Are computer systems needed to complete the project? Are new computer programs or hardware needed to complete the project? Is there a potential for loss of software, data, or computer hardware? Is there a contingency plan to ensure the integrity of data and computer systems?

4. *Regulatory Risk*: What is the level of regulation (local, state or federal)? Are regulatory staff needed on site (Fire Marshall, FEMA, OSHA, etc)? Have the rules, statutes, and law regulating the sector been examined? Are external contractors used? If yes, are they bonded? Are liability plans in place?

5. *Internal Control Environment Risk*: Is there any potential for fraud? Have there been problems in the past? If so, how many and what were the outcomes? What procedures were added to ensure that the potential for fraud was reduced/eliminated?

6. *Asset/Revenue Management Risk*: If a service is rendered, what sort of accounting system will be used when the project is completed? How are funds dispersed and collected? Does the potential for cost overruns exist?

7. *Consumer Impact*: Who is the client base? How will clients or the public be affected by the project? That is, how will they be affected by the construction of the project as well as the services provided by the project?

8. *Equipment Risk*: What sort of equipment is needed? Is new equipment needed? Will the new equipment be used for other projects?

9. *Other Hazards or Issue*: Is there anything else that is not covered in the categories listed above?

Appendix 7B

Economic Ordering Quality Formula: $P = b\,(T/c) + vT + i\,(c/2)$

Step 1: Calculate the Optimal Initial Cash Balance and Transfer Size

Step 2: Calculate the Total Cost of Cash Management

Appendix 7C

Life-Cycle Cost Problem

	Duncan Company 1	Haley Company 2	Heath Company 3
Bid Price	$67,980.00	$69,000.00	$72,000.00
Trade in Value	$3,100.00	$2,900.00	$3,500.00
Expected Use	65,000 miles	65,000 miles	65,000 miles
Life Expectancy	5 years	5 years	5 years
Efficiency Rating	82%	80%	89%
Energy cost	(12 mpg)	(11 mpg)	(14 mpg)
Resale Value	$6,000.00	$5,200.00	$6,500.00
Maintenance Cost	$24,000.00	$22,000.00	$20,000.00
Life-Cycle Cost			

Life-Cycle Cost Difference =

Appendix 7D

City of Lawrence
Debt Management and Fiscal Policy
General Policy

The Debt Management Policy Statement sets forth comprehensive guidelines for the financing of capital expenditures. It is the objective of the policies that (1) the City obtain financing only when desirable, (2) the process for identifying the timing and amount of debt financing be as efficient as possible and (3) the most favorable interest rate and other related costs be obtained. Debt financing, to include general obligation bonds, special assessment bonds, revenue bonds, temporary notes, lease/purchase agreements, and other City obligations permitted to be issued or incurred under Kansas law, shall only be used to purchase capital assets that will not be acquired from current resources.

The useful life of the asset or project shall exceed the payout schedule of any debt the City assumes. This allows for a closer match between those who benefit from the asset and those that pay for it. To enhance creditworthiness and prudent financial management, the City is committed to systematic capital planning, intergovernmental cooperation and coordination, and long-term financial planning. Evidence of this commitment to capital planning will be demonstrated through adoption and periodic adjustment of the City's Capital Improvement Plan and the annual adoption of a multi-year Capital Improvement Budget.

Responsibility for Debt Management
The primary responsibility for making debt-financing recommendations rests with the Director of Finance. In developing such recommendations, the Finance Director shall be assisted by other City staff. The responsibilities of City staff shall be to: Consider the need for financing and assess progress on the current Capital Improvement Budget and any other program/improvement deemed necessary by the City Manager; Test adherence to this policy statement and to review applicable debt ratios listed in the Debt Issuance Guidelines,

❑Review changes in federal and state legislation that affect the City's ability to issue debt and report such findings to the City Manager as appropriate;
❑Review annually the provisions of ordinances authorizing issuance of general obligation bonds of the City;
❑Review the opportunities for refinancing current debt; and,
❑Recommend services by a financial advisor, bond trustees, bond counsel, paying agents and other debt financing service providers when appropriate. In developing financing recommendations, the City staff shall consider:
❑Options for interim financing including short term and inter-fund borrowing, taking into consideration federal and state reimbursements;
❑Effects of proposed actions on the tax rate and user charges;
❑Trends in bond markets structures;
❑Trends in interest rates; and,
☐Other factors as deemed appropriate.

Use of Debt Financing

Debt financing will not be considered appropriate for any recurring purpose such as current operating and maintenance expenditures. The City will use debt financing only for one-time capital improvement projects and unusual equipment purchases under the following circumstances: The project is included in the City's capital improvement budget and is in conformance with the City's general plan; The project is the result of growth-related activities within the community that require unanticipated and unplanned infrastructure or capital improvements by the City; The project's useful life, or the projected service life of the equipment, will be equal to or exceed the term of the financing; There are revenues sufficient to service the debt, whether from future property taxes, user fees, or other specified and reserved resources, debt supported by user fees, special assessments or special charges shall be preferred, The debt shall be primarily used to finance capital projects with a relatively long life, typically ten years or longer.

The equipment is an item that is purchased infrequently, has an expected useful life of at least five years, and costs in excess of $100,000.

Structure and Term of Debt Financing

Debt will be structured to match projected cash flows, minimize the impact on future property tax levies, and maintain a relatively rapid payment of principal. As a benchmark, the City shall strive to repay at least 50% of the initial principal amount within ten years.

General Obligation Bonds

The City shall use an objective analytical approach to determine whether it desires to issue new general obligation bonds. Generally, this process will compare ratios of key economic data. The goal will be for the City to maintain or enhance its existing credit rating. These ratios shall include, at a minimum, debt per capita, debt as a percent of statutory debt limit, debt as a percent of appraised valuation, debt service payments as a percent of governmental expenditures, and the level of overlapping net debt of all local taxing jurisdictions. A set of ratios shall be adopted and itemized in the City's Debt Issuance Guidelines. The decision on whether or not to issue new general obligation bonds shall, in part, be based on (a) costs and benefits, (b) the current conditions of the municipal bond market, and (c) the City's ability to issue new general obligation bonds as determined by the aforementioned benchmarks.

Revenue Bonds

For the City to issue new revenue bonds, projected annual revenues as defined by the ordinance authorizing such issuance, shall be a minimum of 125% of the issue's average annual revenue bond service or at a higher amount if required by the bond indentures. If necessary, annual adjustments to the City's rate structures will be considered in order to maintain the required coverage factor. Revenue bonds will be the preferred financing option for enterprise funds.

Special Assessment Bonds

The City shall maintain a watchful attitude over the issuance of special assessment bonds for benefit district improvements. The City's share of any benefit district project may not exceed more than 95% of any proposed costs related to a benefit district. The developer shall be required to deposit 25% of the costs allocated to the benefit district prior to authorization. In most cases, the debt will have a maximum term of ten years, however, a longer term may be allowed provided it does not exceed the life of the improvements included in the benefit district. The benefit district will be assigned costs such as administration, engineering, financing and legal associated with the formation of the district and issuance of any debt.

Debt Issuance With Intergovernmental Agencies
The City will typically not use of its debt capacity for projects by entities or other special purpose units of government that have the ability to issue tax exempt debt. The City's issuance of debt will be made only (1) after the prior commitment of the full assets and resources of the authority to debt service; (2) if project revenues, or development authority revenues pledged to debt service, are at least 115% of debt service; (3) if debt service reserves provided by the authority's own resources are equal to at least six months debt service; and, (4) if all other viable means financing have been examined. The City will also enter into arrangements with other governmental entities where a portion of the project costs will be reimbursed by the other government. An agreement as to how the project costs will be allocated and reimbursements made must be approved by the governing bodies.

Structure of Debt Obligations
The City normally shall issue bonds with an average life of 10 years or less for general obligation and special assessment bonds and 10-20 years for revenue bonds. The typical structure of general obligation bonds will result in even principal and interest payments over the term of the debt. There shall be no "balloon" bond repayment schedules, which consist of low annual payments and one large payment of the balance due at the end of the term. There shall always be at least interest paid in the first fiscal year after a bond sale. In cases where related revenues may not occur for several years, it may be desirable to capitalize the interest by increasing the size of the issue and deferring the principal payments so that only interest is paid on the debt for the first few years.

Call Provisions
Call provisions for bond issues will be evaluated based upon current market conditions. All bonds shall be callable only at par.

Variable Rate Long-Term Obligations
The City may choose to issue bonds that pay a rate of interest that varies according to pre-determined formula or results from a periodic remarketing of the securities, consistent with state law and covenants of pre-existing bonds, and depending on market conditions.

Debt Administration and Financing

Capital Improvement Budget
A Capital Improvement Budget shall be prepared and submitted to the City Commission annually. The budget shall provide a list of projects and the means of financing. The budget should cover a five-year period of time. The projects included in the budget

should be part of the City's Capital Improvement Plan. Projects must be in either the Capital Improvement Budget or Plan to be authorized.

Bond Fund
Generally, payment of general obligation bonds and special assessment bonds shall be from the City's Bond & Interest Fund. However, in situations where General Obligation bonds are to be paid from user fees or sales taxes, bond payments should be made from the fund that receives the revenue. The minimum fund balance in the Bond & Interest Fund will be maintained at a level equal to or greater than 50% of the total principal and interest payable from that Fund for the upcoming year.

Reserve Funds
Adequate operating reserves are important to insure the functions of the City during economic downturns. The City shall budget a contingency reserve in the General Fund of no less than $150,000. The City will maintain working capital in an enterprise fund sufficient to finance 120 days of operations, if the fund supports debt payments. In addition, all reserves specified by bond indentures must be maintained. The Equipment Reserve Fund will be funded sufficiently to ensure that adequate funds are available to purchase replacement equipment on a timely basis.

Finance Department
It shall be the responsibility of the Finance Department to prepare the Preliminary and final Official Statements. The City Clerk is responsible for collecting and maintaining all supporting documentation such as minutes of the City Commission meetings and relevant resolutions and ordinances. In the case of general obligation bonds, an estimate of the mill levy required to pay off the debt should be provided to the City Commission. The department will also be responsible following applicable secondary disclosure requirements.

Investments
The bond proceeds will be invested in accordance with the City's investment policy. Adherence to the guidelines on arbitrage shall be followed, which at times, may require that the investment yield be restricted. In most cases, the investment will be selected to maximize interest with the assumption that the City will meet the IRS spend down requirement that allows for an exemption from arbitrage calculations.

Bond Counsel
The City will utilize external bond counsel for all debt issues. All debt issued by the City will include a written opinion by Bond Counsel affirming that the City is authorized to issue the debt, stating that the City has met all Federal and State constitutional and statutory requirements necessary for issuance, and determining the debt's federal income tax status. The City's Bond Counsel will be selected on a competitive basis.

Underwriter's Counsel
City payments for Underwriters Counsel will be authorized for negotiated sales by the Department of Finance on a case-by-case basis depending on the nature and complexity of the transaction and the needs expressed by the underwriters.

Financial Advisor
The City may utilize an external financial advisor. The utilization of the financial advisor for debt issuance will be at the discretion of the Director of Finance on a case-by-case basis. For each City bond sale, the financial advisor will provide the City with information on structure, pricing and underwriting fees for comparable sales by other issuers. The Financial Advisor will be selected on a competitive basis for a period not to exceed five years.

Temporary Notes
Use of short-term borrowing, such as temporary notes, will be undertaken until the final cost of the project is known or can be accurately projected. In some cases, projects might be funded with internal funds that will be reimbursed with bond funds at a future date.

Credit Enhancements
Credit enhancement (letters of credit, bond insurance, etc.) may be used if the costs of such enhancements will reduce the debt service payments on the bonds or if such an enhancement is necessary to market the bonds.

Competitive Sale of Debt
The City, as a matter of policy, shall seek to issue its temporary notes, general and revenue bond obligations through a competitive sale. In such instances where the City, through a competitive bidding for its bonds, deems the bids received as unsatisfactory or does not receive bids, it may, at the election of the City Commission, enter into negotiation for sale of the bonds. In cases where the circumstances of the bond issuance are complex or out of the ordinary, a negotiated sale may be recommended if allowed by State statute.

Refunding of Debt
Periodic reviews of all outstanding debt will be undertaken to determine refunding opportunities. Refunding will be considered (within federal tax law constraints) if and when there is a net economic benefit from the refunding or the refunding is needed in order to modernize covenants essential to operations and management or to restructure the payment of existing debt. City staff and the financial advisor shall monitor the municipal bond market for opportunities to obtain interest savings by refunding outstanding debt. As a general rule, the present value savings of a particular refunding will exceed 3%. Refunding issues that produce a net present value savings of less than 3% percent will be considered on a case-by-case basis. Refunding issues with negative savings will not be considered unless there is a compelling public policy objective.

Conduit Financings
The City may sponsor conduit financings in the form of Industrial Revenue Bonds for those activities (i.e., economic development, housing, health facilities, etc.) that have a general public purpose and are consistent with the City's overall service and policy objectives as determined by the City Commission. All conduit financings must insulate the City completely from any credit risk or exposure and must first be approved by the City Manager before being submitted to the City Commission for consideration. The City should review the selection of the underwriter and bond counsel, require compliance with disclosure and arbitrage requirements, and establish minimum credit ratings acceptable

for the conduit debt. Credit enhancement, such as insurance, may be required for certain issues.

Arbitrage Liability Management

Federal arbitrage legislation is intended to discourage entities from issuing tax-exempt obligations unnecessarily. In compliance with the spirit of this legislation, the City will not issue obligations except for identifiable projects with good prospects of timely initiation. Temporary notes and subsequent general obligation bonds will be issued timely so that debt proceeds will be spent quickly. Because of the complexity of arbitrage rebate regulations and the severity of non-compliance penalties, the City will be engage outside consultants to calculate potential arbitrage liability.

Credit Ratings

Rating Agency Relationships

The Director of Finance shall be responsible for maintaining relationships with the rating agencies that assign ratings to the City's debt. This effort shall include providing periodic updates on the City's general financial condition along with coordinating meetings and presentations in conjunction with a new debt issuance.

Use of Rating Agencies

The City will obtain a rating from Moody's Investors Service. The Finance Director will recommend whether or not an additional rating shall be requested on a particular financing and which of the major rating agencies shall be asked to provide such a rating.

Rating Agency Presentations

Full disclosure of operations and open lines of communication shall be made to rating agencies used by the City. The Finance Director, with assistance of City staff, shall prepare the necessary materials and presentation to the rating agencies.

Financial Disclosure

The City is committed to full and complete financial disclosure, and to cooperating fully with rating agencies, institutional and individual investors, City departments and agencies, other levels of government, and the general public to share clear, comprehensible, and accurate financial information. The City is committed to meeting secondary disclosure requirements on a timely and comprehensive basis. Official statements accompanying debt issues, Comprehensive Annual Financial Reports, and continuous disclosure statements will meet (at a minimum), the standards articulated by the Government Accounting Standards Board (GASB), the National Federation of Municipal Analysts, and Generally Accepted Accounting Principles (GAAP). The Finance Director shall be responsible for ongoing disclosure to established national information repositories and for maintaining compliance with disclosure standards promulgated by state and national regulatory bodies.

Appendix 7E
City of Lawrence
Debt Management Policy

Terminology

Arbitrage. Arbitrage refers to the rebate amount due to the Internal Revenue Service where funds received from the issuance of tax-exempt debt have been invested and excess interest earnings have occurred.

General Obligation Bonds. Bonds backed by the full faith and credit of the City. The taxing power may be an unlimited ad valorem tax or a limited tax, usually on real estate and personal property. A special tax rate levied for the Bond & Interest Fund annually to pay for general obligation LTO service. Because it is secured by an unlimited tax levy, this structure has strong marketability and lower interest costs.

Revenue Bonds. Bonds secured by revenues generated by the facility from dedicated user fees. Planning for such issues generally are more complex because future costs and revenues directly affect each other. Credit enhancements (e.g., insurance or letter of credit) may be needed because of the limited source of LTO service payments that may be available in outlying years.

Special Assessment Bonds. Bonds issued to develop facilities and basic infrastructure for the benefit of properties within the assessment district. Assessments are levied on properties benefited by the project. The issuer's recourse for nonpayment is foreclosure and the remaining LTO becomes the City's direct obligation.

Temporary Notes. Notes are issued to provide temporary financing, to be repaid by long-term financing. This type of bridge financing has a maximum maturity of four years under Kansas law.

Source:http://www.lawrenceks.org/policies/debtmanagementpolicy.pdf

Chapter 8
Effectively Communicating Data

Chapter Eight Overview

Given the limited amount of time that policy makers spend reviewing budgets and accompanying paper work, it is important that analysts use the time that they have effectively and efficiently. The main purpose of this chapter is to show you how to effectively display data. The chapter begins with a discussion of data quality, sources of data, and data appropriateness. Then, commonly used methods to displaying data as well as the advantages and disadvantages of each tool are described. Each of these methods employs the use of spreadsheet and/or data processing programs as well as Power Point.

Data Quality, Sources and Appropriateness

Finding data in general is not necessarily a difficult task for someone in a budget office. Data can generally be found in the budget director's office, at the various agencies, and from the chief executive. However, finding reliable comparative data for a different city or state could be a problem. There are two basic types of data: primary and secondary. For the purposes of this chapter, we focus on primary data. Primary data can be collected first hand out of department databases or via surveys or interviews (telephone, mail, in person, or the internet). There are several advantages and disadvantages to using this method when you consider the specific ways to collect primary data. The chief advantage of using this method lies in the fact that you can get the data that you want in the form that you want it, in order to best address your research question. That is, you can design the charts, graphs, and address budget or finance questions exactly the way that you want them. Hence, it is imperative that you use the best data available to address the issue at hand. However, this does not suggest that secondary data sets cannot address your research in a similar fashion.[53]

Displaying Data

A general rule of thumb for tables and graphs is that they should be under-

standable to the decision-makers. Hence, it is important that the title of the figures and labels used to describe the data are effective, appropriate, and timely.
The data/figure should essentially be self-explanatory. That is, the user should
not have to read a paragraph of text to understand the contents of the table. All
charts, tables, and graphs should include the source of the data as well as any
explanatory notes.

Tables

Tables are the most common way to visually describe data. Therefore, it is
very important that the analyst use the space that he/she has effectively and efficiently. Basically, a table should be completely self-explanatory. Thus, the analyst should pay close attention to not only the data in the table, but the labels as
well.

For example, Table 8.1 provides enrollment and expenditure data for the
State Children's Health Insurance Program for 2001. This is *raw data* or un-
processed data. Note how the analyst: used a title that clearly describes the data
in the table, provided the reader with labels that accurately portray the data in as
few words as possible, provided the source of the data and lastly informed the
reader of the number of programs included in the study. If the table is not self-
explanatory the analyst should make sure that a description of all the data and
symbols used are included in a note at the bottom of the table.

Table 8.1 SCHIP Programs by Enrollments and Expenditures (2001)*

	Total Enroll.	Total Expenditure	Average Enroll.	Average Expenditure	Average Expend./Person
Medicaid Expansion	704,922	$526,515,000	41,466	$30,971,471	$747 (n=17)
Separate Program	834,192	$473,727,000	52,137	$29,607,938	$568 (n=16)
Combination Program	3,061,975	$1,725,334,000	170,110	$98,851,889	$563 (n=18)
All Programs	4,601,089	$2,725,576,000	90,217	$53,442,667	$592 (n=51)

Source: Center for Medicaid and Medicare Services.

* Only states with both expenditures and enrollments are included in this table.

Table 8.2 is a *trend analysis*. Trend analysis is essentially a table that shows
the change in a variable over time. It is one of the easiest forecasting methods.
This method works best for revenues and expenditures that are stable. It assumes

that future revenues and expenditures will be comparable to those in the past. For example, the data in Table 8.1 provides the reader with raw revenue and enrollment data for SCHIP Program. Although the table should stand alone, it should be accompanied by narratives that describe what is in the table.

The trend analysis in Table 8.2 shows that the Town of Joyner had a steady flow of revenue with marginal increases up through FY 2007 when the tax based increased dramatically. Since the city did have a substantial increase in revenue in fiscal years 2005 and 2007 the analyst should make sure that he/she can explain the cause of that increase and whether or not the city can expect the trend to continue. This is particularly notable given the estimates for FY 2008. Again, it is important that the narratives thoroughly explain the contents of the tables. The narratives should explain where the increase came from and why it occurred. Further, the narrative should explain why other sources of revenue remained stable over the period. This may entail the analyst doing some additional research.

Table 8.2 Revenue Collection for the Town of Joyner, FY 2005-FY 2009

Revenue	2005 (act)	2006 (act)	2007 (act)	2008 (act)	2009 (est.)
Sales Taxes	$9,345,932.00	$9,995,232.67	$10,346,132.11	$12,685,380.99	$15,945,952.00
Property Taxes	7,389,129.23	8,984,326.63	9,482,027.14	11,942,246.72	13,862,892.42
Franchise Fees	9,456.12	9,978.76	11,736.22	13,157.87	17,757.72
Business Licenses	13,456.12	14,958.56	15,467.98	16,111.84	25,986.55
Street Meters	22,988.89	23,984.21	25,890.09	27,093.28	24,901.08
TOTAL	$16,780,962.36	$19,028,480.83	$19,881,253.54	$24,683,990.70	$29,877,489.77

While the data in Table 8.2 is useful, it is limited. For example, it may be more useful for a policy maker or a budget analyst to know the percentage change in the variable for each year rather than the numerical amount. For example, the data in Table 8.3 shows the percent change in the revenue amounts listed in Table 8.2 from one fiscal year to the next (formula needed to calculate the change is: [2006 actual - 2005 actual) / 2005 actual = Percent Change]).

Table 8.3 Percent Changes in Revenue Collections for the Town of Joyner, FY 06-FY 09

Revenue	FY 2006	FY 2007	FY 2008	FY 2009 (est.)
Sales Taxes	7%	3%	18%	20%
Property Taxes	22	5	21	14

Franchise Fees	6	15	11	26
Bus. Licenses	11	3	4	38
Street Meters	4	7	4	-9
AVERAGE	13.4%	4.5%	24.2%	21.0%

When using modern technology, this is a relatively easy function once the raw data is entered into a standard spreadsheet program. Let's look at an example. The Town of Joyner collected $9,456.12 in Franchise Fees in 2005 and $9,978.76 in 2006. In order to determine the percentage change in the amount, we simply subtract $9,456.12 from $9,978.76 and then divide that sum by $9,456.12. This calculation reveals that Franchise Fees increased 5.53% (rounded to 6%) from 2005 to 2006. Overall, revenues increased 13.39% (rounded to 13.4%) from FY 2005 to FY 2006.

Nollenberger (2004) list four steps that are useful when constructing a trend analysis.

1. After analyzing the revenue structure, split the structure into categories. Then, consider using two sub categories: most stable and least stable revenues.
2. After analyzing the expenditure structure, split it into two categories, salary and non- salary. Then, break non-salary into its component parts. Lastly, analyze the profile of debt separately.
3. Create a historical picture of both revenues and expenditures over the period used with plots, tables and graphs. Make sure that the consumer is knowledgeable of any changes made in the data as a result of policy changes. For example, if political leaders lowered property tax assessments on commercial property, it is likely to affect property tax revenues.
4. Predict how each revenue and expenditure will change based on available data and information. Three possible scenarios should be considered: a.) The item will not change. b.) The item will change by the same average amount as it did in past years. c.) The item will maintain the same rate of change as it did in past years.

As with most forecasting methods, there are always some drawbacks. The main drawback to trend analysis is that it cannot predict how major events or the economy will affect revenue or expenditure streams. The model assumes that nothing has changed in the model. Further, trend analysis cannot answer the "what if" questions. For example, what would happen if the shoe company down the street that employs 300 residents moved south to Mexico? Despite this weakness, trend analysis remains a very useful tool for local governments with stable resources and expenditures (Nollenberger 2004).

Charts and Figures

There are several different ways to display data using charts. Charts are used quite frequently in budgeting and finance and other disciplines to visually show the relationship between variables. The main advantage of a chart is that the reader can look at the data and determine the relationship in seconds. Hence, it is important that the chart clearly convey the message that the analyst is trying to distinguish right away. That is, the chart must be completely self-contained. The reader should be able to look at the chart and understand the labels and data with minimum explanations from written text or verbal communication. One other item to note is that the statistical packages that create charts do not use exact numbers in the labels or legend unless the user requests the exact number. In most cases, data presented in the legend are rounded to the nearest hundredth or thousandth.

There are several different types of charts and each of them provide the analyst with options depending on what he/she is attempting to convey to the consumer. These include: scattergrams, line graphs, pie charts, bar graphs, and column graphs.

Scattergrams

Scattergrams are frequently used to show a pattern or relationship between two variables. They are fairly easy to construct in a spreadsheet program and are very easy to understand. For example, the data in Exhibit 8.1 shows that personal income is more likely to increase as years of college education increases. Note that the independent variable is on the horizontal axis and the dependent variable is on the vertical axis. This format is always used when creating charts with two variables.

Line Graphs

Line graphs are very useful for showing patterns over time or simply displaying data. The only real difference between a line graph and a scattergram is the addition of a line that plots the data rather than individual data points. Exhibit 8.2 is an example of a line graph with two variables. It shows the relationship between years of college education for residents above 25 years of age and growth in personal income. As shown, the percentage of personal income tends to rise as years of education rises.

Exhibit 8.1 Personal Income and Education for City Employees, FY 2009

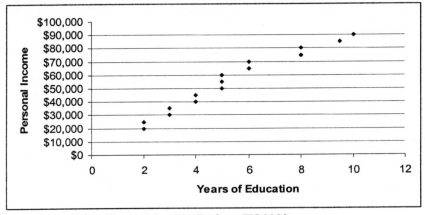

Source: Employee Files and the City Budget, FY 2009.

Exhibit 8.2 Personal Income and Years of College Education for all Residents 25 and Older, Merigold, No Where, 2009

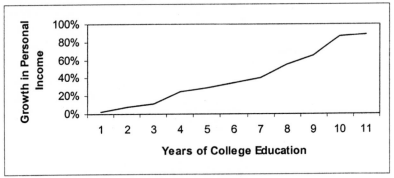

Source: United States Census Department, 2009.

Exhibit 8.3 is also a line graph. It shows revenue collections for the City of Jonestown for fiscal years 2002-2006 and estimates for fiscal years 2007-2009. The difference between this table and the previous table is the use of raw data. In some instances it is a good idea to use raw data. This is particularly true when decision makers want an overall picture of the budget.

Exhibit 8.4 is also a line graph that plots the percentage increase in property tax and sale tax collections over a five year period. This and similar graphs are very useful when comparing multiple revenue streams. Note that the amount of the revenue collection is not the key to the graph. As seen the collection rate of both revenue streams are fairly consistent over time.[54]

Exhibit 8.3 Revenue Collections and Estimates for the City of Jonestown

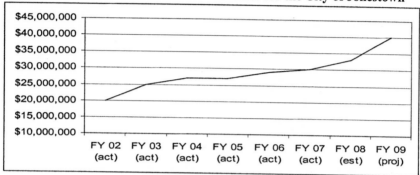

Source: City of Jonestown Budget Office. Data collected from budgets.

Exhibit 8.4 Property and Sales Tax Collections, FY 2004-FY 2009

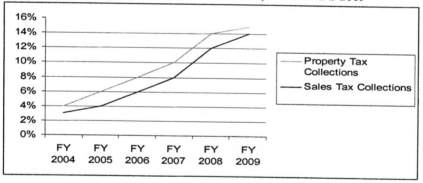

Pie Charts

A pie chart shows the contribution of values to a whole. They are useful when the data is represented in percentages. It is more difficult to use raw data in a pie chart and bar graph, particularly when there are disparate differences in the data. Pie charts are not useful in describing data that has negative changes.

In Exhibit 8.4, the revenue collections for the City of Patrick are shown for fiscal year 2009. As shown, the city received 60% of its revenue from property tax collections, 25% from sales taxes, 9% from franchise fees, and 6% from business licenses. The consumer can see at a glance that the majority of the revenue for the city came from property taxes and sales taxes and that franchise fees and business licenses make up a smaller part of the budget in FY 2009.

Exhibit 8.4 Revenue Collections for the City of Patrick, FY 2009

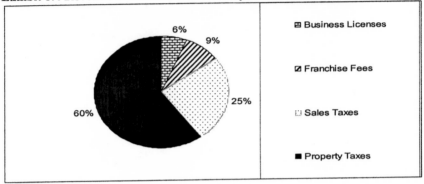

The pie chart in Exhibit 8.5 is a three-dimensional exploded pie chart that shows the contributions of each revenue source to the overall budget for Joyner. This format is useful when there are several revenue categories that are small.

Exhibit 8.5 Revenue Collections for the Town of Joyner, FY 2009

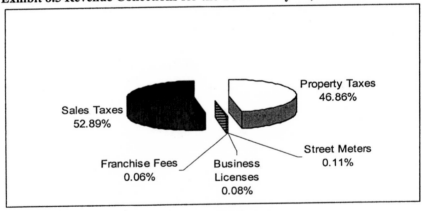

Bar/Column Charts

Bar and column charts are very similar to pie charts in that they are not very useful for negative numbers. However, unlike a pie chart, it is possible to show negative growth using a bar chart. Let's look at the example in Exhibit 8.6. The City of Jules had increases in every revenue category except franchise fees.

The chart indicates that Franchise Fees decreased by 14% in FY 2009. The chart also shows the substantive increases in street meters and property taxes. The disadvantage of this chart as well as the pie charts above is the lack of a dollar amount. The user does not know how much revenue is included in each of these categories.

Exhibit 8.6 Revenue Collections for the City of Jules, FY 2009

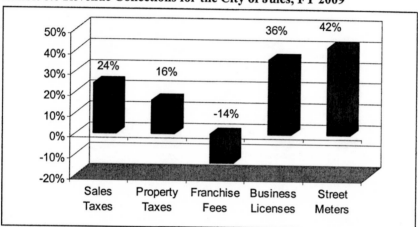

Power Point Presentations

Handouts and paper presentations are remnants of the past when it comes to professional presentations.[55] Paper copies can still be used, but their roles are somewhat cursory in formal presentations. Therefore, it is important that you become proficient in constructing Power Point presentations.

When you open the Power Point software, you will notice that it very user friendly. The program has quite a few preset templates that you can use when constructing your presentation. You should examine these basic rules when constructing your presentation.

Basic Rules For Constructing Power Point Presentations

Step 1: Determine the substantive contents of the presentation. Do not go overboard with tables and figures. If possible, determine what is expected in the presentation prior to beginning the presentation.

Step 2: Determine your design template. This step is more important than you might think. You do not want to use a gaudy design that is inappropriate and takes away from your presentation. I would strongly caution you not to use a lot of cartons in your presentations.

Step 3: Determine the format of your text and tables. Most Power Point presentation do not have text written in paragraphs. You may have a brief introductory page, with a stated purpose, and a conclusion with bullits, but not much in the middle. It is your job as the presenter to have notes to fill in the blanks for explanation.

Step 4: Decide if you want your presentation to be interactive and linked to a web cite or another program. That is, do you want to leave your presentation and visit a website or some other location that may have additional information? If so, ensure that those links are vital and working prior to the presentation. This function can be quite useful in situations where the audience may want or need more information on the spot. However, you should remember that presentations come with time constraints. Hence, do not waste time waiting for a web pages to load or searching for a website.

Conclusion

As mentioned at the beginning of the chapter, there are a number of techniques that are useful in assisting budget analysts and politicians in understanding how to present data. The more time that you spend creating charts and learning new programs, the more proficient you will become in using them. Remember, you want to get the most from any opportunity that you have to get your points across as well as address the questions that have been posed to you. When politicians and administrations meet, time and clarity is the essence to success.

Important Terms and Phrases

Bar Graph	Raw Data
Chart	Revenue Collections
Line Graph	Revenue Estimates
Pie Chart	Scattergram
Power Point Presentation	Secondary Data
Primary Data	Trend Analysis

Chapter 8 Homework Exercises

Directions: Complete questions 1-5 in Excel and paste the answers into a word processing program. The data for questions 1-5 are located in the Appendix and the website. Question five should be printed out in power point.

1. Read the following two hypotheses and create a scattegram using the two variables listed. Explain the results of the chart. Based on the position of the points, can you accept the hypothesis? Explain the results.

a. Hypothesis: Poverty rates (POVR00) have an affect on high school graduation rates (EDR00). Label the scattergram as Question 1a. Label the variables as "H.S. Graduation Rates" and "Poverty Rates."

b. Null Hypothesis: Race (WPOPR00: percentage of the white population) has no impact on the unemployment rate (EMR00). Label the scattergram as Question 1b. Label the variables as "White Population Rates" and "Unemployment Rates."

2. Using the region variable (REG2) in Appendix C8, create a pie chart showing the percentage (round to whole number) of each state in the region and a bar graph showing the number of states in each region. Which one of the techniques best describes the data? Variable Coding: 1=Northeast, 2=Midwest, 3= South, 4=West. Label the pie chart and bar graph as Question 2a and Question 2b respectively. Explain the results. Hint: You have to recode the data prior to creating the chart and graph.

3. Using the data in Appendix C8, create a line graph for total Medicaid enrollment (MEDENR03=FY 2003 Medicaid Enrollment) over the FY 2003-2008 period. Code the data in fiscal years. Describe the line graph. The Medicaid enrollment axis should begin at 18 million. Label the line graph as Question 3.

4. Explain revenue collections over the period FY 2005-FY 2009.

a. Using the data listed below, calculate the percentage change for each revenue source from one fiscal year to the next fiscal year. Describe the findings using only percentages (round the percentages to one digit to the right of the decimal) in your table. A copy of the data is found in APP8B.

Revenue Collection for the City of Walker, FY 2005-FY 2009

Revenue	2005 (act)	2006 (act)	2007 (act)	2008 (act)	2009 (est.)
Property Taxes	$1,389,129.23	$1,484,326.63	$1,585,027.14	$1,752,246.72	$1,962,892.42

Sales Taxes	895,932.00	995,232.67	1,234,132.67	1,385,132.11	1,445,952.00
Franchise Fees	2,456.31	3,056.54	3,456.12	4,756.89	5,001.90
Business Licenses	6,456.12	7,018.56	7,467.98	7,911.84	8,486.55
Street Meters	12,988.89	13,124.21	6,490.09	18,193.28	19,991.08

b. Using the data listed above, calculate the percentage of the budget that is represented by each revenue source for each fiscal year. Each fiscal year should total 100%.

c. Using the percentages that you calculated in 4a, create a line graph describing the growth or decline in revenue collection by source and the percentages associated with each revenue source. Note: The revenue source should be in the legend, not the year. All of these revenue sources should be completed in one graph.

5. Phillip Davis, the city manager for the City of Walker, has requested that you present the cities' revenue collection and expenditures over the past five fiscal years to the city council. Your job is to create a power point presentation describing the data (The raw data is located in APP8C) that is used in question 4 as well as the data that is in the appendix. Your power point presentation should include the following slides in the order that they are listed. Place four slides on each printed page. Each slide should have a label based on the information listed below:

- Slide 1: Title of presentation as well as your name and title.
- Slide 2: Write a general overview/introduction of revenue collections and expenditures over the period (text only).
- Slide 3: Write an outline of each chart/diagram/table used in the presentation.
- Slide 4: Create a bar graph of total revenue growth over the period FY 05 through FY 09. Format the axis to begin at $2,000,000.00. Format the chart area to be white.
- Slide 5: Create an exploded pie chart of all the revenue sources for the Sanitation Department for FY 09 with the percents for each revenue source.
- Slide 6: Create a line graph of property and sales tax collections for the Sanitation Department FY 05 through FY 09.
- Slide 7: Create a line graph of total expenditures over the FY 05 through FY 09. Format the starting axis to the smallest expendi-

ture amount.

- Slide 8: Create a stacked column chart with 3-D visual effects for Capital Expenditures for FY 05 through FY 09.
- Slide 9: Create a clustered bar chart with a 3-D visual effect for expenditures by department for FY 09.
- Slide 10: Write a brief conclusion to your findings.
- Print out your presentation (four power point pages per sheet of paper). Save the presentation on a diskette and bring the diskette to class.

References

Nollenberger, Karl, Sanford M. Groves and Maureen G. Valente. 2003. *Evaluating Financial Condition: A Handbook for Local Government.* ICMA: Washington, D.C.

Appendix 8A

ST	Povr00	Emr00	Edr00	wpopr00	Reg2	Medenr03	Medenr04	Medenr05	Medenr06	Medenr07	Medenr08
AL	14.4	4.6	77.5	70%	3	293,952	296,107	356,478	364,832	378,678	387,482
AK	8.2	6.6	90.4	68%	4	49,300	49,784	49,760	52,428	62,589	72,558
AZ	12.0	3.9	85.1	64%	4	420,470	412,013	431,637	412,367	406,838	436,164
AR	17.8	4.4	81.7	79%	3	128,943	133,189	211,509	236,727	274,327	289,370
CA	12.8	4.9	81.2	47%	4	3,234,820	3,605,477	3,541,295	3,438,056	3,437,996	3,849,152
CO	8.1	2.7	89.7	75%	4	176,488	175,643	203,049	200,408	204,423	221,109
CT	6.6	2.3	88.2	78%	1	198,728	201,085	212,059	213,695	222,517	230,067
DE	9.1	4.0	86.1	72%	3	47,795	48,566	58,334	58,513	61,903	66,316
FL	10.6	3.6	84.0	65%	3	1,144,010	1,509,686	1,194,290	1,137,381	1,173,002	1,245,949
GA	11.2	3.7	82.6	63%	3	670,782	691,067	773,398	746,845	780,978	780,146
HA	9.9	4.3	87.4	23%	4			149	87,249	95,240	
ID	12.9	5	86.2	88%	4	72,334	72,505	73,195	74,589	59,954	101,006
IL	11.5	4.4	85.5	68%	2	955,963	937,590	1,108,986	1,045,873	1,006,133	1,042,649
IN	8.7	3.2	84.6	86%	2	365,380	344,361	358,739	371,973	416,329	478,900
IO	7.2	2.6	89.7	93%	2	158,995	153,117	170,970	172,238	167,978	172,243
KS	9.6	3.7	88.1	83%	2	147,088	143,270	152,788	144,723	153,171	162,695
KY	11.9	4.1	78.7	89%	3	322,044	304,924	343,438	335,619	358,897	401,986
LA	17.3	5.5	80.8	63%	3	398,534	387,847	459,408	430,065	469,531	513,346
ME	8.4	3.5	89.3	96%	1	85,742	84,714	94,030	95,689	99,918	103,265
MD	7.6	3.9	85.7	62%	3	321,877	281,282	220,095	338,566	368,826	427,123
MA	10.1	2.6	85.1	82%	1	364,115	356,014	389,315	564,560	483,551	499,912
MI	10.0	3.6	86.2	79%	2	713,408	697,523	785,525	781,009	795,687	809,521
MN	6.0	3.3	90.8	88%	2	294,775	350,859	353,734	333,186	328,473	330,045
MS	12.9	5.7	80.3	61%	3	280,920	278,342	307,460	298,274	312,055	350,486
MO	8.0	3.5	86.6	84%	2	418,607	420,058	465,834	467,499	514,586	572,899
MT	15.7	4.9	89.6	90%	4	39,367	39,045	53,019	51,466	52,468	53,453
NE	9.0	3.0	90.4	87%	2	45,306	46,058	124,091	132,063	138,060	151,741
NV	8.5	4.1	82.8	65%	4	75,712	82,542	79,714	80,747	93,791	94,746
NH	5.2	2.8	88.1	95%	1	56,361	56,829	60,678	58,861	63,717	67,541
NJ	8.0	3.8	87.3	66%	1	422,781	417,519	456,720	460,440	468,602	491,360
NM	16.8	4.9	82.2	45%	4	206,654	215,370	233,321	231,378	251,177	270,588
NY	13.4	4.6	82.5	62%	3	1,472,627	1,459,578	1,693,941	1,621,869	1,467,669	1,525,759
NC	12.1	3.6	79.2	70%	3	569,026	569,203	670,968	674,006	671,206	688,420
ND	1.0	3.0	85.5	92%	2	31,060	29,335	33,792	32,657	33,350	33,364
OH	10.0	4.1	87.0	84%	2	866,324	815,020	820,116	796,056	808,462	822,277
OK	15.4	3.0	86.1	74%	3	243,399	230,654	247,644		328,526	384,761
OR	11.2	4.9	88.1	84%	4	126,965	114,841	262,650	255,894	257,209	263,455
PA	8.9	4.2	85.7	84%	1	847,024	838,075	895,506	882,877	880,489	861,341
RI	9.1	4.1	81.3	82%	1	70,200	68,429	76,544	77,751	78,240	92,938
SC	10.6	3.9	83.0	66%	3	264,919	268,428	327,629	369,983	415,376	453,295
SD	9.6	2.3	91.8	88%	2	45,284	47,697	53,660	52,925	57,372	62,572
TN	14.7	3.9	79.9	79%	3	462,817	459,331	653,484	669,063	700,599	709,954
TX	14.7	4.2	79.2	52%	3	1,672,446	1,665,087	1,794,065	1,689,961	1,691,655	1,706,960
UT	9.6	3.2	90.7	85%	4	120,659	118,172	125,784	126,290	130,118	131,408
VT	11.3	2.9	90.0	96%	1	56,556	57,914	61,989	62,282	66,480	69,596
VA	7.7	2.2	86.6	70%	3	394,268	394,180	431,054	412,235	410,210	398,334
WA	8.9	5.2	91.8	79%	4	463,743	515,458	561,023	572,927	561,904	568,245
WV	14.0	5.5	77.1	95%	3	208,437	216,486	220,237	209,341	209,869	196,345
WI	9.6	3.5	86.7	87%	2	239,672	209,405	320,044	299,364	310,592	331,047
WY	11.0	3.9	90.0	89%	4	31,441	31,363	33,560	31,697	31,356	32,193

Appendix 8B

City of Walker
Revenue Collections
(Fys 05-09)

	FY 05	FY 06	FY 07	FY 08	FY 09
Property Tax	$1,389,129.23	$1,484,326.63	$1,585,027.14	$1,752,246.72	$1,962,892.42
Sales Tax	895,932.00	995,232.67	1,234,132.11	1,385,380.99	1,445,952.00
Franchise Fees	2,456.31	3,056.54	3,456.12	4,756.89	5,001.90
Bus Licenses	6,456.12	7,018.56	7,467.98	7,911.84	8,486.55
Street Meters	12,988.89	13,124.21	16,490.09	18,193.28	19,991.08
TOTAL Revenue	$2,306,962.55	$2,502,758.61	$2,846,573.44	$3,168,489.72	$3,442,323.95

Question 4A	FY 05	FY 06	FY 07	FY 08	FY 09
Property Tax					
Sales Tax					
Franchise Fees					
Bus Licenses					
Street Meters					
Average Change					

Question 4B	FY 05	FY 06	FY 07	FY 08	FY 09
Property Tax					
Sales Tax					
Franchise Fees					
Bus Licenses					
Street Meters					
TOTAL Revenue					

Appendix 8C

Expenditures

	FY 05	FY 06	FY 07	FY 08	FY 09
General Government	$1,074,100	$1,180,789	$1,283,123	$1,345,897	$1,637,298
Public Safety	$459,129	$495,999	$501,456	$539,985	$589,532
Public Works	$234,908	$245,874	$259,081	$278,902	$290,247
Sanitation	$109,239	$112,897	$125,987	$139,980	$159,436
Water & Sewer	$90,876	$115,987	$121,987	$138,912	$158,943
Capital Expenditures	$335,908	$349,876	$547,987	$578,135	$589,421
TOTAL	$2,304,160	$2,501,422	$2,839,621	$3,021,811	$3,424,877

Sanitation Dept.

	Sales	Property	Street Meters	Sanitation Fee	
FY 05	$26,000	$29,000	$5,000	$49,239	$109,239
FY 06	$24,000	$32,000	$5,000	$51,897	$112,897
FY 07	$29,000	$34,500	$5,500	$56,987	$125,987
FY 08	$32,000	$35,800	$6,200	$65,980	$139,980
FY 09	$35,000	$36,436	$5,200	$82,800	$159,436

Appendix

Writing a Research Proposal

1. *Research Question/Hypothesis*: The first thing that you need to do is to articulate the subject of the paper in the form of a research question or hypothesis.

2. *Cursory Review of Literature*: Conduct a cursory review of the literature (3-4 articles, book, etc) to determine what other scholars have found relative to your subject. Pay close attention to the issues and the variables used to test their hypothesis/research questions. You can use this literature to justify the need or to verify that there is a gap in the literature that you intend to fill. You can also use this review to extend research that has been conducted. What is true today may not be true tomorrow.

3. *Data and Methods*: Find the secondary data that you need for the paper or determine or decide that you are going to collect primary data yourself via surveys, etc. Be specific as to the location of the data, i.e. websites, etc. Then, decide what sort of research design that you will use. For example, cross sectional, time series, or meta analysis. Last, what are you going to do with the data? That is, what sort of statistical analysis will you run on the data [univariate, bivariate (crosstabs), regression, etc] that will allow you to answer your hypothesis/research questions.

Note: The proposal should be no more than two pages.

Writing a Research Paper

1. *Title/Title Page*: The title of your paper should fit the main theme of the paper. It should be centered in bold print (16-18 font) and should not be more than ten words. Place your name one or two line spaces directly under the title in a smaller font size. The date of submission and the class in which the assignment was made should also be included.

If you are presenting the paper at a conference, put your mailing address as well your phone number and email address under your name. Lastly, put the name, date and location of the conference under your demographic information.

Side note: You might want to construct a rough outline of the main headings in the paper highlighting the main point or items that you want to cover as you move along. This becomes more relevant as the length of the paper increases (for example, not necessary for a five page paper, but important for papers over 10 pages in length).

2. *Abstract*: This is a one or two paragraph synopsis of your paper. First and foremost, the abstract should identify your hypothesis/research question in the first or second line.

Then, detail the procedure/application that you used to test your hypothesis/research question (survey data, archival study, regression analysis, content analysis, etc). This sentence [s] should also identify your main data sources (i.e. Survey data, Census data, etc). Lastly, the abstract should provide the reader with your main research findings if you have completed the research. Frequently, proposals for research are just that. If you have completed the research, provide the major findings in one or two sentences. If you have not completed the research, then leave this part out of your proposal. When you finish the research you can go back and rewrite this section with the exact findings. This step is critical because you should be able to polish and refine your statement at this point. An abstract should not be longer than 130 words or 3/4^{ths} of a page.

3. *Introduction*: The introduction to the paper provides the main point of departure for your subject matter. The main objective is not only to clearly convey your hypothesis/research question, but also to validate your study relative to other studies. However, you do not want to delve too deep into the research of other scholars in this section. The literature review section contains this information. Do not force the reader to read more than one paragraph to find your hypothesis/research question. The purpose of your study should be crystal clear to the reader. Researchers frequently begin the introduction with several cursory sentences providing some interesting points or data concerning the subject matter. The introduction can range from half a page to two pages depending on how much background information you include. Ensure that you stay focused when writing this section.

Main Points Summarized:

- Present relevant background or contextual material

- Define terms or concepts when necessary

- Explain the focus of the paper and your specific purpose

- Validate your thesis or purpose statement by showing why it is important

- Reveal your plan of organization for the paper

4. *Literature Review/Previous Literature*: In short, this is a summation of the works of other scholars who have conducted research on your dependent variable/main subject. The bulk of your literature review should be based on scholarly refereed research. Generally speaking, web based articles are still only moderately acceptable in research. This does not include refereed journals that are available online. I am specifically referring to articles that were written and did not go through the process of having several other professional researches read it and provide some sort of stamp of approval (commonly called non refereed research). Literature can be ranked in terms of level of acceptance (most acceptable to least acceptable): 1. university press books and refereed articles, 2. non university press books and text books, 3. articles from research institutes, government agencies, or think tanks such as the Urban Institute, Brookings, Congressional Budget Office, and OMB, 4. web sites, news magazines (Newsweek, U.S. News and World Report, etc.), and newspaper articles. There is also some disparity among web sites, newspapers, and news magazines, so be careful when citing them.

A literature review is normally written by date or subject matter. In some instances, there may be two areas of research that cover your subject, so it would be wise to split them into two sections with an appropriate heading for each and then discuss them by date. The most recent material should appear first. This is not necessarily true if there is a classic pioneering article or book in the field. If everyone else is citing the piece, then you should as well. Your goal is not to summarize the research, but to cite the research design and the findings as it applies to your work. If multiple authors have the same findings, then cite them together in one sentence. The literature review can range from two to four pages depending on how much work has been conducted in your area. Carefully cite the research you are building from, synthesizing the information as much as possible rather than just describing each individual research piece. Academic reviewers often go to this section first to see what basis the research is basing their theoretical/research design upon since this section demonstrates the writer's knowledge and understanding of the state of the current research in the area.

Main Points Summarized:

- Use your outline and prospectus as flexible guides

- Build your paper around points you want to make (i.e., don't let your sources organize your paper)

- Integrate your sources into your discussion

- Summarize, analyze, explain, and evaluate published work rather than merely reporting it

- Move up and down the "ladder of abstraction" from generalization to varying levels of detail back to generalization

5. *Data and Methods*: The main objective of this section is to inform the reader of your data sources, research application and model. It is not necessary to list the exact location of your data sources. For example, if you use data from the U.S. Census Bureau's web site, you should simply list the main web site. The reader simply needs to have enough information to find the location of the data if they look for it. You should also indicate the time frame covered in the research.

It is easier to describe secondary data than primary data. When using primary data, you must detail the exact collection method as well as any other nuances that you employed when collecting the data. This is particularly true with content analysis studies and primary survey data. Review the article "Advancing E-Government at the Grassroots: Tortoise or Hare?" in the January/February 2005, v 6 p 64-75 issue of *Public Administration Review* for an example of writing the data and methods section for a survey research article. Review the article "The Media's Portrayal of Urban and Rural School Violence: A Preliminary Analysis" in the September/October 2001, v 22 #5 issue of *Deviant Behavior* for an example of content analysis. The article that is listed on our website with this handout also uses secondary data analysis. Methodology refers to the statistical application that you use in your study. This includes chi square analysis, regression analysis, correlations, factors analysis, etc.

Lastly, you should put your model in this section. This includes items such as illustrations describing your model or regression models. Each of the terms that you use to describe your illustration or variables in your model must be described in detail. For example, you may have an education variable in your model. It is necessary to inform the reader how you measure education: in years?, grades?, or degrees completed? Depending on how many variables that you have in your paper, it may be necessary to include an appendix or footnotes/endnotes with the full description of the variable along with any coding that you used.

Main Points Summarized:

- Provide the location of data sources
- Describe the variables used in your paper (in the paper or in the appendix)
- Describe the methodology used and it limitations (regression, survey or content analysis, archival studies, etc)
- Present your model/paradigm/etc

6. *Findings/Results*: This section provides the reader with the results of your analysis. No conclusions are drawn in this section. So, if you test three hypotheses, you might simply list them one by one and provide the results for each. If you have tables and charts describing your findings, place them in this section. Your tables should stand alone. That is, the reader should be able to discern what is in the table or illustration without reading the text. However, the text should clearly explain what is in the table [s]. You should not refer extensively to the literature review in the findings. The tables and charts must be carefully constructed so that the reader can readily understand labels, headings, sources or data, etc.
Main Points Summarized:

- Repeat research question/hypothesis followed by the findings
- Present tables, charts and graphs
- Do not draw any conclusions based on previous research

7. *Conclusions*: The first thing that you want to do in your conclusion is remind the reader of your hypotheses/research questions. Then, confirm or reject those propositions as well as compare them to the findings of other scholars. It is okay to indicate that you did not find what you expected to find. Scholars frequently indicate how their research was limited and what they would do or recommend to future researchers. It is not necessary to reinvent the wheel in this section. It is a summary, not a regurgitation of the findings. Depending on the number of hypothesis tested, your conclusion can range from a paragraph to a couple of pages in length.

After you have drafted your conclusion section, go back to the introduction and make sure that the two are still linked! Did you do what you said you were going to do? Is the paper organized the way you said it would be? Does your concluding paragraph (s) clearly address the purpose of the paper?

Main Points Summarized:

- If the argument or point of your paper is complex, you may need to summarize the argument for your reader.

- If prior to your conclusion you have not yet explained the significance of your findings or if you are proceeding inductively, use the end of your paper to add your points up, to explain their significance.

- Move from a detailed to a general level of consideration that returns the topic to the context provided by the introduction.

- Perhaps suggest what about this topic needs further research

8. *References/Bibliography*: Please consult a style manual for proper citation methods. There are three main techniques (APA, MLA, and Chicago Style) and they do change over time. So, you should consult the most recent version of the technique that you are using.

9. *Endnotes/Footnotes*: These are short explanatory sentences that are conservatively used throughout your paper. For the most part, they are used to offer additional explanation, definitions or other pieces of information that may be useful to the reader. Do not put things in the notes that can be included in the paper. If you are using quantitative analysis in your paper it may be better if you use an appendix along with notes. Use notes sparingly.

10. *Appendices/Footnotes/Endnotes*: The appendix contains information that is not needed directly in the text. This would include items such as the coding scheme for your models, definitions of terms, and additional information about your data. There is no set amount or type of information that should be included in your appendix.

Notes: The items that are included in this summary should be included in a basic run of the mill research paper. There is no exact model to follow when writing a research paper. Different journals use different models and professors often want different things. The more you read scholarly research and write research papers the more adept you will become in your writing skills.

You may also include other items such as a background section discussing a policy or a definition that your paper focuses on. However, it is recommended that you do not go overboard in this process.

The information contained in this summary is not applicable and should not be mistaken for "research papers" that are really literature reviews. It is possible to conduct a content analysis or an archival study on the work of other scholars. However, to simply go to the library and find articles and books on a subject and write a paper is not a research paper, but a literature review disguised as a research paper. The term research suggests that you have gone beyond what other writers have done and conducted some sort of analysis that presumably has not been done before.

Research papers frequently use a Times Roman 12 point font and are double spaced. Unless indicated otherwise, there is no real page limit. However, research papers do not tend to extend beyond 40 pages. The following websites offers additional information on writing using the APA style http://webster.commnet.edu/apa/ or http://www.apastyle.org.

Aids to Writing Research Papers

Guidelines for writing a research report.

Harbrace college handbook.

Making sense : a student's guide to research and writing : social sciences.

MLA handbook for writers of research papers.

Model research papers from across the disciplines.

Put it in writing: learn how to write clearly, quickly and persuasively.

Research and report writing [video recording].

Research paper smart: where to find it, how to write it, how to cite it.

Understanding style : practical ways to improve your writing.

Webster's new world student writing handbook.

Writing handbook.

Writing research papers: a Norton guide.

End Notes

1. With the exception of Georgia and the federal government during the Carter administration, no government has ever used zero-based budgeting.

2. See Gianakis and McCue 1999; Novick 2002; Mikesell 2003; and Solano 2004 for additional information on program budgets.

3. In reality, the government would provide line-item detail within the program. A legislator is not going to accept a single number without backup. The government would also present information by subprogram, such as street paving, striping, snow removal, etc.

4. See Mikesell 2003 and Smith and Lynch 2004 for additional information on performance budgets.

5. See Riley and Colby 1991; Carney and Schoenfeld 1996; and Smith and Lynch 2004 for additional information regarding the common elements of a budget.

6. Chapter 5, "Funding the Budget," has a complete description of revenue source along with the advantages and disadvantages of each source. See Robert L. Bland's, "A Revenue Guide for Local Government" for a detailed explanation of revenue sources.

7. Review Riley and Colby 1991; Bland and Rubin 1997; Smith and Lynch 2004; Holder 2004; Solano 2004 and Kittredge and Ouart 2005, for additional information on governmental accounting methods and fund accounting.

8. See Riley and Colby 1991; Bland and Rubin 1997; Mikesell 2003; Smith and Lynch 2004; and Solano 2004 for additional readings on enterprise and internal service funds.

9. See Bland and Rubin 1997; Smith and Lynch 2004; Rogers and Brown 1999; and Solano 2004 for additional information on budget cycles.

10. The director (and staff) issues the guidelines, reviews requests, formulates revenue projections, and provides written analysis to the chief executive. The budget director attends the budget hearings.

11. Note: All of the parties are not necessarily involved at the same time. The first thing the agency head has to do is sell the chief executive on the budget via the budget director. If you are unsuccessful at that stage, your idea is not likely to succeed. The agency head could "back door" the request by lobbying the legislator, but that might get the agency head fired. The legislator is not involved until the budget gets to him/her. That is, when the outside parties are also involved.

12. Although income taxes are considered a part of the personal budget, they are intentionally excluded from this chapter because the payment of income taxes completely falls upon the burden of the employee. The tax rate can change for different individuals based on a number of different items that are not directly correlated with this discussion. These taxes are however discussed in detail in chapter 5, "Funding the Budget."

13. Despite the fact that these two items frequently comprise more than 50% of the budget, it is very difficult to cut the personnel budget. This is particular true during periods of low economic activity. Personal service is the only portion of a budget that is likely to increase every fiscal year (COLAs or cost of living adjustments). Along with this increase is also an increase in fringe benefits.

14. See Robert L. Bland's *A Revenue Guide for Local Government*, 2nd Edition, for more information. See also Friedman 1983 for a discussion of calculating compensation costs.

15. In 2004, the State of Oregon issued $2.1 billion to cover the shortfall in their retirement system.

16. A performance budget is similar. See Exhibit 1.3 for an example. The only thing that would change is the items listed under operating expenses.

17. Large governments may prepare budgets to the nearest thousand dollars, omitting the last 000s.

18. Review Bland and Clarke 1999; Mikesell 2003; Aronson and Schwartz 2004; Smith and Lynch 2004; Solano 2004; and Vogt 2004 for additional information on capital budgets and capital improvement plans.

19. Review Axelrod 1995 p. 104-105; Bland and Rubin 1997, p. 169-174; and Bland and Clarke 1999, p. 654 for additional material discussing capital budget and budget projections.

20. Capital budgets include financing provisions and must be balanced. However, there are a number of things that can and do occur on capital projects that cause cost overruns.

21. This material was taken from Nice 2002, p. 123-127; Bland and Rubin 1997, p. 171-175; and Riley and Colby 1983, p. 105-106; and Mikesell 2003.

22. This includes experienced managers, service professionals, budget and finance staff, governing board members, other officials, and citizens.

23. Excerpted from A John Vogt's chapter titled "Prioritizing Capital Projects" in *Capital Budgeting and Finance: A Guide for Local Government*. ICMA Washington, D.C.

24. Many governments are not allowed to issue debt. So, instead they use other means such as certificates of participation and lease-purchase arrangements.

25. See the debt administration section of Chapter 7 for more information on financing debt using bonds.

26. Review chapters 6, 7, and 8 of Vogt 2004 for a thorough discussion of these items.

27. If using Excel, first copy the spreadsheet and then click on "edit" in MS Word. Second, click on "paste special." Third, click on "Pictures (Windows Metafile). The table without the lines should appear. If you need to make changes in the file, you will have to go back into Excel and make the changes.

28. A progressive tax provides for rates that increase as the tax base (the value of the property or the amount of income being taxed) increases. A regressive tax remains constant or declines as the tax base increases.

29. For example, cities in Ohio, Pennsylvania and Maryland can collect income taxes on earnings.

30. According to the Census Bureau, in 2002 insurance trust revenue made up less than 10% of total state and local government revenue. Furthermore, charges and fees just for hospitals, sewerage, utility and liquor made up over 11% of the total revenue.

31. See Gianakis and McCue 1999; and Smith and Lynch 2004 for additional information.

32. The yield on property tax is based on the value of the house, not the income of the owner. There are many senior citizens who are house-poor. They live on fixed incomes but live in houses with high property taxes. So, this would invalidate the progressive claim.

33. In many New England local governments, the property tax is the balancing factor. They first determine all other sources of revenue. Whatever is needed becomes the property tax levy.

34. Another way to think about millage rates is in terms of assessments. If we apply the one mill being one tenth of a percent-meaning one mill rate equals $1 of revenue for every $1,000 of assessed value- then a property tax rate of 67.5 mills as applied to a $110,000 property assessed at 25% percent of market value would yield $1,856.25 (110 X .25 X 67.5 = $1,856.25).

35. Alaska, Florida, Nevada, South Dakota, Texas, Washington and Wyoming had no state income tax as of January 1, 2002. Tennessee and New Hampshire have a state income tax that is limited to dividend and interest income. Http://www.taxadmin.org/fta/rate/ind_inc.html.

36. See Lynch 1995; Gianakis and McCue 1999; Smith and Lynch 2004; and Gruber 2005 for a discussion of payroll taxes.

37. Review Gianakis and McCue 1999; Mikesell 2003, 2004; Smith and Lynch 2004; Kittredge and Ouart 2005, and Rubin 2006 for a discussion of sale taxes.

38. See also Downing 1983 and Mikesell 1999, 2003; and Rubin 2006 for a discussion of user fees and charges.

39. Review Mikesell 1999; Clynch, Feig and Kaatz 2001; and Nice 2002 for additional information on gaming revenues.

40. Equity is defined in terms of the impact on small businesses versus all businesses.

41. Higher education normally translates to higher paying jobs. Hence, higher incomes equal more taxes.

42. Cities that have a substantial retirement community on fixed incomes should pay particular attention to this point.

43. Review Lynch 1995; Lee and Johnson 1998; Gianakis and McCue 1999; and Gruber 2005 for a discussion on cost-benefit and cost-effectiveness analysis.

44. The following items require further analysis if the arrow is in the downward slope indicating a decrease in the item: population density, personal income per capita, property value, home ownership, number of jobs in the community, % elastic revenues, tax revenues, % user charges, enterprise operating position, % fund balances, % liquidity, % pensions assets, maintenance effort and capital outlay. The remaining items would require further analysis if the arrow indicates an increase. The only exception is the population and revenues per capita factor.

45. Chapter 8 provides details on displaying data.

46. Review Bland and Rubin 1997; Mikesell 2003; Nollenberger, et al 2003; and Rubin 2006 for a discussion of pensions and the pay-as-you-go method.

47. See Khan 1996; Lee and Johnson 1998; Smith and Lynch 2004; and Keown, Martin, Petty and Scott 2005 for a review of cash management.

48. See Lee and Johnson 1998; Larson 2004; and Smith and Lynch 2004 for additional information on internal cash management.

49. Note that the life expected use of the truck in bid 1 is not exactly 100,000 miles in the final analysis. The data was forced to reflect whole numbers rather than cents. This is an acceptable practice given the amount of miles expected over the life of the vehicles.

50. If there are more than two bids, you should subtract the two lowest life-cycle cost differences from each other.

51. Laws have to be in place in order for this to occur.

52. See Chapter 4 for a discussion of financing debt.

53. Secondary data are existing data sets collected for another purpose by someone else. There are a number of factors such as timeliness of the data, aggregating data, searching for data, purchasing data, as well as the source of secondary data that will affect your decision to use the data. Secondary data is particularly useful when conducting comparative or longitudinal studies. This data can be found in libraries, reference books, databases, government agencies, internet, etc). However, all data is not equal. That is, data is only as good as the entity that collected it. For example, there are a number of entities that collect statistics on various federal agencies. However, the U.S. Census Bureau is one of the most respected institutions responsible for collecting data on the U.S.

population on a variety of different subjects from agriculture issues to vital statistics that is used world wide. Therefore, I would want to stick to the official source, rather than using data from a less credible source.

54. When using excel, make sure that you understand how to use the "series" button to move and add variables to the graph.

55. See the appendix in chapter 8 for an outline of a full fledge research paper.

About the Author

Charles Menifield is an associate professor and graduate admissions coordinator at the University of Memphis in the Division of Public and Nonprofit Administration where he teaches graduate courses in budgeting and financial management, public management information systems, research methods, and statistics. His areas of research include the use of lotteries to fund public education, public health and welfare issues, and minority politics. He was previously employed at Murray State University, Mississippi State University and the Congressional Budget Office. He received his doctorate from the University of Missouri-Columbia.